Practical Arduino Engineering

End to End Development with the Arduino, Fusion 360, 3D Printing, and Eagle

Second Edition

Harold Timmis

Apress®

Practical Arduino Engineering: End to End Development with the Arduino,
Fusion 360, 3D Printing, and Eagle

Harold Timmis
Jacksonville, FL, USA

ISBN-13 (pbk): 978-1-4842-6851-3
https://doi.org/10.1007/978-1-4842-6852-0

ISBN-13 (electronic): 978-1-4842-6852-0

Managing Director, Apress Media LLC: Welmoed Spahr
Acquisitions Editor: Susan McDermott
Development Editor: James Markham
Coordinating Editor: Jessica Vakili

Distributed to the book trade worldwide by Springer Science+Business Media New York, 1 NY Plaza, New York, NY 10004. Phone 1-800-SPRINGER, fax (201) 348-4505, e-mail orders-ny@springer-sbm. com, or visit www.springeronline.com. Apress Media, LLC is a California LLC and the sole member (owner) is Springer Science + Business Media Finance Inc (SSBM Finance Inc). SSBM Finance Inc is a **Delaware** corporation.

For information on translations, please e-mail booktranslations@springernature.com; for reprint, paperback, or audio rights, please e-mail bookpermissions@springernature.com.

Apress titles may be purchased in bulk for academic, corporate, or promotional use. eBook versions and licenses are also available for most titles. For more information, reference our Print and eBook Bulk Sales web page at http://www.apress.com/bulk-sales.

Any source code or other supplementary material referenced by the author in this book is available to readers on GitHub via the book's product page, located at www.apress.com/978-1-4842-6851-3. For more detailed information, please visit http://www.apress.com/source-code.

Printed on acid-free paper

To my friend AJ. I love you and miss you.
May you rest in peace.

Table of Contents

About the Author

 **Harold Timmis**, since he was a small child, has fostered a curiosity for technology, taking apart everything in his parents' house just to see how it all worked. This fueled his thirst for knowledge of computer science, programming, and its uses. He has worked with LabVIEW and Arduino for the past 13 years. During that time, he has been involved in several professional projects using LabVIEW, as well as many hobbyist projects utilizing both Arduino and LabVIEW. Harold attended the Florida Institute of Technology, where he studied computer engineering and was introduced to LabVIEW and Arduino. Later, he worked at the Harris Corporation and General Electric, where he created several LabVIEW projects for trains and became very interested in the Arduino, data acquisition, and control theory.

About the Technical Reviewer

Sai Yamanoor is an embedded systems engineer working for an industrial gases company in Buffalo, NY. His interests, deeply rooted in DIY and Open Source Hardware, include developing gadgets that aid behavior modification. He has published two books with his brother, and in his spare time, he likes to contribute to build things that improve quality of life. You can find his project portfolio at http://saiyamanoor.com.

Acknowledgments

I would like to thank my beautiful wife Alexandria for being very patient with me while I wrote this book. I also want to thank my daughter Natalie for inspiring me every day. As always, I want to thank my mom (Bonnie), dad (George), sister (Amanda), and brother (George) for always believing in me.

I want to thank the Apress team for helping me complete this book. It was rough with COVID, but we finally finished the book! I want to personally thank Natalie Pao and Jessica Vakili. They helped me navigate through this process again effectively and efficiently. Also, I want to thank my Technical Editor Sai Yamanoor. His thoughts were insightful and made this book much better.

I want to thank the Arduino Team for developing a truly revolutionary product. I want to thank SparkFun, Pololu, PCBWay, Autodesk, Simplify3D, National Instruments, and Adafruit. You all make making so much more enjoyable and attainable.

Preface

Hello reader! Welcome to the wonderful world of engineering. First off, this book is divided into two main sections: the first section will teach you about the various bits of software and hardware that we will be using in this book. The topics in this section include

- The Engineering Process

- An Arduino Software Review

- 3D Modeling with Autodesk Fusion 360

- PCB Design with Autodesk Eagle

- First Section Final Project

Once those are completed, we move to the final project where you will be given a requirements document that you will need to interpret and understand to make the final project all while using the skills you obtained in the previous section of this book. The topics in this section are

- Final Project PCB

- Final Project 3D Model

- Final Project Software

- Final Project Putting It All Together

Once completed, you will have a unique robot that you can modify and elaborate on for future projects. So without further ado, let's get started with the engineering process.

CHAPTER 1

The Process of Arduino Engineering

In this chapter, we will discuss the engineering process and how you can use it to streamline your prototypes by avoiding problems with hardware and software and keeping to a fixed schedule. Throughout this book, you will have projects that will be organized into a sequence I like to call the "engineering process." Here's a quick summary of the sequence:

1. Requirements gathering

2. Creating the requirements document

3. Gathering hardware

4. Configuring the hardware

5. Writing the software

6. Debugging the Arduino software

7. Troubleshooting the hardware

8. Finished prototype

As you can imagine, even this summary of the engineering process is very effective when prototyping, which is why we will use it with the Arduino in this book. What is the Arduino? The Arduino is a very customizable microcontroller used by hobbyists and engineers alike. Also, it is open source, which means that the source code is available to you for

© Harold Timmis 2021
H. Timmis, *Practical Arduino Engineering*, https://doi.org/10.1007/978-1-4842-6852-0_1

your programming needs; the integrated development environment (IDE) (where you will be writing your software) is free, and most resources you can find are open source. The only thing you have to buy is the Arduino microcontroller itself. The Arduino is supported very well on the Web and in books, which makes it very easy to research how-to topics; a few sites that will help you get started are `www.arduino.cc` and `http://tronixstuff.wordpress.com/tutorials/`. But this book is more than simply a how-to reference; this book is going to teach you the engineering process—a skill that is useful for making projects more readable, efficient, and reliable. This book will also focus on end to end development, another useful skill (or skills as the name implies) that will allow you to create robust prototypes and/or fully developed hardware and software, but first we will take a look at the engineering process.

Gathering Your Hardware

Before we examine the engineering process steps, it's important to know some of the parts and materials you'll need. Throughout this book, you will need the following pieces of hardware to complete the various projects we'll be working on (for a complete list of hardware used in this book):

- Arduino: Since the first edition of this book, there have been many new developments in the Arduino product line (a lot from other vendors as well); there are many flavors of the "Arduino" out in the wild. For the purposes of this book, the MEGA 2560 Pro will be used. This is because it has a very small form factor, and it has a ton of IO (inputs/outputs). Really though as we are designing through this book, you may want to experiment with other Arduino boards; that is fine and encouraged since most of the code in this book will work with the standard Arduino UNO form factor; that is not to say other form factors will not work as well. See Figure 1-1.

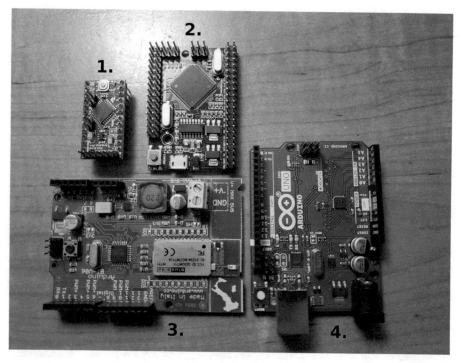

Figure 1-1. *1. Arduino Pro Mini, 2. MEGA 2560 Pro, 3. Bluetooth Arduino, and 4. Arduino UNO*

- Bluetooth Mate Silver or RN-42: Since this book will focus on end to end development while still keeping in mind the engineering process to prototype your circuit, you may want to purchase a Bluetooth Mate Silver, but when we design actual PCBs (Printed Circuit Boards), we will need to use a module that we can quickly and effectively use just like the Bluetooth Mate Silver, which is the RN-42. This module has a small footprint which will be nice because we want to use as little space on the PCB as possible. See Figure 1-2.

Figure 1-2. *1. RN-42 Bluetooth Module, 2. Bluetooth Mate Silver*

- Solderless breadboard: Another very important piece of hardware is the solderless breadboard (see Figure 1-3), which is used to implement your circuitry. For this book, you need to have a midsize solderless breadboard. It will be used in both the design and troubleshooting phases of the projects and will allow you to create a proof of concept for when we create the PCB in Eagle.

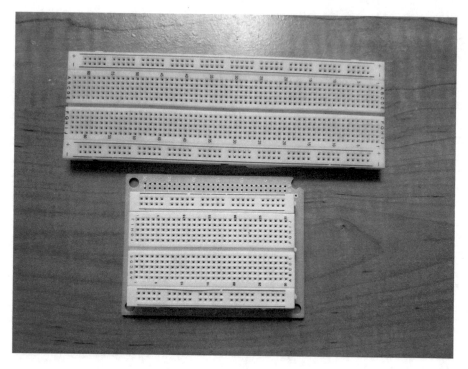

Figure 1-3. *An example of some solderless breadboards*

- Wire: We will use a large quantity of wire in this book; you can get a wire jumper kit at almost any electronics store.

- Arduino shields: Unlike the first edition of this book, we will not focus too much on shields; they are very useful and can make validating firmware a breeze, but this edition will focus on creating a couple of shields for the MEGA 2560 Pro. See Figure 1-4 for a couple of examples of shields, and underneath that picture, you will find a few descriptions of useful shields for this book. Please note that it is not necessary to purchase these shields, but they are still valuable tools.

Figure 1-4. *1. Motor shield, 2. GPS shield, 3. GSM shield*

- Motor shield: This shield is used to control motors up to 18V. It includes a surface mount H-bridge, which allows for a higher power motor to be used as well as for control of two motors.

- GPS shield: This shield is used to get positioning information from GPS satellites. It uses the National Marine Electronics Association (NMEA) standard, which can be parsed to tell you any number of things such as longitude and latitude, whether the GPS has a fix, what type of fix, a timestamp, and the signal-to-noise ratio.

- Sensors: These are very important because they give your projects life. Some sensor examples are PIR (Passive Infrared), sonar, and temperature (see Figure 1-5).

Figure 1-5. *1. GPS module with breakout board, 2. accelerometer, 3. photoresistor, 4. temperature sensor, 5. flex sensor, 6. PIR sensor, 7. tilt sensor, 8. humidity sensor, 9. FSR (force sensitive resistor)*

- PIR sensor: This is an outstanding sensor for detecting changes in infrared light and can detect changes in temperature. It is also great at detecting motion, and that's what we will use it for.

- Sonar sensor (not pictured): Sonar sensors are good at detecting objects in their surroundings. The sonar sensor we will use is a Parallax sensor that uses digital pinging to tell how far away an object is.

- Temperature sensor: These sensors are used to read temperature. To use them, you first scale the voltage to the temperatures you want to record.

- Accelerometer: This sensor can detect acceleration in multiple directions, that is, in the X, Y, and Z directions. There are accelerometers that have more degrees of freedom. These sensors can be used to measure motion, vibration, or shock. For example, accelerometers are used in Fitbits and other exercise tracking hardware to keep track of your step count or even what exercise you are doing. We will be using an accelerometer later in this book on the main shield that we will create.

- GPS module: The GPS module that will be used in this book is the EM-506; it has a UART interface which will make it very easy to interface with the Arduino.

- Photoresistor: These sensors are used to sense brightness and dimness.

- Tilt sensor: This sensor is used to detect if a system has flipped over which can be useful if you don't have access to an accelerometer.

- Flex sensor: As this sensor is flexed, the resistance increases, which can then be read by the Arduino on one of its ADCs (Analog to Digital Converters) to keep track of how much flex a system has.

- Humidity sensor: The RHT03 humidity sensor can read both temperature and relative humidity and is accurate (+/–2%RH for humidity and +/–0.5C for temperature) for a low-cost sensor.

- FSR (force sensitive resistor): This sensor is great to detect force. A good use for this sensor may be a scale or to detect pressure points.

- Servos and motors: We will be using motors and servos to control many aspects of the projects (see Figure 1-6).

Figure 1-6. *1. 12V DC motor, 2. 9g servo motor, 3. 24V DC pancake stepper motor*

- Miscellaneous: These are the most common components, such as resistors, capacitors, LEDs, diodes, headers, push buttons, and transistors. You can buy many kits that will supply you for a while on all this hardware at a low cost (see Figure 1-7).

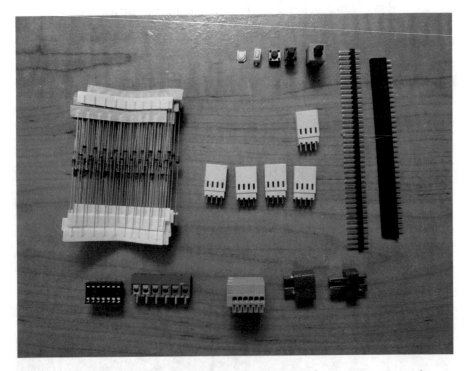

Figure 1-7. *Miscellaneous pieces of hardware (various terminal blocks/connectors, diodes, headers, push buttons)*

Gathering Your Tools

You will also use a variety of tools; this section will briefly describe them. An (*) will be placed next to the hardware that is not required, but is a good tool to have.

Electronic Hardware

- Soldering iron: This tool is used to connect circuits to each other; we will use it mostly to connect wire to circuits (see Figure 1-8).

- Solder: You will use this in conjunction with the soldering iron; it is the metal that connects the circuits together. Solder has a very low melting point.

- Needle-nose pliers: These pliers are very important; they are used to hold wire and circuits in place, wrap wire around circuitry, and so on.

- *Third hand: This is a very useful tool when you are trying to solder a PCB together (see Figure 1-12 #2).

- Cutters: These are used to cut wires (see Figure 1-12 #1).

- Wire stripper: This tool is used to take off wire insulation (see Figure 1-12 #3).

- Multimeter: Possibly the most important tool you can own; this tool allows you to read voltage (AC (alternate current) and DC (direct current)), amps (ampere), and ohms (see Figure 1-10).

- *Scientific calculator: This allows you to do various calculations (Ohm's law, voltage divider, etc.).

- *Adjustable DC power supply: With a power supply, you can give your projects continuous power; this is normally only used for testing circuits (see Figure 1-9).

- *Microscope: Can be very useful for checking leads on circuits to make sure they are soldered properly (see Figure 1-11).

- *Logic analyzer: Another very useful tool; a logic analyzer will read back data coming off of various IO lines. For example, the one pictured in Figure 1-13 #1 can read eight lines of IO simultaneously; these IO lines could be UART, I2C, SPI, and so on. We will discuss these protocols later in this book.

- *AVR programmer (AVRISP mkII): This programmer can be used to upload code into various Atmel uC (microcontrollers). It is also able to upload the Arduino Bootloader onto the ATMEGA2560 or ATMEGA328p.

- *FTDI programmer: Another programmer, if the board you are working on does not have an ISP (in-system programmer), it may have a five-pin header that you can connect an FTDI programmer to. Make sure you get the correct voltage level FTDI programmer for your system. Normally, they come in 5V and 3.3V levels (see Figure 1-14).

- *Oscilloscope: The multimeter and the oscilloscope are probably the most important tools when debugging electronics. The Oscope, as it is sometimes referred to as, allows you to measure voltage vs. time. This can be useful when reading back digital or analog signals. For example, you may want to read the output of a digital pin to make sure it is triggering at the correct intervals. This is an example where a multimeter would not be as useful as an Oscope because the Oscope will show you voltage over time (such as transitions from high to low states) for a set interval, and the multimeter will just display the latest voltage output.

Figure 1-8. *A soldering iron and its stand*

Figure 1-9. *Adjustable DC power supply (3, 4.5, 6, 7.5, 9, and 12V)*

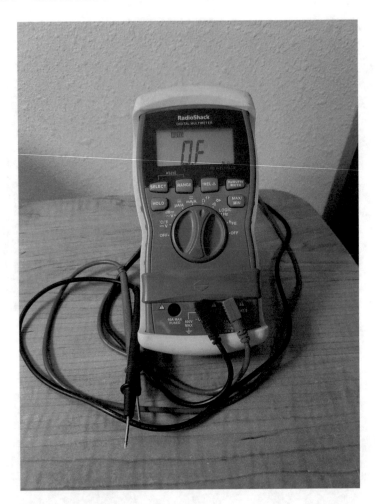

Figure 1-10. *Multimeter*

Figure 1-11. *USB microscope*

Figure 1-12. *1. Cutters, 2. third hand with magnifying glass, 3. wire strippers*

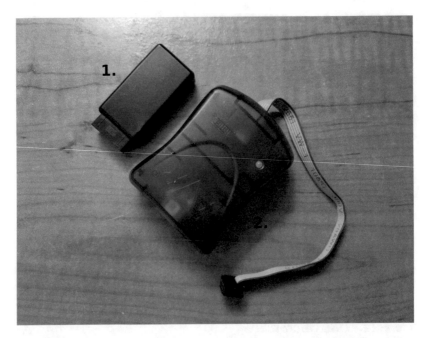

Figure 1-13. *1. Logic analyzer, 2. AVR programmer AVRISP mkII*

Figure 1-14. *FTDI programmer*

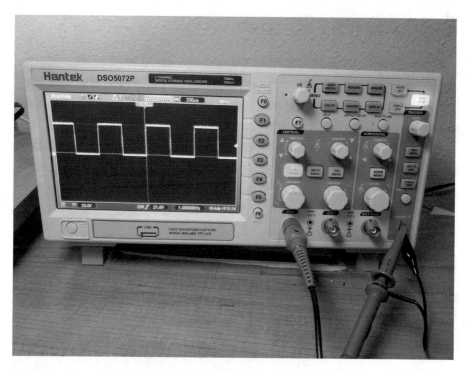

Figure 1-15. *A two-channel 70MHz digital oscilloscope (note how the Oscope is displaying the high to low transitions 0 to 5V at a frequency of 1kHz and a 50% duty cycle)*

Understanding the Engineering Process

The engineering process is very useful in making your designs more efficient, streamlined, and comprehensible. The process consists of gathering requirements, creating the requirements document, gathering the correct hardware, configuring the hardware, writing the software, debugging the software, troubleshooting the hardware, and the signing off on the finished prototype.

Requirements Gathering

One day, when you're an engineer, you may be asked to go to a company and assess its needs for a particular project. This part of the engineering process is crucial; everything will depend on the requirements you gather at this initial meeting. For example, assume you learn that your client needs to **blink an LED at a certain speed**, and for that task, you and the client determine that the Arduino microprocessor is the best choice. To use the Arduino to blink the LED, a customer needs an LED to blink at 100ms intervals.

Creating the Requirements Document

Based on the client's needs and your proposed solution, the following is a very simple requirements document:

- Hardware
    - Arduino
    - LED
    - 9V battery
    - 9V battery connector
    - 330ohm resistor
- Software
    - A program that blinks an LED at 100ms intervals

Mind you, this is a very simple example, but we will be using this format for the rest of this book. One of the reasons you create a requirements document is to stop *feature creep*. This happens when a customer keeps adding features to the software and/or hardware. This is, of course, a problem because you will be working more hours without more pay on a project that may never end. You should create a requirements document, so you and the client know what you are doing and the features you will be creating for your project. After you have created the requirements document, you can create a flowchart that will help you debug the software later in the design process (see Figure 1-16).

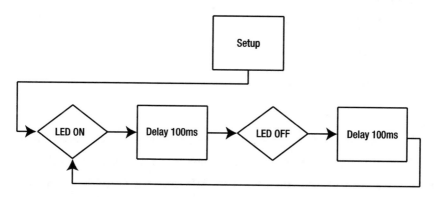

Figure 1-16. *Blinking LED processes*

Gathering the Hardware

The next very important part of the engineering process is making sure you have the right hardware. Your hardware needs should be decided as you gather requirements, but it is important to make sure all your hardware is compatible. If it is not compatible, hardware changes may be necessary, but you should consult the company you are working with to make sure it is satisfied with any hardware changes.

Configuring the Hardware

Once you have the correct hardware, it is time to configure it. Depending on the hardware required for the project, the configuration can change. For example, let's take a look at the hardware configuration for the blinking LED project:

- Arduino

- LED

- 330ohm resistor

- USB cable

To set up the hardware, we need to connect the LED to the solderless breadboard, then attach the 330ohm resistor to the anode (+) of the LED; next, take a male to male wire and attach it from the cathode (-) of the LED to the GND (ground) pin on the Arduino UNO. Finally, take another male to male wire and attach it from the other end of the resistor to pin 13 of the Arduino (see Figures 1-17 and 1-18).

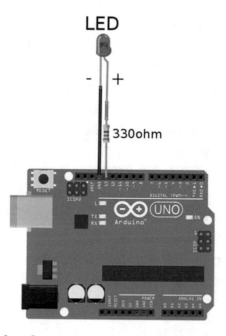

Figure 1-17. *The hardware setup for the blinking LED project*

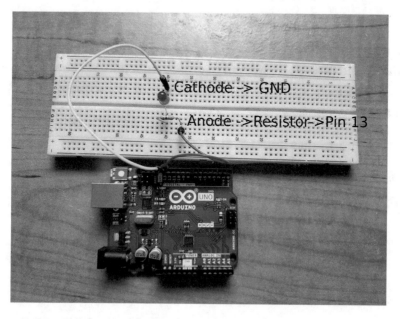

Figure 1-18. *Wiring guide for the Arduino LED project*

Alright, now that the hardware is finished, we need to get the Arduino IDE software up and running on Windows. To do this, go to www.Arduino. cc/en/Main/Software. The Arduino IDE will work with Windows 8 or 10 (it will even work with older versions of Windows as well), Mac OS X, and Linux systems. After the Arduino IDE is downloaded to your desktop, it will be in a zipped format, so unzip the Arduino folder to your desktop. The Arduino IDE is now installed.

Now that you have the Arduino IDE installed on your computer, you need to make sure it is configured correctly. To do this, open the Arduino IDE, and go to Tools ➤ Port; select the serial port your Arduino is connected to. Next, select Tools ➤ Board, and select the Arduino board you are using; for this project and this project only, we will use the Arduino UNO. Later projects will use the MEGA 2560 Pro board. Once your hardware is configured, it is time to write the software.

Writing the Software

Now, let's consider the software we need to write. This part of the engineering process is crucial. Let's take a look at the blinking LED software requirements document to decide what the software will need to do: the LED needs to blink in 100ms intervals. The software might look something like this:

```
// This code blinks an LED at 100ms

const int LEDdelay = 100;  // delay time

void setup()
{
    pinMode(13, OUTPUT);  // makes pin 13 an output
}
```

```
void loop()
{
    digitalWrite(13, HIGH);    // this writes a high bit to pin 13
    delay(LEDdelay);           // delay 100ms
    digitalWrite(13, LOW);
    delay(LEDdelay)            // this will throw a syntax
                               // error due to a missing semicolon

}
```

Note   When you try to compile this program to your Arduino, it gives you an error. This is because of a syntax error that we will debug in the next section.

Debugging the Arduino Software

The last program failed to compile because of a *syntax error*. This type of error is because of incorrectly formatted code, such as a missing semicolon (which is why the last program didn't compile). Here is the revised code:

```
// This code blinks an LED at 100ms

const int LEDdelay = 100;  // delay time

void setup()
{
    pinMode(13, OUTPUT);   // makes pin 13 an output
}
```

```
void loop()
{
    digitalWrite(13, HIGH);    // this writes a high bit to pin 13
    delay(LEDdelay);           // delay 100ms
    digitalWrite(13, LOW);
    delay(LEDdelay);           // the semicolon is now present
                               // and the code will compile

}
```

Syntax errors are not the worst errors out there. The worst errors you can receive are *logical errors*; these errors allow the code to compile, but the end result is unexpected. For example, using a greater-than symbol instead of less-than is a logical error, and if it is in a project with thousands of lines, it can be almost impossible to fix.

Note   A logical error in the blinking LED project would be if you put digitalWrite(13, HIGH); for both digital write functions.

We can debug logical errors in an Arduino program by using a flowchart to figure out where the values are not lining up.

Troubleshooting the Hardware

The number one tool used to troubleshoot hardware is the multimeter. This tool can save your hardware from being damaged. For instance, if your multimeter detects that your power supply is more than is required, the hardware setup for the blinking LED project could use a 330ohm resistor to keep the LED from burning out. Also, an Oscope could be valuable as we can make sure the intervals are correct at 100ms on and 100ms off.

Finished Prototype

Once you have finished debugging the software and troubleshooting the hardware, you should have a completed prototype that will work under most circumstances. In this chapter, we used a very simple project, but in future chapters, the projects will get more complicated, and the engineering process will become even more necessary to make sure our code is efficient, streamlined, and comprehensible.

Summary

In this chapter, you learned the different pieces of hardware and various tools such as the Arduino, Arduino shields, multimeter, and needle-nose pliers, just to name a few that will be used throughout this book. We then went over the engineering process, which is a sequence you can use to solve problems that provides the format for this book. The steps in the process are requirements gathering, creating the requirements document, gathering the hardware, configuring the hardware, writing the software, debugging the Arduino software, troubleshooting the hardware, and finished prototype. I also defined a few new terms that will help you understand the engineering process, and you learned the differences between logical and syntax errors. In the next chapter, we will go over some of the software that we will use throughout this book. We will also use a different programming technique that will allow our code to have multitasking capabilities; this is called a finite-state machine or FSM for short.

CHAPTER 2

Understanding the Arduino Software

In this chapter, we will discuss the various programming components that will be used throughout this book. If you have programmed in C, you will find that programming for the Arduino is very similar. If not, this chapter will teach you the basic concepts. Why is it important for you to learn the basics of programming the Arduino? In the long run, this will help keep your code clean and readable. Also, learning the basic loops and structures initially will allow us to focus more on the libraries later. Libraries can be sets of classes, types, or functions and can be called by using keywords in your program. The purpose of a library is to readily add more functionality to your program by using code that has been created previously; this promotes code reuse. We will also take a look at the new TinyGPS++ library.

© Harold Timmis 2021
H. Timmis, *Practical Arduino Engineering*, https://doi.org/10.1007/978-1-4842-6852-0_2

Getting Started with setup( ) and loop( )

All Arduino programs must have two main components to work properly—
setup() and loop()—and they are implemented like this:

```
// Basic Arduino Program

void setup()
{
    // Set up I/Os here
}

void loop()
{
    // Do something
}
```

setup() is used to set up your I/O ports such as LEDs, sensors, motors, and serial ports. Careful setup is important because in order to use the pins on the Arduino, we need to tell the Arduino that they are going to be used.

loop() holds all of the code that controls your I/O ports. For instance, here, you'd tell your motor to go a certain speed. I will explain how to set up and control your I/Os in the next sections.

Arduino programs also have subroutines—very useful extra functions you can call within loop() or its subroutines. To use a subroutine, you must first initialize it at the beginning of your program; this initial mention is called a *function prototype*. Here is an example:

```
// Function Prototype
void delayLED();

void setup()
{

}
```

```
void loop()
{

}

// Subroutine Example

void delayLED()
{
    // This will go after the loop() structure.
}
```

Initializing Variables

Variables are the most basic programming building blocks; they are used to pass data around your program and are used in every program we will write in this book. We can write several types of variables to the Arduino language; Table 2-1 illustrates them.

Table 2-1. *Types of variables*

Type Name	Type Value	Type Range
char	'a'	−128 to 127
byte	1011	0 to 255
Int	-1	−32,768 to 32,767
unsigned int	5	0 to 65,535
long	512	−2,147,483,648 to 2,147,483,647
unsigned long	3,000,000	0 to 4,294,967, 295
float	2.513	−3.4028235E+38 to 3.4028235E+38
double	2.513	−3.4028235E+38 to 3.4028235E+38

Now that you know what types of variables are out there, you need to know how to declare those variables. In order to declare them, you need to know in what *scope* those variables can be used and then specify (or *declare*) the scope that meets your needs. In this book, we will declare two scopes for variables: local variables and global variables. A *local variable* only works in its given scope. For instance, a for loop keeps its declared variables only within its parentheses, so those variables are local to the for loop. A *global variable* can be called at any point in your program. To define a global variable, initialize it at the beginning of your program. The following program illustrates how to initialize local and global variables:

```
// Initialize Variable

int x;   // This variable is declared globally and is available
              for access throughout this program.

void setup()
{

}

void loop()
{
    x = 1 + 2;   // Assigns the value 3 to x
    for(int i; i <= 100; i++)
    {
        // i is a local variable and can only be called in this
            for loop.
    }

}
```

The rest of the declarations are set up the same way until you start using arrays. *Arrays* allow you to pass multiple values of the same type, for example, if you want to pass multiple digital pins without having to declare each one individually:

```
int pins[] = {13,9,8};
```

It is a good idea to declare the size of the array, as in the following example:

```
const int NumOfPins = 3;
int pins[NumOfPins] = {13,9,8};
```

This will allow you to access your array's information, and then you can pass that information to a digital pin or whatever else you want. Now that you have declared variables, how do you use them? This will be discussed in the next few sections of this chapter.

Note   *Whitespacing* means that you've added blank lines and spaces in your code to make it more readable.

Writing Conditional Statements

Conditional statements can be used to control the flow of your program. For instance, say you want to turn a motor on only when a button is pressed; you can do so using a conditional statement. We will discuss the following conditional statements: if, if-elseif, if-else, and switch statements.

An if statement is a very important conditional statement; it can be used in any Boolean capacity for a variety of reasons, such as limiting testing. Here is an example of an if statement:

```
int i;
if (i < 10)
{
    i++;
}
```

You can also add elseif statements to the end of your if statement to add other conditions to your program and create an if-elseif statement, for example:

```
int i;
if (i < 10)
{
    i++;
}
else if (i > 10)
{
    i--;
}
```

A practical use of a conditional statement would be to read a value from a potentiometer, as in the following example:

```
potValue = analogRead(potPin);

if (potValue <= 500)
{
    digitalWrite(motorpin, 1);
}
```

```
else
{
    digitalWrite(motorpin, 0);
}
```

Note   You must remember to set up your Arduino's pins before you
call them in a loop.

A switch statement is used if you have multiple conditions because it
cleans up your code. Here is an example of a switch statement:

```
switch (potValue){
case 500;
    digitalWrite(motorPin,1);
case 501;
    digitalWrite(ledPin,1);
    break;
default:
    digitalWrite(motorPin,0);
    digitalWrite(ledPin,0);
```

In this example, if potValue is equal to 500, the motor will turn on, and
if potValue is equal to 501, an LED will turn on. The default case is true
when the potValue equals neither 500 nor 501, and in that case, the motor
and LED are both turned off.

Timers vs. Delays

When you are writing code, you may get used to using delays to pause
when an LED turns on or off. This is not very efficient; what we should be
using is timers instead. The reason behind this is so that your code is not

stuck in a delay and can move on with other tasks. For example, say you want to blink an LED at a 10-second interval and turn a motor on and off at a 2-second interval. You may think that this code would suffice:

```
int LED = 13;
int motorPin = 5;

void setup()
{
    pinMode(led, OUTPUT);
    pinMode(motorPin, OUTPUT);
}

void loop()
{
    // turn on LED for 5s and then turn off LED for 5s
    DigitalWrite(LED, HIGH);
    delay(5000);
    DigitalWrite(LED, LOW);
    delay(5000);

    // turn on motor for 1s and then turn off motor for 1s
    DigitalWrite(motorPin, HIGH);
    delay(1000);
    DigitalWrite(motorPin, LOW);
    delay(1000);

}
```

The code does compile, and the LED does turn on and off in 10s intervals, but you may notice that the motor has to wait until the LED code finishes; this is because we used a delay and can be fixed by using a timer instead. Let's take a look at some of the functions we can use to accomplish this task:

- millis() function: This function will return the amount of milliseconds that have passed since the Arduino program started. It is also important to note that this function will overflow in 50 days as an unsigned long can only hold 0 to 4,294,967,296.

- micros() function: This function will return the amount of microseconds that have passed since the Arduino program started. It is also important to note that this function will overflow in 70 minutes as an unsigned long can only hold 0 to 4,294,967,296.

We will need to handle overflow (this is when a value returns to 0) of the micros() and millis(), and we will do this in the new LED/motor example:

```
// initialize the led and motor pins
int LEDPin = 13;
int motorPin = 5;

// keep track of the current state of the led and motor
int LEDState = 0;
int motorState = 0;

// store led and motor previous time value
unsigned long prevLEDTime = 0;
unsigned long prevMotorTime = 0;

// interval declaration can be changed if needed
const long LEDInterval = 5000;
const long motorInterval = 1000;
```

```
void setup() {

  // set up motor and led pins to be outputs
  pinMode(LEDPin, OUTPUT);
  pinMode(motorPin, OUTPUT);

}

void loop() {

  // get current time for the led and motor pin
  unsigned long curLEDTime = millis();
  unsigned long curMotorTime = millis();

  // this is a delta of the current time and previous time for
     the led circuit
  // this will also handle overflow
  if (curLEDTime - prevLEDTime >= LEDInterval)
  {
    // set the previous time to the current time to keep track
       of the led's state
    prevLEDTime = curLEDTime;

    // set the led state to high or low depending on what its
       previous state was.
    if(LEDState == LOW)
    {
      LEDState = HIGH;
    }
    else
    {
      LEDState = LOW;
    }
```

```
  // turn on or off the led
  digitalWrite(LEDPin, LEDState);
}

// this is a delta of the current time and previous time for
    the motor circuit
// this will also handle overflow
if (curMotorTime - prevMotorTime >= motorInterval)
{
  // set the previous time to the current time to keep track
      of the motor's state prevMotorTime = curMotorTime;

  // set the motor state to high or low depending on what its
      previous state was.
  if(motorState == LOW)
  {
    motorState = HIGH;
  }
  else
  {
    motorState = LOW;
  }

  // turn on or off the motor
  digitalWrite(motorPin, motorState);
}

}
```

With this new code, we are running true timers that will keep track of the LED and motor states with no delay in between; that is, the LED conditional statement will occur, and then the motor conditional statement will occur in quick succession rather than like the previous code where the motor had to wait 10 seconds before it could turn on and off. This is the power of timers, and we will continue to use them throughout this book.

Finite-State Machine

With a finite-state machine (FSM for short), you can make your code more readable and split your tasks into much smaller blocks while still accomplishing the multitasking like we did in the previous section with the millis() function. Take a look at the following code:

```
// initialize the led and motor pins
int LEDPin = 13;
int motorPin = 5;

// Keep track of Prev States of the LED and Motor
int prevLEDState = 0;
int prevMotorState = 0;

// Keep track of the current states of the LED and Motor
int currLEDState = 0;
int currMotorState = 0;

// store led and motor previous time value
unsigned long initLEDTime = 0;
unsigned long initMotorTime = 0;

// store led and motor previous time value
unsigned long currLEDTime = 0;
unsigned long currMotorTime = 0;

// interval declaration can be changed if needed
const long LEDInterval = 5000;
const long motorInterval = 1000;
```

```
void setup() {

  // set up motor and led pins to be outputs
  pinMode(LEDPin, OUTPUT);
  pinMode(motorPin, OUTPUT);

}

void loop() {
  // Run State Machines
  LED_State_Machine();
  MOT_State_Machine();

}

void LED_State_Machine(){
  prevLEDState = currLEDState;

  // current state will always be preserved, so when in
     currLEDState = 2 the
  // switch statment will always go back to that state until
     set to a new state
  // in this case state 3.
  switch(currLEDState){
    case 0: // Init State
      currLEDState = 1;
    break;
    case 1: // Set State 1
      // Set initial time and Set the LED to High
      initLEDTime = millis();
      digitalWrite(LEDPin, HIGH);
      currLEDState = 2;
    break;
```

```
    case 2: // Update State 1
      // get current time and compare time to interval
      currLEDTime = millis();
      if (currLEDTime - initLEDTime > LEDInterval)
      {
        currLEDState = 3;
      }
    break;
    case 3: // Set State 2
      // Set initial time and Set the LED to Low
      initLEDTime = millis();
      digitalWrite(LEDPin, LOW);
      currLEDState = 4;
    break;
    case 4: // Update State 2
      // get current time and compare time to interval
      currLEDTime = millis();
      if (currLEDTime - initLEDTime > LEDInterval)
      {
        currLEDState = 0;
      }
    break;

  }
}

void MOT_State_Machine(){
  prevMotorState = currMotorState;

  // current state will always be preserved, so when in
     currMotorState = 2 the
  // switch statment will always go back to that state until
     set to a new state
```

```
// in this case state 3.
switch(currMotorState){
  case 0: // Init State
    currMotorState = 1;
  break;
  case 1: // Set State 1
    // Set initial time and Set the Motor to High
    initMotorTime = millis();
    digitalWrite(motorPin, HIGH);
    currMotorState = 2;
  break;
  case 2: // Update State 1
    // get current time and compare time to interval
    currMotorTime = millis();
    if (currMotorTime - initMotorTime > motorInterval)
    {
      currMotorState = 3;
    }
  break;
  case 3: // Set State 2
    // Set initial time and Set the Motor to Low
    initMotorTime = millis();
    digitalWrite(motorPin, LOW);
    currMotorState = 4;
  break;
  case 4: // Update State 2
    // get current time and compare time to interval
    currMotorTime = millis();
    if (currMotorTime - initMotorTime > motorInterval)
```

```
    {
        currMotorState = 0;
    }
    break;

  }
}
```

You will notice a few differences between the previous sketch and this sketch; first off, the loop function has been taken from several lines to two lines of code. Also, there are two functions that now control the state of the LED (LED_State_Machine()) and motor (MOT_State_Machine()). Finally, the if statements have been replaced with a switch statement that has cases of values 0 through 4. You will also notice that each case has very simple blocks of code; this is where the readability comes into play. If you run this code, you will notice that both the LED and the motor will update independently just like the previous example. We will be utilizing the FSM in later projects.

Working with Loops

Loops have many uses including getting rid of redundant code and iterating through arrays. The loops we will use are for, while, and do... while. These loops will allow us to run through code while a condition is true (or false, in some circumstances).

- for loop: This loop is used to repeat a block of code a fixed number of times. The for loop's basic setup is

```
for(int i = 0; i <= 10; i++)
{
        // Place statements here
}
```

- A practical application for a for loop is to use it to
  update multiple pinMode settings:

```
int pins[] = {13,9,8};

void setup()
{
    for(int i = 0; i<=2;i++)  // Sets up each pin
    {
        pinMode(pin[i], OUTPUT);
    }
}
void loop()
{
    // Put code here
}
```

Note   pinMode is used to set up your I/O pins on the Arduino.

- while loop: This loop will run until a condition has
  been met; if its first condition is false, it will not run at
  all. For example, you'd use a while loop if you wanted to
  run code until a certain value came from a sensor. The
  following example illustrates this principle:

```
int potPin = A1;
int motorPin = 9;
int potVal;
```

```
void setup()
{
     pinMode(motorPin,OUTPUT);
     pinMode(potPin,INPUT);

}
void loop()
{
     potVal = analogRead(potPin);
     while(potVal <= 100)   // Runs until potVal is
                                greater than 100

     {
          digitalWrite(motorPin,1);
     }

}
```

- The first thing this code does is initialize the potentiometer and motor pins; then, it declares potVal, our variable that holds the potentiometer value. Next, we set the motorPin to an output and the potPin to an input. Finally, we use a while loop with a condition potVal <= 100, and while that condition is true, the motor will be on.

- do...while loop: This is the same as the while loop except that the conditional statement is checked at the end of the loop, so this loop will run at least one time. Here's an example:

```
do
{
     i++;   // Increment i
}while(i <= 100);
```

Communicating Digitally

Throughout this book, we will be communicating different types of
I/O through the digital pins, so it is important to understand how that
communication works. Specifically, we use the digitalWrite(pin,HIGH/
LOW) and digitalRead(pin) commands to communicate with the digital
pins. An example of this is shown in Listing 2-1.

Listing 2-1. Digital commands

```
int button = 12;
int led = 13;
int buttonState;

void setup()
{
    pinMode(button,INPUT);
    pinMode(led,OUTPUT);

}
void loop()
{
    buttonState = digitalRead(button);  // Assigns button to
                                                buttonState
    if(buttonState == 1)
    {
        digitalWrite(led,HIGH);  // Writes a 1 to pin 13
    }
    Else
    {
        digitalWrite(led,LOW);  // Writes 0 to pin 13
    }
}
```

This program uses digitalWrite() and digitalRead() to get the value of the button pin and writes a new value to it (in this case, high or low).

Note   Use the PWM digital pins to control motor speed and LED brightness.

Communicating with Analog Components

You can also use analog communication with sensors and motors, meaning you can connect potentiometers to control motor speed through a pulse width modulation (PWM) pin on the Arduino. The functions for analog communication are analogRead(value) and analogWrite(pin,value). The only thing you need to remember is that a potentiometer will give a value of 0 to 1024, so you will have to scale analogWrite from 0 to 255, for example:

```
analogWrite(LED,ledValue/4); // 1024/4 = 255
```

Serial Communication

We will be using serial communication throughout this book. Serial communication allows us to communicate with a computer, LCD, and many other devices, as you will see in the next several chapters. Some serial commands are Serial.begin(baud), Serial.Println("anything you want to write to the serial pin"), Serial.read(), Serial.write(Binary data), Serial. available(), and Serial.end(). These commands allow us to read and write to any serial peripheral we want. Here is a brief description of each of these serial commands:

- Serial.begin(baud): You will put this command inside your setup() structure and put the appropriate baud rate for the device with which the serial will be communicating, for example:

```
void setup()
{
    Serial.begin(9600); // 9600 baud rate to
                            communicate with a computer
}
```

- Serial.println(): Use this command to write values to the serial port, for example:

```
void loop()
{
    Serial.println("Hello, World");   // Writes Hello,
                                        World to the
                                        serial port

}
```

Or...

```
void loop()
{
    Serial.println(potVal);  // Writes potVal to the
                                serial port

}
```

- Serial.read(): This reads in a value from the serial port. For example, you could use this to read something from your computer that you'd then want to write to an LCD on the Arduino.

```
void loop()
{
    char var = Serial.read();  // Read incoming byte
                                  from serial port

}
```

- Serial.write(): Use this to write binary data to a serial
  port, for example:

```
void loop()
{
while(Serial.available() > 0)
    {
        char var = Serial.read();  // Reads incoming
                                      byte from
                                      serial
        Serial.write(var);  // Writes binary data to
                               serial

    }

}
```

Note   In this book, most of the time, you will use Serial.println( ) because we will be writing int or string values to the serial monitor. The Serial.write( ) function is used to send binary data to the serial monitor or any other serial port program.

- Serial.available(): This function checks to see if there are any incoming bytes at the serial port, for example:

```
void loop()
{
    while(Serial.available() > 0)
// This makes sure there is at least one byte at the
                                    // serial port.
    {
        // Put code here
    }

}
```

- Serial.end(): This disables serial communication.

Now that you have seen the command set for serial communication, we can use them in our programs. Listing 2-2 illustrates most of the functions we have been discussing.

Listing 2-2. Serial communication

```
int incomingByte;
const int ledPin = 13;
void setup() {

    Serial.begin(9600);         // Opens serial port, sets data
                                    rate to 9600 bps

    pinMode(ledPin, OUTPUT);

}
```

```
void loop()
{

  while(Serial.available() > 0)
  {

    incomingByte = Serial.read();          // Reads incoming byte
    Serial.println(incomingByte, BYTE);    // Prints incoming
                                           // byte to serial port
    digitalWrite(ledPin, incomingByte);    // Write to LED pin

  }

}
```

This program is the foundation of serial communication: it initializes incomingByte and ledPin. Next in the setup structure, the baud rate is set to 9600. When we get inside the loop structure, the while loop is checking to see if anything is at the serial port. If there is, it assigns the information on the serial port to incomingByte. Finally, the program prints the data to the serial port and writes data to ledPin (in this case, 1 or 0).

SerialEvent

SerialEvents are pretty cool if you need some code to run whenever you send data to the Arduino via the serial port. Here is how it is used:

```
Void setup()
{
    // code here
}

Void loop()
{
    // code here
}
```

```
void serialEvent() {
  // code here
}
```

What this will allow you to do is trigger an event if the serial port reads any data. You can then take that data and pass it into various functions such as a parser, or you can turn different hardware on, and so on. We can use this, for instance, to read a certain NMEA string from a GPS with a code sent over the Arduino's serial port; more on this later. Oh! One more thing, since we will be using the MEGA 2560 Pro, we will have multiple UARTs which means we can use the serialEvents for each of these ports; all you need to do is add the functions for each UART you will use: serialEvent1, serialEvent2, serialEvent3.

Using Arduino Libraries

Now that you know the basics of Arduino programming, I want to at least describe one important library in this chapter called the TinyGPS++ library, and in later chapters I will expand on other libraries as we add more components to our design. To use the TinyGPS++ library, you will need to download it and unzip it into the Libraries folder in the Arduino directory. After you do that, you should be able to do this with many other libraries.

TinyGPS++

This library parses NMEA data, such as longitude, latitude, elevation, and speed, into a user-friendly style. All you need to do now is download the TinyGPS++ library from http://arduiniana.org/libraries/tinygpsplus (we need to thank Mikal Hart).

Putting Together the Arduino Language Basics

You should now know how to create the most basic Arduino program, so let's take a moment to recap some of the key programming points just discussed. You can use this recap to help you program throughout this book and through creating your own projects. Here is an example of that program:

```
void setup()
{
    // Setup I/Os here
}
void loop()
{
    // Put code here
}
```

We also went over declaring variables and using them globally, as in the following example:

```
char ch = 'A';
int pin = 13;
```

These values have types of character and integer.

You also learned about if and if-else statements and how to use them:

```
if (condition)
{
    // Put code here
}
else
    // Put code here
```

Also, you can now add elseif statements to create if-elseif statements to add more conditions, if you need them:

```
else if(condition)
{
    // Put code here
}
```

We then went over the switch statement, another type of conditional statement that is used sometimes to clean up larger if statements; it has this format:

```
switch(value)
{
    case value:
        // Put code here
        break;
    case: value:
        // Put code here
        break;
    default:
        // Put code here
        break;
}
```

After the conditional statements were explained, we discussed timers vs. delays and how to use the millis() and micros() functions to accomplish multitasking within the Arduino. That then leads us to the finite-state machine (FSM) which made multitasking and readability much better compared to the nested if statement version. We then went over the various loop structures you can use to parse or iterate through code. The first loop we discussed was the for loop:

```
for(initialization;condition;Variable Manipulation
{
    // Put code here
}
```

We then went over the while loop and its functions:

```
while(condition)
{
    // Put code here
}
```

After that, you learned about a close relative of the while loop called the do...while loop; it has the following format:

```
do
{
    // Put code here
}while(condition);
```

Next, you needed to learn about different ways to communicate with sensors and other peripherals, so we discussed the digitalRead() and digitalWrite() functions, which follow:

```
digitalRead();
digitalWrite(pin,state);
```

We then discussed communicating with the analog pins on the Arduino. The analog pins use these commands:

```
analogRead();
analogWrite(pin,value);
```

After learning about the different ways to communicate with sensors, we needed a way to communicate with serial communication. Here are the commands for serial communication:

```
Serial.begin(baud);
Serial.println(value);
Serial.read();
Serial.write(value);
Serial.available();
Serial.end();
```

We also discussed the SerialEvent function and how it can be used to trigger code based off of data received by the serial port. Finally, you learned a little about the TinyGPS++ library that will be used throughout this book.

Summary

In this chapter, you learned about the Arduino language. Specifically, you learned how to get your programs set up and how to use conditional statements, the differences of timers and delays, and how to utilize a finite-state machine and loops to refine them. You also learned how to communicate with different types of hardware pins using digital, analog, and serial communication. Finally, we discussed the TinyGPS++ library and its use. In the next chapter, we will be switching gears from the Arduino to 3D Modeling using Fusion 360.

CHAPTER 3

Modeling with Fusion 360

Here we go!!! Now we will learn about 3D CAD; I will first introduce a few different pieces of software that you can use to create 3D objects that can then be sent to your 3D printer. The 3D CAD software used in this book will be Fusion 360; this is a very powerful piece of software that will allow you to make pretty much anything you can think of. After going over some of the basics of Fusion 360, such as menus, how to navigate around a model, and so on, we will go through a project that will have you make your first 3D object from sketch to a 3D model; this will include a section on how to constrain your model which will also help when using the parametric paradigm. We will be using the parametric 3D Modeling paradigm throughout this book, which will allow us to make quick changes to our 3D model by adjusting sketches or features of the model. Here are a couple more examples of other 3D CAD software used in the industry:

> Solidworks: This is probably the most used industrial 3D CAD software on the market. One of the main reasons it is not used in this book is because it can be a bit pricey; that is not to say it is not worth the price; I just want to make sure all the readers of this book can utilize 3D Modeling without breaking the bank.

© Harold Timmis 2021
H. Timmis, *Practical Arduino Engineering*, https://doi.org/10.1007/978-1-4842-6852-0_3

DesignSpark Mechanical: This software is specifically made for 3D printing; it includes a lot of nice features and is also free to use. It uses more of a direct modeling approach as opposed to the parametric 3D Modeling paradigm. DesignSpark Mechanical is a good piece of software, but it does not have the number of features that Fusion 360 has with the same price tag.

Onshape: This is another powerful piece of 3D CAD software; it is also free to use, but it is a web browser program which means you need to be connected to the Internet to use it. Also, if you want to store your files locally, you must pay.

There are many other pieces of software out there that will allow you to create 3D objects and then save them as STL files (see Chapter 4).

Installing and Setting Up Fusion 360

First things first, we need to download and install Fusion 360; this is an easy process and works just like any other program you would install on your PC other than the fact that you need to create an Autodesk account, which is still pretty straightforward. So, let's get started.

Download Fusion 360

Now we can go ahead and download Fusion 360 from this URL: *www. autodesk.com/products/fusion-360*. Let's start by creating an account. Click the "SIGN IN" button at the top-right corner of the screen; a drop-down menu will display; click the "Sign In" portion of the drop-down menu. See Figures 3-1 and 3-2.

Figure 3-1.   *Click the SIGN IN link*

Figure 3-2.   *SIGN IN drop-down menu*

Next, click the "CREATE ACCOUNT" hyperlink under the email address text box, or if you think you have an account, type it in and click "NEXT." If you have an account, great! Move to Figure 3-5. Otherwise, see Figure 3-3.

Figure 3-3. *Autodesk login screen*

Now you will need to supply a few things: your first and last name, email address, and the password you want to use. After you add the previous data, make sure you read the Privacy Statement and click the "I Agree" checkbox. See Figure 3-4.

Figure 3-4. *Click the "CREATE ACCOUNT" button*

After that, click the "CREATE ACCOUNT" button. This will then send you an email asking you to verify your account; click the "VERIFY EMAIL" button in the email you received from Autodesk, which will bring you back to Autodesk and tell you whether you were successful or not.

Alright! Now that you have an account, you can download Fusion 360. Go back to this URL: www.autodesk.com/products/fusion-360; you should already be signed in, but if you are not, go ahead and sign in to your account. Now go ahead and click the "FREE TRIAL" button, and it will bring you to a new site (Figure 3-6). Click the "NON-COMMERCIAL USE" button, and again you will go to a new page. You should be able to click the "Get started" button. This will bring you to a new page and start downloading the client that will be used to download and then install Fusion 360. See Figures 3-5, 3-6, and 3-7.

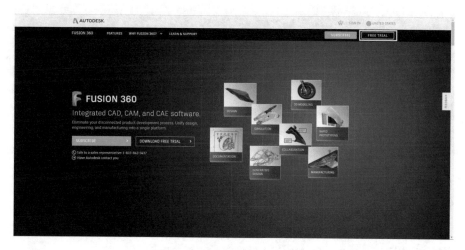

Figure 3-5. *Click the "FREE TRIAL" link*

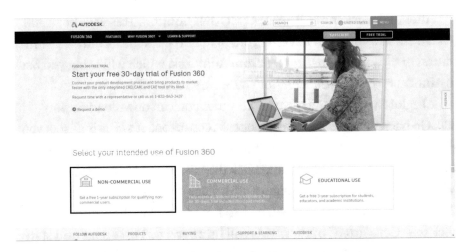

Figure 3-6. *Click the "NON-COMMERCIAL USE" link*

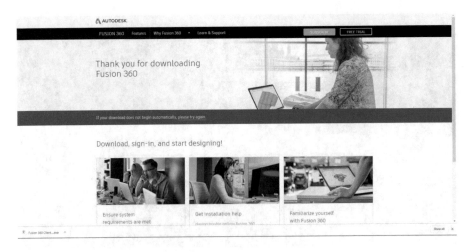

Figure 3-7. *Fusion 360 will begin to download*

Now that the download is completed, you will need to install Fusion 360 which will be discussed in the next section.

Installation Procedures for Fusion 360

Okay, so let's start by going to our downloads folder and double-click the "Fusion 360 Client Downloader." See Figures 3-8 and 3-9. Fusion 360 will begin to set up its files.

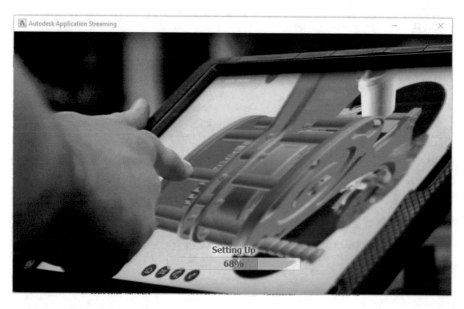

Figure 3-8. *Install Fusion 360*

Figure 3-9. *When Fusion 360 is done installing, sign in and the main screen will appear*

Once that is done, Fusion 360 should start up automatically. You may notice a lot of buttons and menus on the screen now; these will be discussed in the next section.

Getting to Know Fusion 360

Before we get into designing 3D objects in Fusion 360, it is important to know the various interfaces/controls that you will be using in order to manipulate your models. This section will go over several areas in Fusion 360; it won't be a complete reference to Fusion 360 as that could be and has been the talk of many books, but it will get you started, so that you can begin to work with Fusion 360.

Fusion 360's User Interface

Figure 3-10 will give you a basic understanding of the layout of Fusion 360. This may be useful later if you need a reference of the various menus, controls, and so on (see Figure 3-10).

Figure 3-10. *Layout of Fusion 360*

Let's first talk about the mouse gestures you will need in order to maneuver around in Fusion 360.

Right mouse click: This will pop up the quick menu in Fusion 360, which will allow to navigate through Fusion quicker, but for now we will use the regular menus to get around. See Figure 3-11.

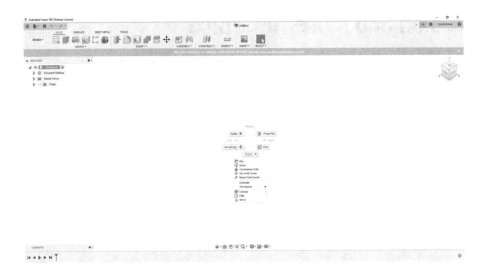

Figure 3-11. *Right mouse click*

Left mouse click from the top left to the bottom right: This will create a blue box around an object and select just the object that is completely in the window when the left mouse button is released. See Figures 3-12 and 3-13.

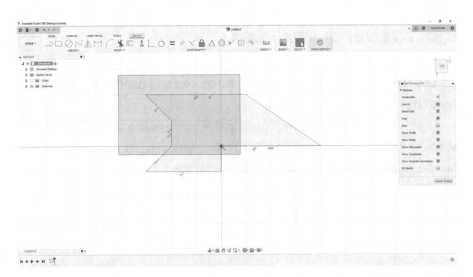

Figure 3-12. *Make selection with left mouse click and drag top left to bottom right*

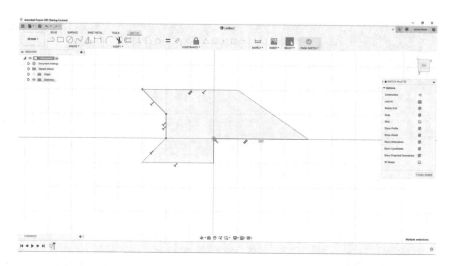

Figure 3-13. *Only lines completely in the window will be selected*

Left mouse click from the top right to the bottom left: This will create a dashed box around an object, but when the mouse button is released, it will select all objects within the box even if the object is only partially selected. See Figures 3-14 and 3-15.

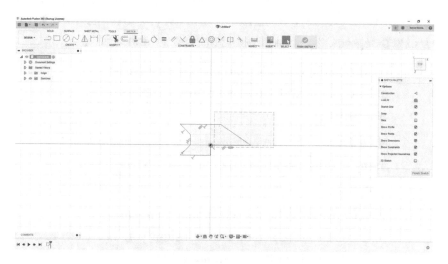

Figure 3-14. *Make selection with left mouse click and drag top right to bottom left*

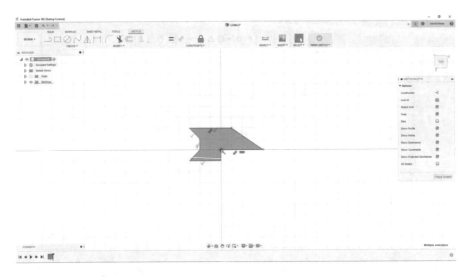

Figure 3-15. *Will select entire shape*

Center mouse button: Usually, the wheel on the mouse is also a center mouse button; when you click this in Fusion 360, you can pan the object. This will be denoted by this ✥ pointer image.

Center mouse button + Shift: Holding down the center mouse button while also holding down the Shift key will allow you to rotate the field of view in 360 degrees. It will be denoted by this ⊕ mouse pointer.

> Mouse roller: Use this to zoom in and out of an object. Roll forward to zoom in and roll backward to zoom out.

> Now that that is over, we can start to talk about the many menus and icons on the Fusion 360. Let's start with the ViewCube.

> ViewCube: This visual aid is located in the top-right corner of the screen and will show you the current view of the object or plane; you can select Top, Bottom, Front, Back, Right, and Left, and the

view will switch immediately to the selected view. Also, you will see arrows that allow you to turn the object clockwise or counterclockwise. Then there is a Home button that will take you to the Top-Front-Right corner of the object or plane. Finally, there is a drop-down menu that will allow you to change how you see your objects, and you can also set a new home for the 3D object. See Figure 3-16.

Figure 3-16. *ViewCube*

Browser: This menu will allow you to create a new component which will have sketches and bodies that can be manipulated. Also, the planes are located here under the Origin submenu and if selected will display a demo of the plane. The final thing I want to say about the Browser menu is that under the Document Settings submenu, you will find the Units control which will allow you to switch from inches to millimeters or vice versa. This will be used throughout this book, so you will get plenty of practice with navigating its options. See Figure 3-17.

Figure 3-17. *Browser*

Design History Bar: This is very important when it comes to parametric 3D Modeling as this will allow you to move back and forth from one feature to the next. For example, say you want to modify a sketch at the very beginning of a component and you also want the features that you have done to also apply to these new dimensions; you would use the Design History Bar to move back to that sketch, modify the dimensions needed, and then move the bar back to the last feature, and that's it! The model will use those new dimensions and apply all the features you have already created. You can also move features and sketches around and delete features as needed. See Figure 3-18.

Figure 3-18. *Design History Bar*

Navigation Bar: Instead of using the mouse, you can use this menu to select ways to move around a component or sketch. The selections are

Orbit: Allows you to rotate around a component

Look At: Select a face or sketch, and the view will be switched to that face.

Pan: When this is selected, hold the left mouse button and move the mouse to view an object in the left, right, up, and down directions.

Zoom: When selected, zooms in and out of a component.

Zoom Window: This will allow you to zoom in to a region of a component or sketch.

Display Settings: This allows you to change effects, environment, visual style, object visibility, and so on; the most used feature here is the visual style which will allow you to change to a wireframe to see hard-to-see areas of a component.

Grid and Snaps: Allows you to change where components or sketches snap to; initially, this is set to 10mm, which is what we will use for this book.

Viewports: This will allow you to see a component from multiple angles.

Fusion 360 Sketch Tools

Now we can get down to the nitty-gritty of parametric design. By using sketches and sketch features, we can create a 2D model that can be extruded, revolved, loft, and so on to create a 3D object, so that later on if we need to make changes to the model, we only need to change the dimensions on the sketch. For now, we will go over the basics and move to more sophisticated tools in later chapters.

All these functions are under the "CREATE" tab:

Create Sketch: This is the first thing you will do after making/naming components needed for the model. This will put you into sketch mode automatically, and the only thing you need to do to begin drawing is to select a plane.

Line: This allows you to create a line on the plane you selected; just left-click where you want the line to start and then left-click again to select where you want the line to end. Later, we will use the dimensioning tool to constrain our sketches. Equally important to note is that there are two types of line; one is a regular line, and the other is a construction line. A construction line will not be a part of your overall sketch, and because of that when you extrude your sketch, the dimensions of

the construction lines will not be included. To turn a
line into a construction line, select the line and press
the "x" key on your keyboard. See Figure 3-19 for an
example of a normal line and a construction line.

Figure 3-19. *Normal and construction lines*

Rectangle: There are a few types of rectangles, and
each one has its benefits in certain situations; we
will be going over these different benefits later
in this book. For now, it is important to know the
center rectangle which will create a rectangle from
the inside out. The other rectangle is the two-point
rectangle; this will allow you to select two points
in a plane that will create a length and width for a
rectangle.

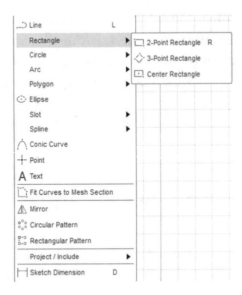

Circle: There are several options here; for the most part, we will stick with the center diameter circle which, just like the center rectangle, will create a circle from the inside out.

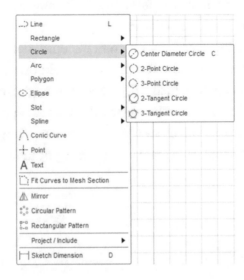

Arc: Mainly, we will be using the three-point arc which will create an arc based on three individual points.

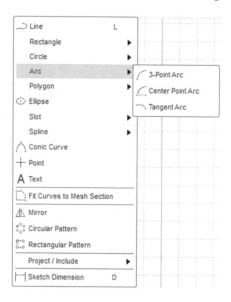

Polygon: Create a specific number of sides sketch, for example, a hexagon.

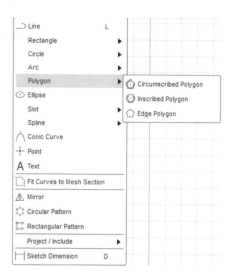

Text: This is a great feature for adding text sketches onto your models, which just recently became available.

Mirror: This is a great time savings tool; it allows you to duplicate lines from one side of a centerline to the other side, so you will only need to create half a sketch if the sketch is symmetric.

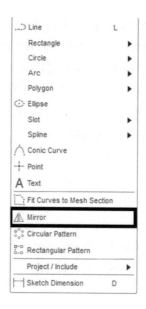

All these functions are found under the "MODIFY" tab:

Fillet: This will create an arc with a specific radius. All you must do is select two coincident lines like a corner of a rectangle.

Trim: This is a very useful tool when you need to clean up your sketch by trimming lines that are not needed, but be careful if those lines are used to constrain your sketch; you might be better off making them a construction line.

Offset: To use this feature, select the outline/lines you want to offset and then put in the dimensions needed; you should then see a demo of what to expect when you accept the offset. This is a great time saver if you need to, for example, make a small border around a sketch or object.

This should be enough to get started with as we will be using most of these functions throughout this book, but don't be discouraged; I will be introducing more features in later projects. This is just a good set of features to start with.

Fusion 360 3D Tools

Alright, now once you finish creating your sketch, you will need tools to make a 2D image a 3D object. This can be done several ways in Fusion 360; we will discuss a few of them in this section, as well as a few features that will allow you to modify a 3D object without using the sketch.

All these functions are found under the "CREATE" section in the "SOLID" tab:

New Component: This is used when you first start to make your model. You should separate your 3D project into several components if it is required, which most of the time it is. Also, give the component a well-defined name, so that you know what that component's 3D model is; you do this by going to the Browser menu on Fusion 360 (see the "Getting to Know Fusion 360" section) and double-clicking the new component and renaming it.

Extrude: Probably the most used method of going from a 2D sketch to a 3D object. This will allow you to extrude a sketch to a desired height. There are also other settings here that will allow you to extrude to another 3D object surface; also, if you want to make a hole, you can extrude into a 3D object, and it will cut out material instead of adding it.

Revolve: This will allow you to select a sketch and revolve it around an axis. Very useful when you want to make a cylindrical object.

Sweep: Create a 3D object by selecting a sketch and a path (a line) for the sketch to follow.

Loft: Create a 3D object by selecting multiple
sketches on multiple planes; this will then create a
3D object with those shapes as profile.

Rectangular Pattern: Just like in the sketch mode,
you can create patterns that will allow you to quickly
replicate 3D objects; this also works for holes. This
function creates a rectangular pattern. You can also

choose how many objects are replicated, which axis to create the sketches on, and what type of pattern to create.

Circular Pattern: Just like in the sketch mode, you can create patterns that will allow you to quickly replicate 3D objects; this also works for holes. This function creates a circular pattern. You can also choose how many objects are replicated, which axis to revolve around, and what type of pattern to create.

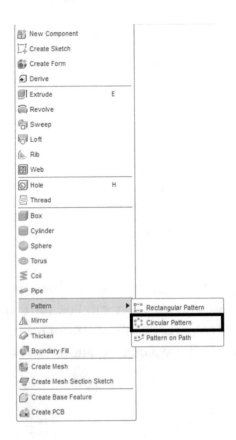

All these functions are found under the "MODIFY" section in the "SOLID" tab:

> Press Pull: This will allow you to extend a face or retract a face. Useful if you need to make a quick modification to a face.

> Fillet: Adds a radius to one or more edges. This can be used to strengthen corners by adding a bit more material between two faces.

Chamfer: Will create a bevel on one or more edges. This can be used just like the fillet; it will create an angled feature as opposed to a round feature.

Shell: This tool is very useful if you need to make a hollow object. All you need to do is select the face to shell and then specify the inside thickness and voila! You have a hollow object.

Combine: If you need to merge two or more objects, this tool will allow you to do that.

Well, I know this might all seem like a lot, but with a little practice and patience, you will be able to create a lot of different models even with this short list of functions. Next up! I will explain a few tools that you can use to measure and review your models.

Fusion 360 Tools

There are a lot of useful functions in the Tools tab; they can be used for many things like checking out a section of a model or measuring distances between two or more points. You will want to get used to using these as it will be important later when you are making your own models or working on someone else's model. Here is a short list of Fusion 360 tools:

All these functions are found under the "INSPECT" section in the "TOOLS" tab:

Measure: Measure the distance, angle, and area of two points.

Section Analysis: Allows you to see your object in a cutaway view; you can move the arrow to view different areas of an object. For example, say you have a hollow box and you want to make sure there are no other structures within the hollow box; you can use this feature to look inside the box and verify no other structures are in it.

Alright, that was short and right to the point. There are many other tools in this menu, but for starters these are the key tools, so I wanted to go over them first. The final portion of this section will go over how to import various files into Fusion 360.

Importing Files

Sometimes, you may need to import a STEP file, a DXF file, or maybe even an SVG file. Here are some functions that will help make adding these files possible:

To add a STEP file to your project:

1. Go to the Data Panel by clicking the Data Panel button at the top left of the screen. See Figure 3-20.

Figure 3-20. *Select Data Panel*

2. Select New Project. See Figure 3-21.

Figure 3-21. *Select New Project*

3. Name the project.

4. Click the "Upload" button. See Figure 3-22.

Figure 3-22. *Select Upload*

5. A pop-up window will appear, and you can drag and drop or select the STEP file you want to use in this project. See Figure 3-23.

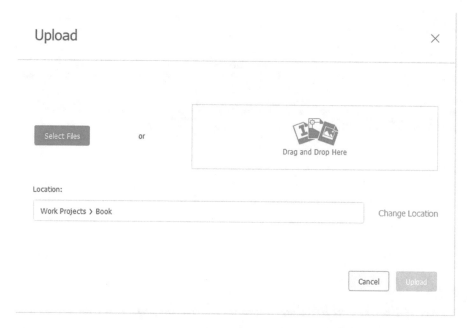

Figure 3-23. *Drag and drop the STEP file or browse to the file*

6. Click the Upload button, and you will see this screen
which will tell you the progress of your import.
When the STEP file is finished, click the "Close"
button. See Figure 3-24.

Figure 3-24. *When finished, click the Close button*

To insert a DXF file:

1. Go to the "SOLID" tab in Fusion 360. See Figure 3-25.

Figure 3-25. *Go to the "SOLID" tab*

2. Go to the "INSERT" drop-down menu. See Figure 3-26.

Figure 3-26. *Click the "INSERT" drop-down menu*

3. Select the "Insert DXF" option. See Figure 3-27.

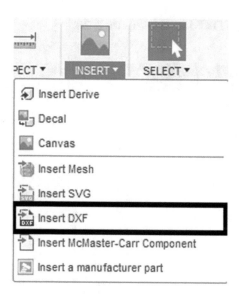

Figure 3-27. *Click the "Insert DXF" button*

4. Select the plane/sketch that you want the DXF image to be placed on to. See Figure 3-28.

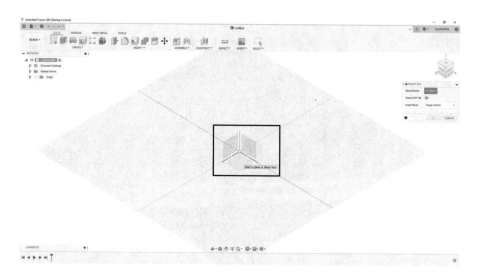

Figure 3-28. *Select the plane that the DXF will display on*

5.   Select the DXF file. See Figure 3-29.

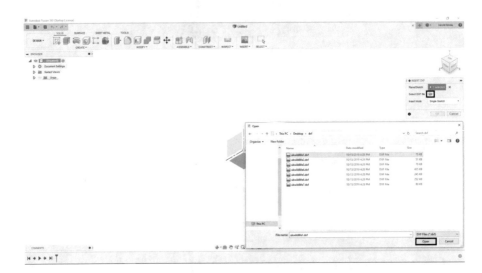

Figure 3-29. *Select the DXF file from your computer*

6.   Then click the "OK" button. See Figure 3-30.

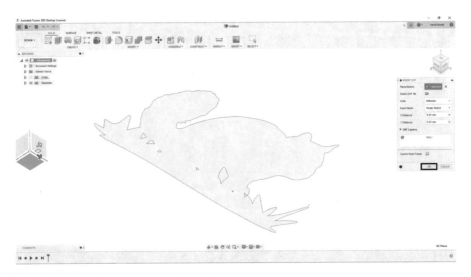

Figure 3-30. *Click the "OK" button*

7. You should now see your DXF file on the plane you chose earlier. See Figure 3-31.

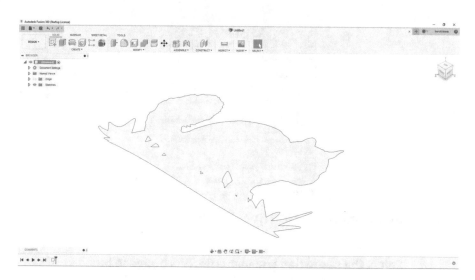

Figure 3-31. *DXF is loaded into Fusion 360*

To insert an SVG file:

1. Go to the "SOLID" tab in Fusion 360. See Figure 3-32.

Figure 3-32. *Go to the "SOLID" tab*

2. Go to the "INSERT" drop-down menu. See Figure 3-33.

Figure 3-33. *Click the "INSERT" drop-down menu*

3.   Select the "Insert SVG" option. See Figure 3-34.

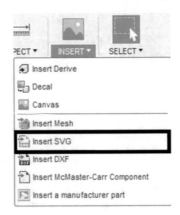

Figure 3-34. *Click the "Insert SVG" button*

4.   Select the plane that you want the SVG image to be placed on to. See Figure 3-35.

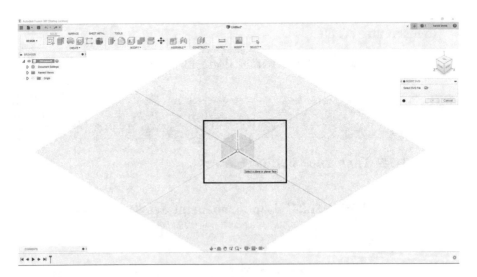

Figure 3-35. *Select plane*

5.   Select the SVG file. See Figure 3-36.

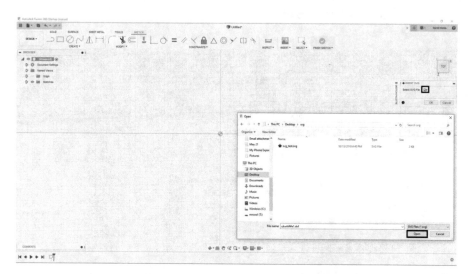

Figure 3-36. *Select the SVG file from your computer*

6.   Then click the "OK" button. See Figure 3-37.

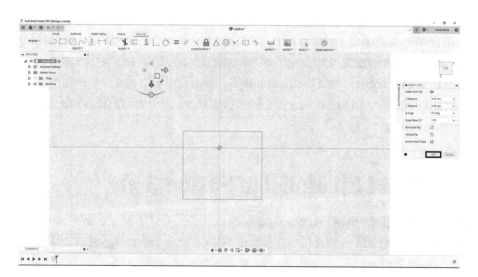

Figure 3-37. *SVG will be added to Fusion 360*

7.   You should now see your SVG file on the plane you
     chose earlier. See Figure 3-38.

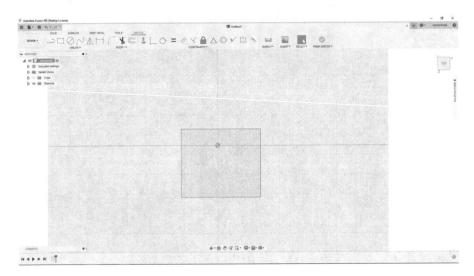

Figure 3-38. *SVG is ready to be extruded*

Alright, now that you have a little understanding of Fusion 360, you
can move on to the exciting part, making your first 3D model. After reading
through this chapter, you may feel you are not ready to make a model yet,
but don't worry; it won't be that complicated, and you can always look
back if you need to know where a function is, so without further ado let's
get modeling!

Your First 3D Model in Fusion 360

Alright, let's get started with a simple 3D model, and then we will move to a
more complex 3D model (don't worry; it won't be too complex). Go ahead
and open Fusion 360 so we can create our first sketch.

Creating a Sketch

1. Save this project as "Cube" by pressing Ctrl-S.

2. Click the "Create Sketch" icon under the "SOLID"
    tab. See Figure 3-39.

Figure 3-39. *Left-click "CREATE SKETCH"*

3. Select a plane to draw your sketch on. In this
    example, I chose the XZ plane. See Figure 3-40.

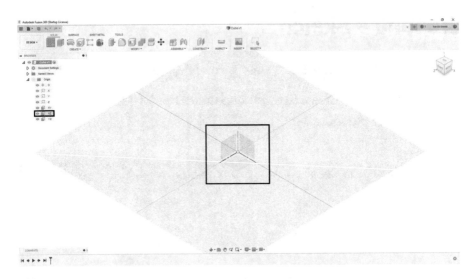

Figure 3-40. *Select plane from the grid or the Browser menu*

4. Now select the Rectangle tool under the "SKETCH" tab. See Figure 3-41.

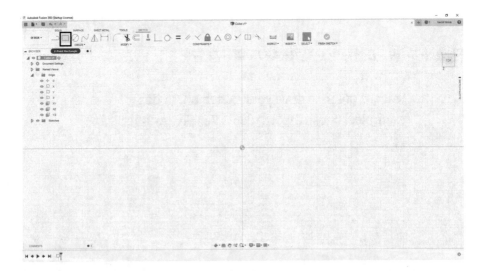

Figure 3-41. *Select a two-point rectangle from the "SKETCH" tab*

5. Put a rectangle anywhere on the grid; don't worry
    about the dimensions yet. Press "Enter" when you
    are finished. See Figure 3-42.

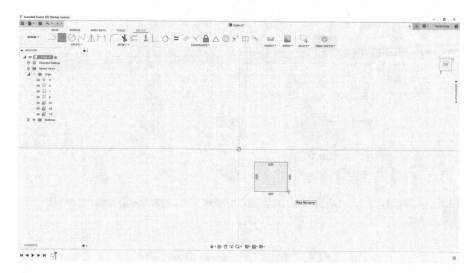

Figure 3-42. *Add a rectangle to the grid*

Now I want to give this next part a bit of context. You may notice
that the square's lines are all blue; blue lines mean that the sides are
not constrained, which can be a problem if you are trying to make
a maintainable 3D model. You can constrain sketches using several
different methods, for example, by defining the square's dimensions and
referencing the origin. Let's give that a try and see what happens.

6. Click a single point of your sketch and the origin.
    See Figure 3-43.

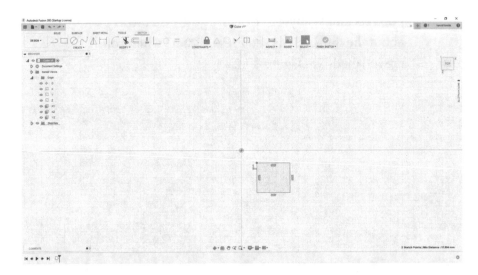

Figure 3-43. *Left-click a single point on the rectangle and a point on the origin*

7. Go to the "CONSTRAINTS" menu under the "SKETCH" tab. See Figure 3-44.

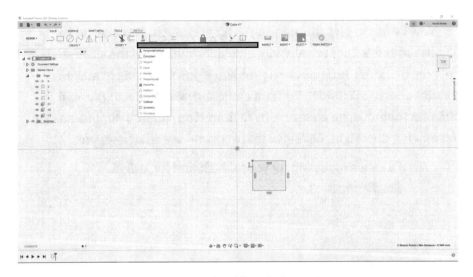

Figure 3-44. *Select the "CONSTRAINT" drop-down menu*

8. Select the "Coincident" selection, then select the
    origin, and you will notice that your square has
    moved to the origin and two of the four sides of your
    square have turned black which indicates those
    sides are now constrained. See Figure 3-45.

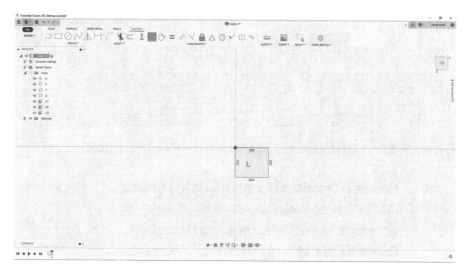

Figure 3-45. *Select Coincident from the drop-down menu*

9. Now let's constrain the other two sides. Press the
    "D" key. Select one of the blue sides and enter
    the value 5. (I am using millimeters; this can be
    switched in the Browser menu under Document
    Setting ➤ Units). Now three sides are constrained.
    See Figure 3-46.

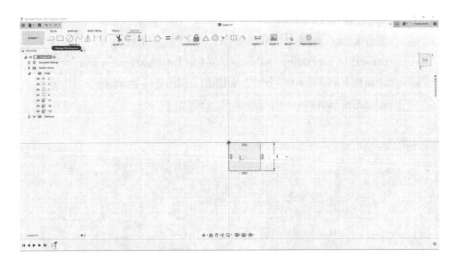

Figure 3-46. *Add dimensions for one side of the rectangle*

10. Finally, let's constrain the last side by pressing the "D" key and selecting the final blue side and entering a 5 into the text box. See Figure 3-47. Congratulations! Your sketch is fully constrained now.

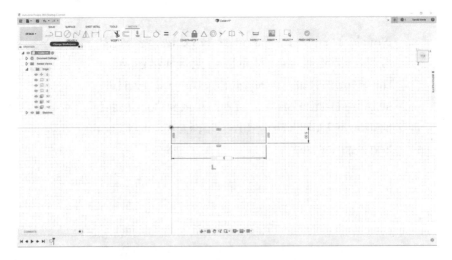

Figure 3-47. *Add dimensions to the last side of the rectangle*

11. Select the "FINISH SKETCH" button to get out of
     sketch mode. See Figure 3-48.

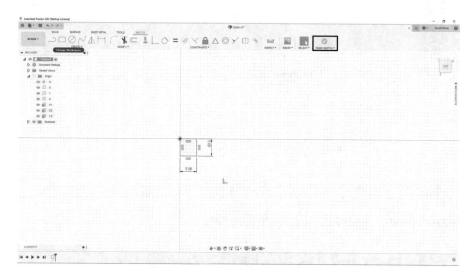

Figure 3-48. *Click "FINISH SKETCH"*

Okay, now that the sketch is done, you can move on to the next part
which will have you create a 3D model from the sketch you just completed.

Using the Extrude Function

1. Select the "Extrude" function from the "SOLID" tab.
    See Figure 3-49.

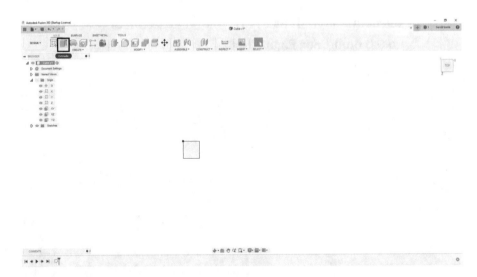

Figure 3-49. *Select the Extrude function*

2. The "Extrude" function has a lot of options, but for now let's just move to the distance text box and enter "5" and press enter. See Figure 3-50.

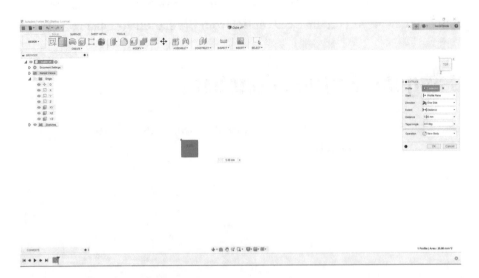

Figure 3-50. *Extrude out 5mm*

3. You can get a better angle on the 3D model by pressing the Shift key and holding down your mouse's center button and moving the mouse toward your computer screen. You could also select the "Home" button next to the ViewCube. See Figure 3-51.

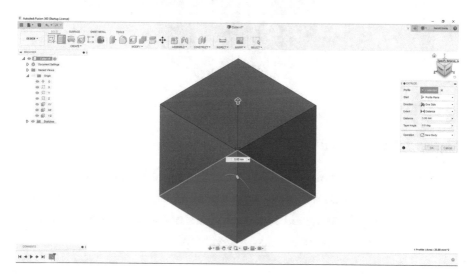

Figure 3-51. *Select "HOME" on ViewCube*

4. If everything looks fine, press the Enter key or click the "OK" button under the "EXTRUDE" menu. See Figure 3-52.

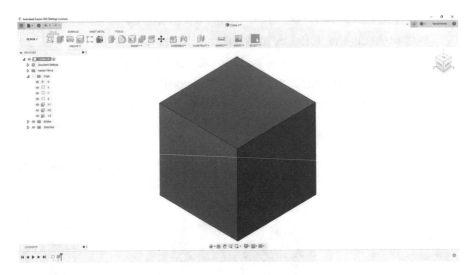

Figure 3-52. *Final cube*

Alright! That was your first 3D model. Great job! Now I want to move on to a bit of a more complex example that will be used in the following chapter. Also, it will be a good segue into parametric 3D Modeling as we will use the "Cube" project to make a keychain.

Parametric Modeling in Fusion 360

1. Let's start by opening our Cube project. Go to the Data Panel ➤ My Recent Data; the Cube project should be the most recent project. See Figure 3-53.

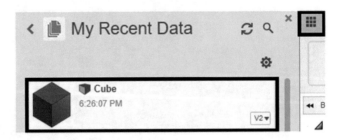

Figure 3-53. *Go back to the Cube project*

2. Double-click the Cube project and close the Data Panel.

3. Go to the Browser menu and go to the folder Sketches and double-click Sketch1. This will take you to the Sketch view, and you can start to modify your sketch. See Figure 3-54.

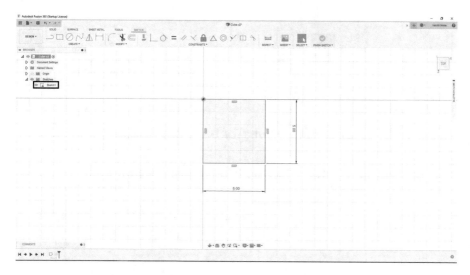

Figure 3-54. *Select Sketch1*

4. We want to change this square into a rectangle; let's change (double left-click) the X axis dimension to 20mm and the Z dimension to 10mm. To do this, press the "D" key and select the X axis dimension and type in 20mm, then change the Z dimension to 10mm. Press "Enter" when you are finished. See Figure 3-55.

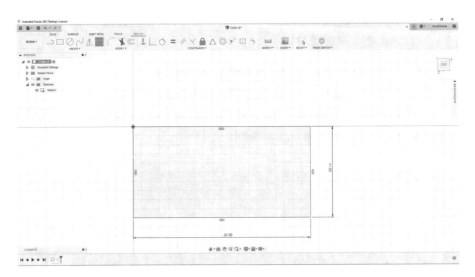

Figure 3-55. *Change dimensions for the X and Z axis*

5.   Click the "FINISH SKETCH" button. See Figure 3-56.

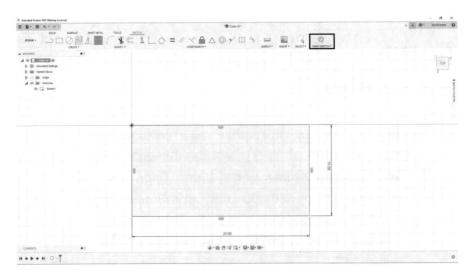

Figure 3-56. *Click the "FINISH SKETCH" button*

6. You will notice that your 3D model has changed to a shape that is 10mm x 20mm x 5mm. This is the power of parametric 3D Modeling; it allows you to make quick changes to your sketch and then applies these dimensions through the rest of the history of the 3D object.

7. Now double-click the Extrude1 icon in the History Bar at the bottom of the screen. See Figure 3-57.

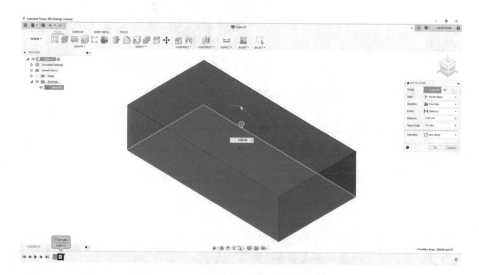

Figure 3-57. *Select the Extrude1 in the Design History Bar*

8. Edit this to be 3mm instead of 5mm in the Distance text box and press enter. See Figure 3-58.

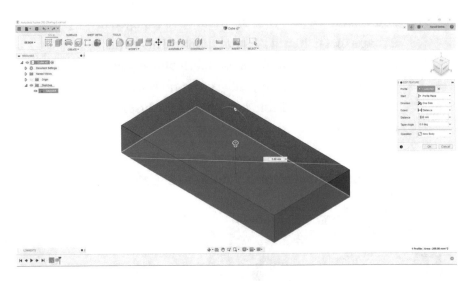

Figure 3-58. *Extrude only 3mm*

9. Click the "Create Sketch" button at the top left under
    the "SOLID" tab.

10. Select the top of the 3D object, and this will put you
    into sketch mode. See Figure 3-59.

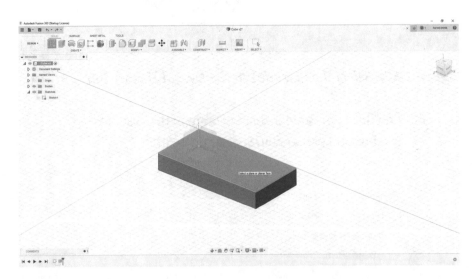

Figure 3-59. *Select the top of the 3D object*

11.   Under the Create menu, select the Offset function
and click the edge of the 3D object. See Figure 3-60.

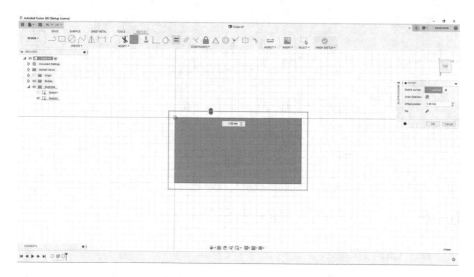

Figure 3-60.   *Select the Offset function*

12.   Notice that there is now a box around your 3D
object. To change this, put –1.00mm into the Offset
position text box, or just click the "Flip image." Press
"Enter" when you are finished. See Figure 3-61.

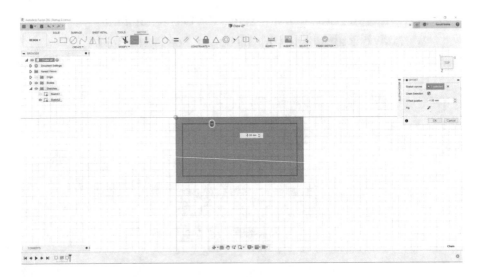

Figure 3-61. *Edit the dimension to –1mm*

13. Click OK.

14. Now select the Center Diameter Circle by going
here: SKETCH ➤ CREATE ➤ Circle ➤ Center
Diameter Circle, or just press the "C" key. See
Figure 3-62.

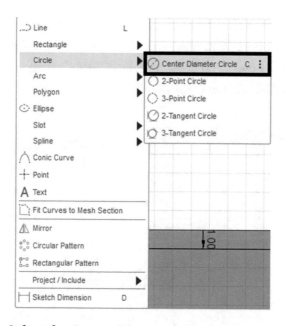

Figure 3-62. *Select the Center Diameter Circle*

15. Place a circle on the top face, just like the offset.
    See Figure 3-63.

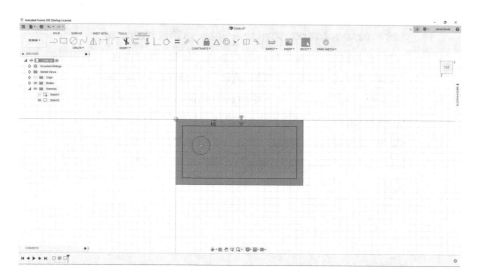

Figure 3-63. *Place a circle on the grid*

16. Now you will notice the circle is not constrained;
    let's fix this. First, press the "D" key and select the
    circle's edge; type in 3mm. Press "Enter" when you
    are finished. See Figure 3-64.

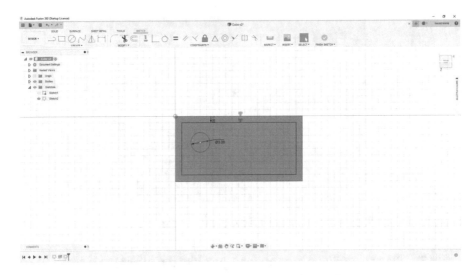

Figure 3-64. Add a dimension to the circle (3mm)

17. Let's make some construction lines, so that we know
    where the center of this rectangle is. First, select the
    Line function from the "CREATE" menu or press the
    "L" key, and place a line from one side of the rectangle
    to the other side. You will see this symbol when you
    have selected the center for an edge; once you see that,
    left-click and move to the other side and left-click
    again. See Figure 3-65.

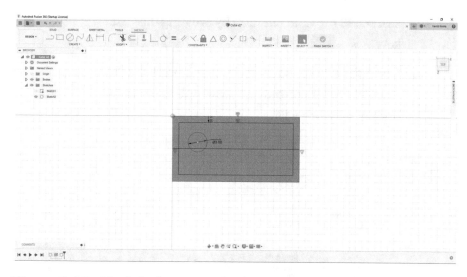

Figure 3-65. *Find the horizontal center of the rectangle*

18. Do the same for the top and bottom of the sketch.
    See Figure 3-66.

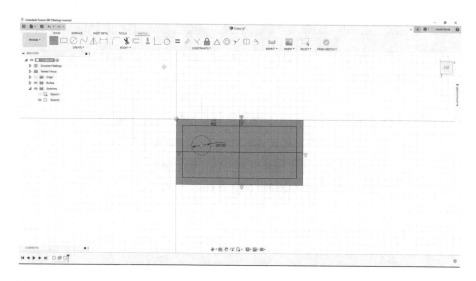

Figure 3-66. *Find the vertical center of the rectangle*

19. Exit out of the Line function by pressing the "Esc" key.

20. Select the two lines you created and press the "x" key. This will make both of those lines construction lines. See Figure 3-67.

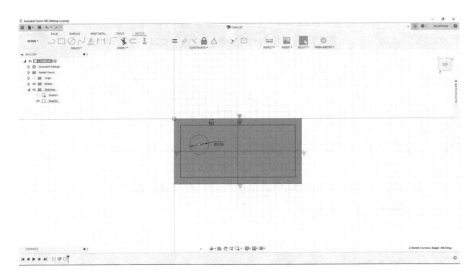

Figure 3-67. *Make both the horizontal and vertical center lines construction lines*

21. Now while pressing the "Ctrl" key, select the center of the circle and the horizontal construction line; then select the coincident constraint from the "CONSTRAINTS" menu. See Figure 3-68.

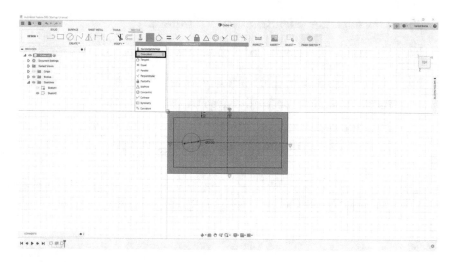

Figure 3-68. *Constrain the circle to the horizontal center line*

22. Next, press the "D" key and select from the center
     of the circle to the edge of the left side of the vertical
     offset and put 3mm into the text field and press
     enter. See Figure 3-69.

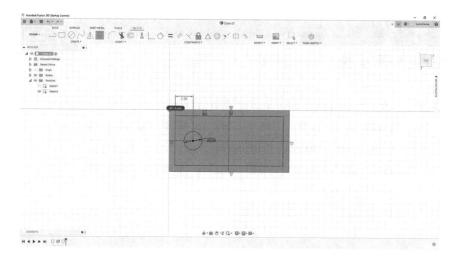

Figure 3-69. *Add the dimension from the left offset to the center of the*
circle to 3mm

23. Now click the "FINISH SKETCH" button.

24. Make sure you press Ctrl-S to save your progress.

25. Now click the Extrude button on the "CREATE" menu and click the border area we created with the Offset function; extrude the border 1mm. Press "Enter" when you are finished. See Figure 3-70.

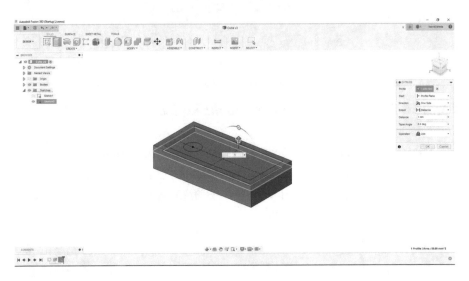

Figure 3-70. *Extrude the border to 1mm*

26. Once you press the "Enter" key, the sketch goes away; to bring the sketch back up, all you need to do is go to the Browser menu and go to Sketches and click this button on Sketch2 to view the sketch. See Figure 3-71.

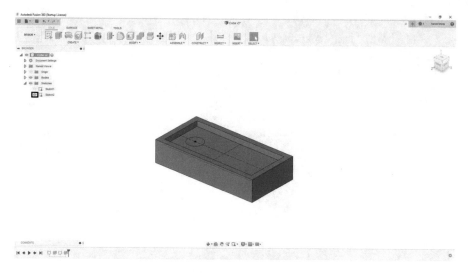

Figure 3-71. *Show Sketch using the Browser menu*

27. Next, select the circle and click the Extrude button. This will be a bit different as you are going to create a hole. Rotate the 3D object so you can see the bottom of the 3D object and left-click the bottom of the 3D object and click OK; this will create a hole that is 3mm in diameter. Press "Enter" when you are finished. See Figure 3-72.

Figure 3-72. *Extrude the circle to the bottom face*

28. You can hide your sketch again by clicking the same icon shown in step 26.

29. Now to make this keychain template more appealing, let's add a fillet to one side. Using the Design History Bar, move the slider right after the Sketch1. See Figure 3-73.

Figure 3-73. *Go to Sketch1 in the Design History Bar*

30. Double-click the Sketch1 icon in the Design History Bar, and you will be able to edit this sketch. See Figure 3-74.

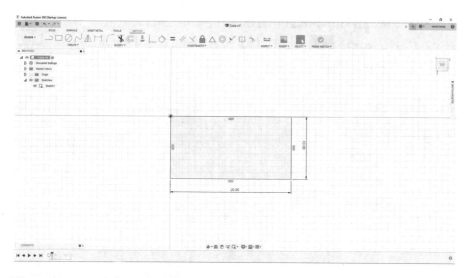

Figure 3-74. *Select Sketch1*

31.   Add a fillet by going to the "MODIFY" tab and
       clicking the Fillet button. See Figure 3-75.

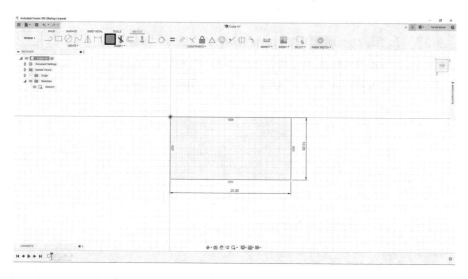

Figure 3-75. *Add fillet*

32.   Click the top horizontal line, then the left vertical line, and finally the bottom horizontal line. See Figure 3-76.

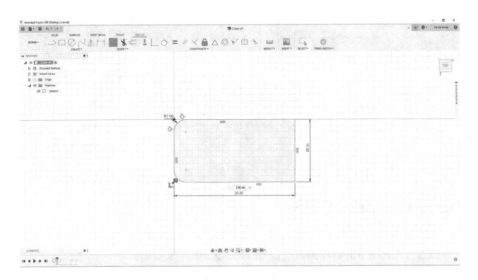

Figure 3-76. *Select left-side outlines*

33.   In the text box, put 2mm and press enter (don't mind the warning that you may get when you do this). Press "Enter" when you are finished. See Figure 3-77.

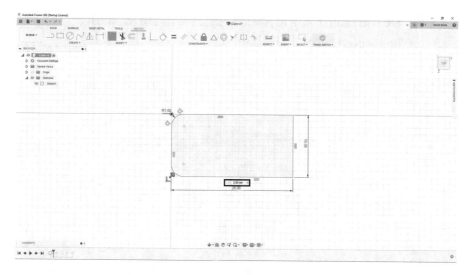

Figure 3-77. *2mm fillets*

34. Click the "FINISH SKETCH" button.

35. Now drag the Design History Bar slider to the right after Sketch2 and double-click the Sketch2 icon in the Design History Bar. See Figure 3-78.

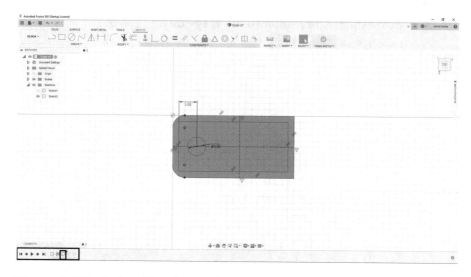

Figure 3-78. *Select Sketch2 in the Design History Bar*

36.   Do the same thing to Sketch2 that we did to Sketch1.
      See Figure 3-79.

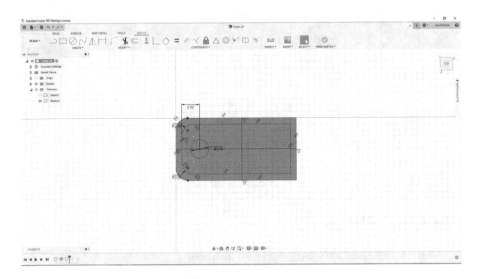

Figure 3-79. *Add 2mm fillets*

37.   Click the "FINISH SKETCH" button.

38.   Move the History slider to the very end and see the
      result! See Figure 3-80.

39.   Make sure you save the project (Ctrl-S).

Figure 3-80. *Move the Design History Bar slider all the way to the right*

So, with parametric 3D Modeling, we were able to change our simple cube into a keychain template very quickly and with only a few modifications to the original model.

Now we have a blank keychain template that we can use as an example in the next chapter to 3D print. We will also add an image to this keychain in that chapter.

Summary

Great job! You now have a better understanding of Fusion 360. This chapter was a bit long, but there was a ton of material to cover. Here is a brief list of what was covered in this chapter; these items will be important moving forward as we will be doing 3D Modeling in several chapters:

- Creating a user account for Autodesk

- Downloading and installing Fusion 360

- Understanding the Fusion 360 user interface

- Fusion 360 sketch tools

  - Create Sketch

  - Line

  - Rectangle

  - Circle

- Fusion 360 3D tools

  - New Component

  - Extrude

  - Revolve

  - Sweep

  - Loft

- Fusion 360 tools

  - Measure

- Importing files into Fusion 360

  - STEP, DXF, SVG

- Creating a sketch

- Extruding a sketch

- Parametric 3D Modeling in Fusion 360

CHAPTER 4

3D Printing

Alright! It is now time to learn a bit about a very cool engineering tool called a 3D printer. We will start with a look at what 3D printing is and what type of 3D printing this book will focus on, which is Fused Filament Fabrication (FFF). After that, we will investigate the tools needed by anyone who wants to use a 3D printer. Then I will discuss the various parts and upgrades a printer can have to allow for faster printing times, easy printing setup, and better print quality. Then we will discuss what a slicer is and the various slicers available on the market. Once we have all that knowledge, we can focus on troubleshooting common issues with 3D printers and prints. Finally, we will update and print the keychain we made in Chapter 3. This chapter will be filled with tons of information; you don't need to memorize it, but you can use this as a reference when using your 3D printer in the future.

What Is 3D Printing

Well, you can think of Fused Filament Fabrication as a hot glue gun with an XYZ table. The extruder will lay down plastic onto the build plate in the X and Y coordinates in a 2D fashion, but then when the first layer has completed, the Z axis will move up a predetermined amount, and another 2D layer will go on top of the previous 2D layer; this will continue until the model is completed, and a 3D object will be the final product. You can also

© Harold Timmis 2021
H. Timmis, *Practical Arduino Engineering*, https://doi.org/10.1007/978-1-4842-6852-0_4

use many types of 3D filament. This book will mainly focus on using PLA plastic as it is easy to get and very easy to use. The only real downside to PLA is it is not very heat resistant, so don't leave the parts in your car on a hot day. See Figure 4-1.

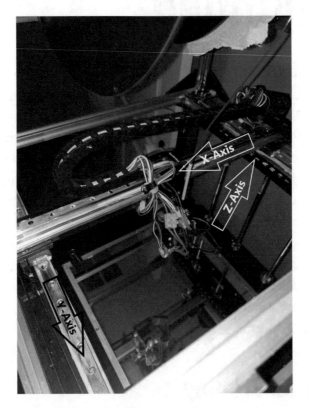

Figure 4-1. *FDM printer with its axes labeled*

Types of 3D Printers

There are many types of 3D printers, but I want to talk about two main types of 3D printing for hobbyists; they are FFF and SLA.

FFF (Fused Filament Fabrication): As stated earlier, this is a process that takes plastic filament and places molten plastic onto a build plate, and when it is finished with that layer, it then melts plastic onto the previous layer, and over time (sometimes hours or days) a completed 3D model is created. FFF printing is great for printing tools, fixtures, and toys, especially when real high resolution is not needed. Normally, you can print at 50 microns with a good FFF printer. See Figure 4-2.

Figure 4-2. Example of an FDM printer

SLA (Stereolithography): This is a process that includes a vat of photochemical (chemicals that harden with light) and a galvanometer. The galvanometer has a laser that uses two mirrors to move around the resin and hardens it over time. Then the Z moves up (like on an FDM printer), and the process starts all over again until you have a 3D model. The 3D model comes up out of the resin and will be printed upside down. An SLA printer is great at fit check assemblies, high-definition models, and anything with high amounts of detail. SLA printers have a very high resolution, usually around 10 microns. See Figure 4-3.

Figure 4-3. *Example of an SLA printer*

We will go into more depth of what is required to doing FFF printing, but for SLA printing I would suggest looking at Formlabs white paper on the subject at this web address: `https://formlabs.com/blog/ultimate-guide-to-stereolithography-sla-3d-printing/`.

For FFF printers, there are also a variety of filament feeding styles; they are direct drive (what this book will focus on) and Bowden style of feeding filament. Direct drive as its name states will push filament directly from the extruder to the cold break. Bowden extruder assemblies will normally be on the back side of the printer, and the cold break and hot end will be on the gantry; this is ideal for speed, but some filaments do not work well with this style of filament feeding. These are the main two types; there is also the Wade style extruder, but it is not used as often.

Now we can talk about the various tools you will need in order to 3D print successfully.

Tools of the Trade

On the journey of becoming a 3D printing guru, you will need many tools; some of the more common tools are as follows.

Needle-nose pliers: Great for removing support material and other excess of plastic the 3D model does not need. See Figure 4-4.

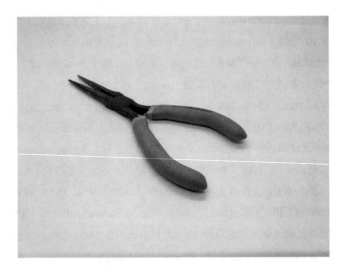

Figure 4-4. *Needle-nose pliers*

Paint spatula: Great for taking 3D models off the build plate. See Figure 4-5.

Figure 4-5. *Paint spatula*

Wire cutters: Again, these can help you take off support material. See Figure 4-6.

Figure 4-6. *Wire cutters*

Allen wrenches: These are a must as you will need to maintain your 3D printer which almost always use hex cap screws. See Figure 4-7.

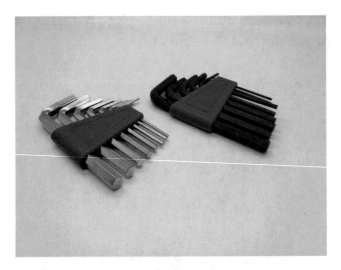

Figure 4-7. *Allen wrenches both SI and metric sets*

Tweezers: Great for cleaning plastic off the extruder's nozzle. See Figure 4-8.

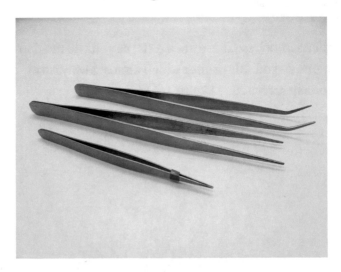

Figure 4-8. *Few types of tweezers*

X-Acto knife: This is a must-have tool when you are cleaning up 3D prints, but be careful. See Figure 4-9.

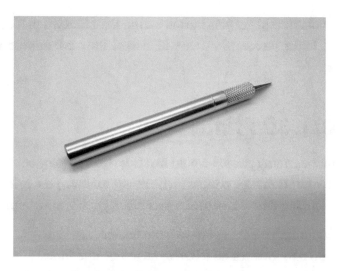

Figure 4-9. *X-Acto knife.* **BE CAREFUL**; *these are very sharp*

Calipers: This tool is used to measure the parts coming off the printer as well as debugging some common issues a printer might have. See Figure 4-10.

Figure 4-10. *Digital calipers*

These tools should get you started on the right foot when it comes to 3D printing. In the next section, we will discuss the most important parts of a 3D printer.

Parts of a 3D Printer

A 3D printer has many parts; I would like to go over the key components. These components make up most of the functionality of the printer; they are the hot end, cold break, extruder assembly, gantry, and control board.

> Hot end: This component has a heater cartridge and a thermistor attached to an aluminum block that has a nozzle at the bottom. This is where plastic is melted and placed on the build plate. Common issues with this include plastic seeping out of the top of the nozzle or at the top of the aluminum block because the nozzle or the block has not been tighten down. See Figure 4-11 for an example of a hot end.

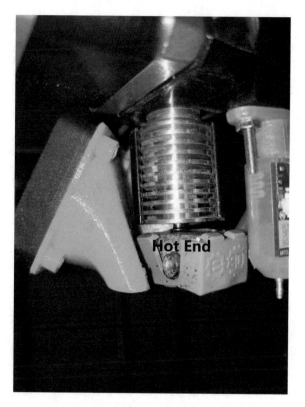

Figure 4-11. *Hot end with silicone cover*

Cold block: This part of the extruder allows pressure
to build up in the hot end, so you never run out
of plastic. It does this by acting as a heat sink and
drawing out the heat that may creep up from the
hot end. One key issue that you can run into is heat
creep; this is when heat from the hot end softens the
plastic too much in the cold block, and a jam occurs.
See Figure 4-12.

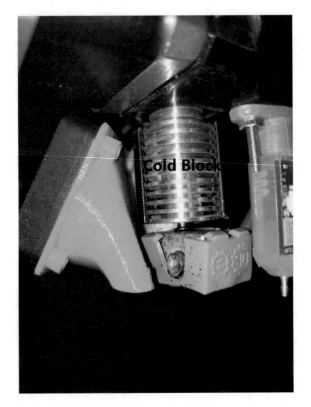

Figure 4-12. *Cold block*

Extruder assembly: The extruder assembly draws plastic in from a spool of plastic filament that is either 1.75mm or 3mm. It does this by using a hob gear and a pully under tension; plastic is fed between these two parts and fed into the cold break. The hob gear is normally mounted to a stepper motor that feeds the plastic filament at a set rate (steps/mm). Common issues with the extruder assembly are jams; sometimes, the hob gear can get plastic bit in its teeth, and because of this, plastic will slip. Also, when loading the plastic, you can sometimes miss the hole to the cold break, and no plastic will ever make it to the hot end. See Figure 4-13.

Figure 4-13. *E3D brand extruder assembly*

Gantry: With some printers, the X and Y axes move on the same apparatus, and the Z moves up and down on an acme screw or a ball screw. Other printers have the X and Z axes mounted together, and the build plate moves along the Y axis. Both styles of machine work well; I personally like the former to the latter, but it is up to you to decide which style of printer is right for you. Common issues with the gantry include screws loosening due to vibrations, axes getting jackknifed or misaligned, very noisy due to lack of lubrication, and/or motor driver being set to high/low on its reference voltage. See Figure 4-14.

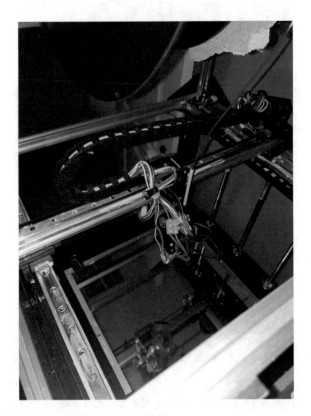

Figure 4-14. *FT5 gantry X, Y, and Z axes*

Control board: This is the brain of the 3D printer; it controls all aspects of the printer. There are a few components on here of note. For starters, the motor drivers are located here; the MOSFETs that control both the build plate and hot end heaters are here, and all the sensors used to home the printer are on the control board as well. Common issues with the control board are: the voltage reference on the motor drivers is not dialed in all the way, loose thermistor wires can cause thermal runaway, and noisy (electrically noisy) power supply can cause your printer to restart at inopportune times. See Figure 4-15.

Figure 4-15. *Duet Wifi 2 control board*

Build plate: This is where the print will be created. The most important thing to know about it is whether it is heated and the build envelope. It is also important to note the different materials used on a build plate. For example, the image in Figure 4-16 shows a mirror being used as a build plate. Other materials that are used for 3D printing build plates are borosilicate glass, aluminum, and PEI. See Figure 4-16.

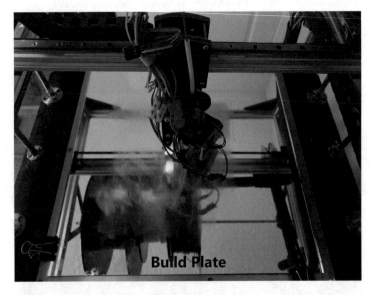

Figure 4-16. *Build plate, with heated bed*

Now that we have a basic understanding of the various components of a 3D printer, we can move on to the software side of things. The software we are going to talk about is very important as it will convert an STL file into G-code.

What Is a Slicer

A slicer is a program that takes a 3D image normally and an STL file (stereolithography file); this file is then converted into layers (slices) of the 3D object. The slicer also contains all kinds of settings that you can use to make your print quality better, print speed faster, and so on. For this book, I will be using Simplify3D; this application does cost 150 USD, but it is worth it in the long run. I also recommend Cura as it is a free slicer and has a ton of settings as well. Let's get started by talking about these two slicers in a little more detail.

Different Slicing Programs

Cura: As stated earlier, it is a free software from Ultimaker that a community of hobbyists, makers, and engineers update on a regular basis, which is nice because you normally get a lot of new features with each release. Now, that being said, Cura offers a lot of features in the magnitude of 100s of settings, so it can be a bit overwhelming, but there is also a lot of forums that you can go to, to get help. Visit `https://community.ultimaker.com/forum/107-ultimaker-software/` for any help with Cura, or if your printer has a forum, I would suggest visiting that forum as well.

Simplify3D: Unlike Cura, Simplify3D is not freeware and costs about 150 USD, but I think it is worth it for one key feature which is it allows you to add and remove support structures (we will go over this in the next section). It also has a forum and regular releases; it works well with most printers, and there are some that have full libraries of material profiles that you can use. The next section will cover everything you need in order to get started with Simplify3D.

Simplify3D

For this book, I will be using Simplify3D; you can use any slicer you would like, but I prefer Simplify3D because it is really easy to use and has some great functionality. First off, I want to explain all the function of the main screen. Then I will go into details of the various settings that you may or may not use when using Simplify3D. Finally, I will import the 3D model we made in the previous chapter to demonstrate the preview mode on Simplify3D. So, let's get started with the Simplify3D's main screen.

The Main Screen

In Figure 4-17, you will see an illustration of the main screen of Simplify3D. This screen has many buttons, drop-down menus, selection boxes, and so on. I want to go over each of these, so you have a better understanding of the software when we use it later in this chapter as well as in chapters to come.

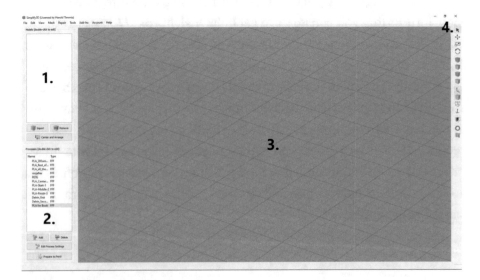

Figure 4-17. *Main Simplify3D screen*

1. Models selection box: This is where you add your STL file to Simplify3D. You can drag and drop your files into this box, or you can use the "Import" button; once you do that, the part will be added to the build area. You can also use the "Remove" button if you want to remove a model from the build area.

2. Processes selection box: This is where all the processes for the various plastics go. They are created by clicking the "Add" button and deleted by clicking the "Delete" button. The next section will have a more in-depth look at the various settings in these processes.

3. Build area: This is where the 3D model will be viewed; you can manipulate the position of the 3D object by double-clicking it and changing the rotation on the X, Y, and Z plane. This menu will also allow you to change the scale and position. If you have a part that is too large for the build area, Simplify3D will tell you, and you can adjust the 3D object accordingly (but only upon inserting the 3D model, not when you scale a model already on the build area).

4. Side bar: This bar has several functions; they are

   - Normal selection: This will allow you to select the various models in the build area.

   - Translate models: Move a model in X, Y, and Z directions.

   - Scale models: Make a model larger or smaller in all directions.

- Rotate models: Allow you to rotate a model.

- Default view: This will take you to the home view.

- Top view: Rotates the view to the top.

- Front view: Rotates the view to the front.

- Side view: Rotates the view to the side.

- Coordinate axes: Toggles the X, Y, and Z coordinate image.

- Solid model: Toggles the solid models on and off.

- Wireframe: Toggles the wireframe of the model.

- Show normals: Will toggle the normal on a 3D model.

- Cross-section view: Very important function; it can be used to see cross-sections of the 3D model in the X, Y, and Z directions. Useful when you want to see support material within the 3D model.

- Machine control panel: Here, you can control your printer over a USB cable. Very useful if you need to debug a problem.

- Support generation: This is a great function; it allows you to add or remove support structures, and it also allows you to change the density of support structure.

In the next section, we will discuss common settings needed in order to create the best print possible.

Common Settings

Click the "Add" button on the main screen under the processes selection box (see Figure 4-18). You may be in the basic setting menu. To get into the advanced menu, click the "Show Advanced" button, and you will see a lot of new settings.

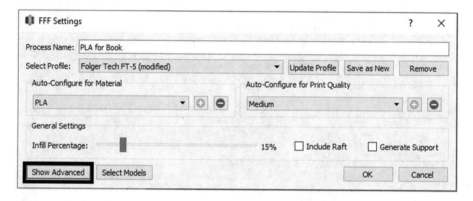

Figure 4-18. *Click the Show Advanced button for more functions*

1. Tab 1: Extruder (see Figure 4-19)

    - Extruder List: This is where you will select which extruder you want these settings to apply to. If you only have a single extruder, only the primary extruder will be available.

    - Nozzle Diameter: This is the diameter of the nozzle at the end of the extruder.

    - Retraction Distance: How much plastic to suck back into the extruder.

- Retraction Vertical Lift: The nozzle will lift up when a retraction occurs. This is very useful when you are printing multiple parts, so the nozzle will not hit other parts.

- Retraction Speed: How fast the extruder will retract.

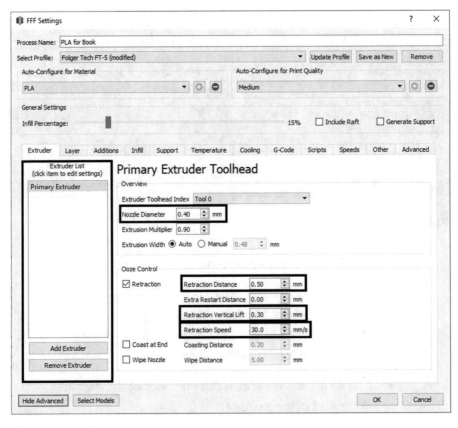

Figure 4-19. *Extruder tab*

2. Tab 2: Layer (see Figure 4-20)

    • Primary Extruder: Select the extruder that these
       settings apply to.

    • Primary Layer Height: Layer height for the z axis.

    • Top Solid Layers: How many top solid layers to
       print.

    • Bottom Solid Layers: How many solid layers to
       print.

    • Outline/Perimeter Shells: How many perimeters to
       print. Good for making bosses for threaded inserts
       or screws.

    • Single outline corkscrew printing mode (vase
       mode): Increment the Z axis so that the print will be
       seamless. Note that this will mean there is no infill.

    • First Layer Speed: Slow down or speed up the first
       layer by a certain percentage.

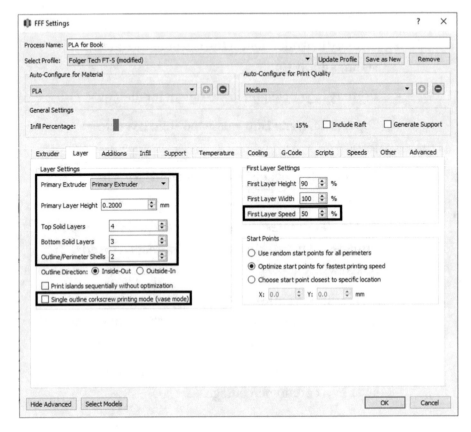

Figure 4-20. *Layer tab*

3. Tab 3: Additions (see Figure 4-21)

- Use Skirt/Brim: This will purge some plastic at the beginning of the print. It will outline the entire print. Normally, this is set to two or three outlines. If you set the "Skirt Offset from Part" to zero, it will create a brim which is useful for keeping a print from warping.

- Use Raft: Raft is very useful when you need to keep a print from warping. Normally, I don't like to use them, and if you have a well-leveled build plate, you should not need to use a raft.

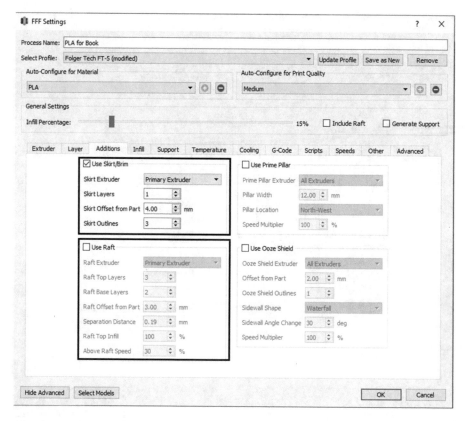

Figure 4-21. *Additions tab*

4. Tab 4: Infill (see Figure 4-22)

- Infill Extruder: Extruder that will be used for infilling the part.

- Internal Fill Pattern: What fill pattern will be used. For now, rectilinear will be used.

- External Fill Pattern: This is the pattern that will be used for the top and bottom fill.

- Interior Fill Percentage: The amount of plastic infill used on the interior of the print.

Figure 4-22. *Infill tab*

5. Tab 5: Support (see Figure 4-23)

    • Generate Support Material: Toggle whether to add
       support material to a print.

    • Support Extruder: Which extruder will be used to
       print the support material.

    • Support Infill Percentage: How dense the support
       material will be.

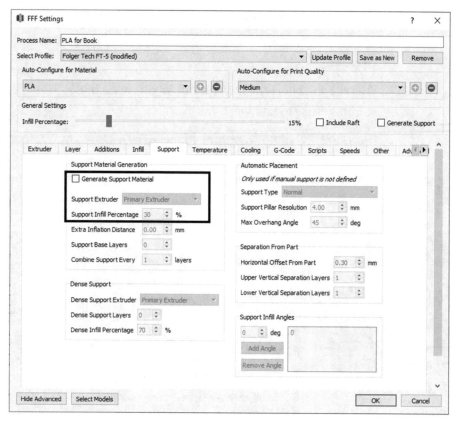

Figure 4-23. *Support tab*

6. Tab 6: Temperature (see Figure 4-24)

    •   Temperature Controller List: List of heaters on the
        3D printer. Select one and update the settings for it.

    •   Temperature Identifier: Identifies the temperature
        controller.

    •   Temperature Controller Type: Select whether the
        type of heater is for an extruder or heated build
        plate.

- Per-Layer Temperature Setpoint List: Displays the various temperature setpoints and which layer it will set.

- Layer Number: What layer number you want the temperature to change.

- Setpoint: What temperature you want to set.

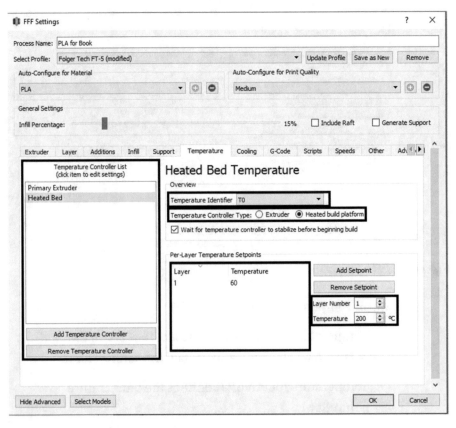

Figure 4-24. *Temperature tab*

7. Tab 7: Cooling (see Figure 4-25)

- Per-Layer Fan Speed List: Displays what percentage the cooling fan will be set and at what layer

- Layer Number: Layer number to set the percentage of the cooling fan speed

- Fan Speed: The percentage to set the cooling fan speed

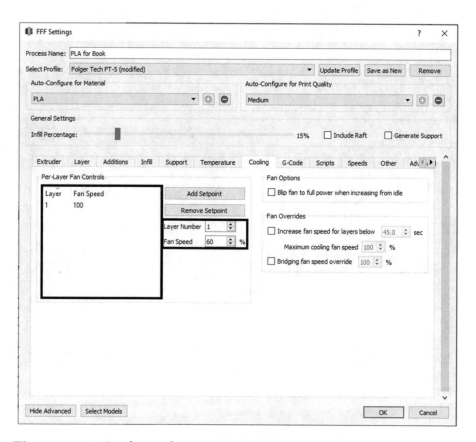

Figure 4-25. *Cooling tab*

8. Tab 8: G-Code (see Figure 4-26)

- Build Volume: You can adjust the build volume of your printer if the configuration assistant had the incorrect build volume or you have updated the printer's build envelope.

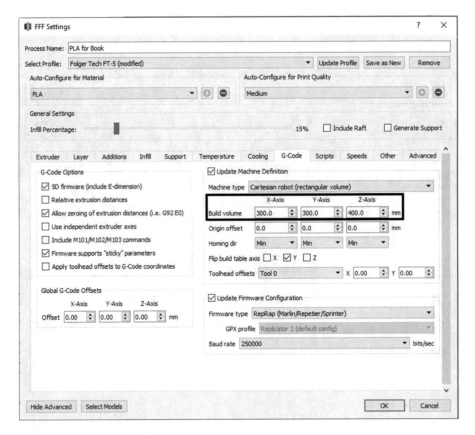

Figure 4-26. *G-Code tab*

9. Tab 9: Scripts (see Figure 4-27)

- Starting Script: This script will run at the very beginning of the print. Useful for setting up auto leveling or purging plastic.

- Ending Script: This script will run at the end of the print. Useful for turning off hot ends and moving the extruder to the home position.

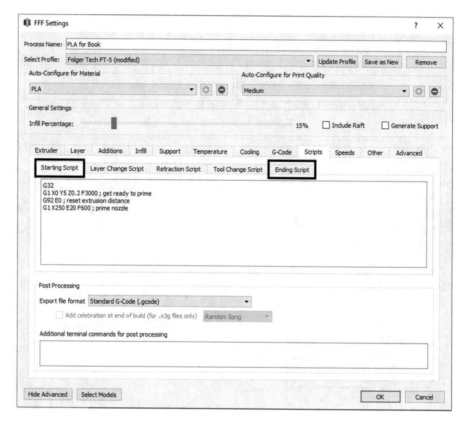

Figure 4-27. *Scripts tab*

10. Tab 10: Speeds (see Figure 4-28)

- Defaulting Printing Speed: Initial speed used for all printing movements.

- Outline Underspeed: Speed that the outline of the print is printed at.

- Solid Infill Underspeed: The infills print speed.

- X/Y Axis Movement Speed: How fast the extruder will move when it is not printing.

- Z Axis Movement Speed: Speed of the Z axis movement.

- Adjust Printing Speed for Layers below: Very useful when you have small features of parts that need a bit more cooldown between layers.

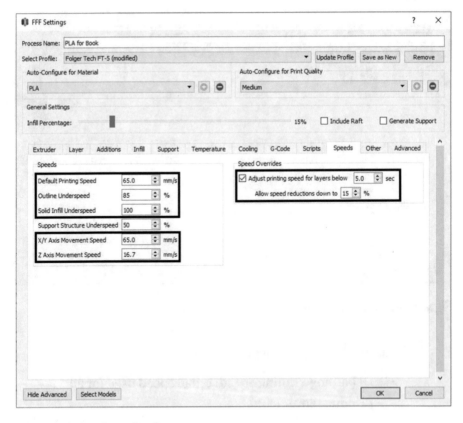

Figure 4-28. *Speed tab*

11. Tab 11: Other (see Figure 4-29)

- Filament Diameter: For most printers set to a value close to 1.75mm, it is best to check the filament with calipers to get an average of the filament diameter and then update this setting.

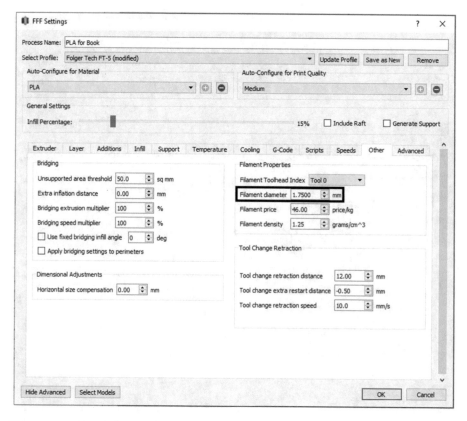

Figure 4-29. *Other tab*

12. Tab 12: Advanced (see Figure 4-30)

- Start Printing at Height: The height that the current process will begin at.

- Stop Printing at Height: The height that the current process will end at.

- Only Retract when Crossing Open Spaces: Will retract when extruder is moving from one part to another.

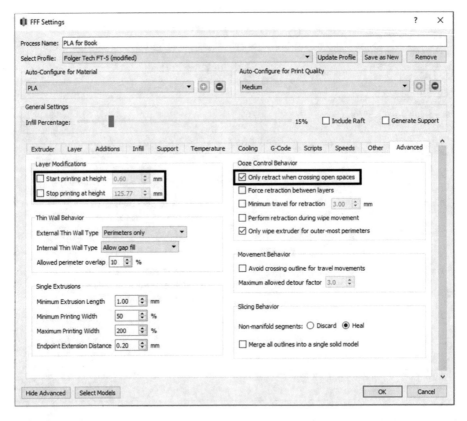

Figure 4-30. *Advanced tab*

Troubleshooting

Alright, let's get started with a simple 3D model, and then we will move to a more complex 3D model (don't worry; it won't be too complex). Go ahead and open Fusion 360 so we can create our first sketch.

Over/Under Extrusion

If you have an over extrusion, it means you have too much plastic being pushed out of the nozzle. If you have an under extrusion, you will notice gaps in the print. You may want to first check the Extrusion Multiplier in the Extruder tab of settings. See Figure 4-31.

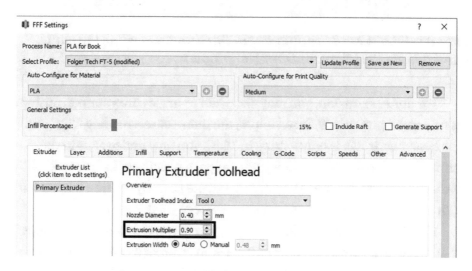

Figure 4-31. *Adjust the Extrusion Multiplier to increase or decrease the flow of plastic*

If that does not help, you may want to make sure the filament is consistent ~1.75mm; if it is not correct, make sure the Filament Diameter setting in the "Other" tab of the processes window is updated to the correct value. See Figure 4-32.

Figure 4-32. *Check the filament in three areas, average the value, and update the Filament Diameter property*

For under extrusion, you may also want to make sure your thermistor is calibrated properly. If, for example, the thermistor is reading 220C and the heater cartridge is only getting to 180C, you may notice gaps in the print due to the printer not being able to push plastic out as smoothly as it should be. You can make sure this is not the issue by taking a laser temp gun and checking the hot end for consistency.

If none of those are working for you, you may need to adjust the steps/ mm in the firmware of the printer. This is an advanced task, so I would make sure none of the other adjustments won't fix the problem before attempting this.

1. Find the steps/mm perimeter in the firmware for your printer, change the value, and upload the firmware to your printer. See Figure 4-33.

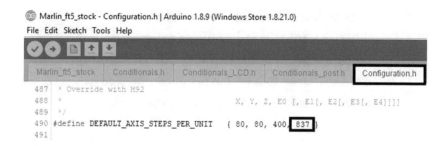

```
487  * Override with M92
488  *                                        X, Y, Z, E0 [, E1[, E2[, E3[, E4]]]]
489  */
490  #define DEFAULT_AXIS_STEPS_PER_UNIT    { 80, 80, 400, 837 }
491
```

Figure 4-33. *Update steps/mm value of the extruder motor*

2. Decrease this value (because you are over extruding or increase the value if the printer is under extruding) and recompile and upload into your printer.

3. Mark a distance of 100mm on the filament going into the extruder. See Figure 4-34.

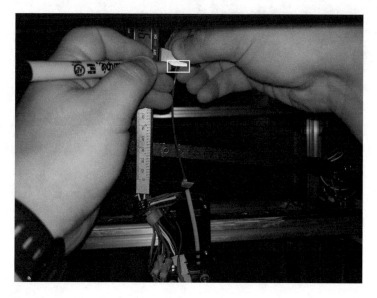

Figure 4-34. *Put a mark at 100mm*

4. Extrude 100mm of material using the machine
    control panel (also, make sure your extruder is
    heated up; otherwise, the extruder will not extrude);
    you will also need to have the printer connected to
    your computer for this process. See Figure 4-35.

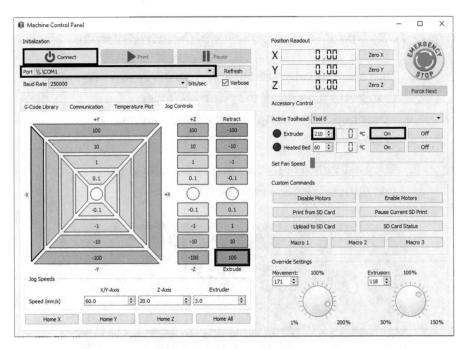

Figure 4-35. *Open the machine control panel to control your printer*

5. If the 100mm mark is above or below the entrance
    into the extruder, then you will need to adjust the
    steps/mm setting again. See Figures 4-36, 4-37,
    and 4-38.

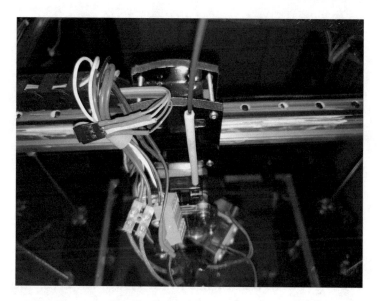

Figure 4-36. *This is what you want to see*

Figure 4-37. *If you see this, decrease the value of the steps/mm*

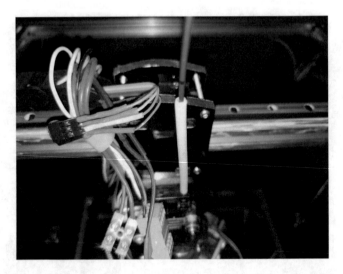

Figure 4-38. *If you see this, increase the value of the steps/mm*

Ghosting

Ghosting is when you see outlines of the print on the exterior of the print; for example, you may see outlines of holes next to a physical hole in your print. See Figure 4-39. The most important setting to adjust here would be the speed at which you are printing.

Figure 4-39. *Ghosting example*

Parts Do Not Stay on Build Plate

The first thing to do is to make sure your build plate is true/level to the extruder's nozzle. Normally, this means moving the nozzle to the Z Offset (or 0) and using a piece of paper at each side and then finally in the center. You want to make it to where the paper just barely drags on the nozzle at all points. To do this, you adjust the thumb screws under the build plate to either lift the build plate or lower the build plate. Today's printers normally have automatic bed leveling, and I would highly recommend the BLTouch as it works great on all build plates. There are also tons of videos on how to level a build plate; if you are having issues leveling your build plate, I recommend going to the companion YouTube channel for this book and watching the "Build Plate Leveling Tutorial."

If that does not work, I would recommend adjusting your Z Offset. Again, this will be a firmware update on most printers. I would recommend going to the companion YouTube channel for this book and watching the "Z Offset Adjustment Tutorial."

Finally, if you are still having issues, make sure you have a nice even amount of Elmer's "Disappearing Purple" glue on the build plate.

Our First Print

So here we are ready to try our first print. The first thing you will want to do is set your printer up in Simplify3D. To do this, you can go through the "Configuration Assistant" in the Help ➤ Configuration Assistant; this will bring up a menu that will have you select your printer, and it should automatically create a profile for your printer. 10 to 1 that your printer will work even if it is not on the list as it is probably a copy of another printer, for example, the Wanhao Duplicator 4S is a remake of the MakerBot Replicator 2X and the FlashForge Creator. Next, we will need to open Fusion 360 and load our project from the previous chapter. See Figure 4-40.

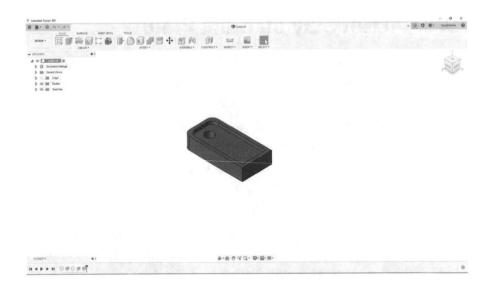

Figure 4-40. *Open the Fusion 360 project from Chapter 3*

1. Go to the Tools ➤ MAKE drop-down menu and
   select "3D Print." See Figure 4-41.

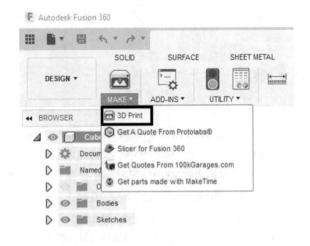

Figure 4-41. *Select the 3D Print function*

2. Select the 3D object you want printed.
    See Figure 4-42.

Figure 4-42. *Select the model you want converted to an STL*

3. If "Send to 3D Print Utility" checkbox is selected,
    remove the check. See Figure 4-43.

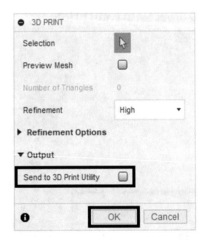

Figure 4-43. *Deselect the "Send to 3D Print Utility" and click OK*

4. Click "OK" and select where you want the STL to go.
   See Figure 4-43.

5. Go back to Simplify3D and click the "Import"
   button. See Figure 4-44.

Figure 4-44. Go back to Simplify3D and click the "Import" button

6. Find the STL file you just created, select it, and then click the "Open" button. See Figure 4-45.

Figure 4-45. *Select the STL file that was created by Fusion 360*

7. You will notice that the tag will be put on its side; this is suboptimal since there is an overhang. To fix this, press Ctrl-L and select the bottom of the tag; this will put the bottom of the tag to the top of the build plate which is a much more efficient orientation for this part to be printed in. See Figure 4-46.

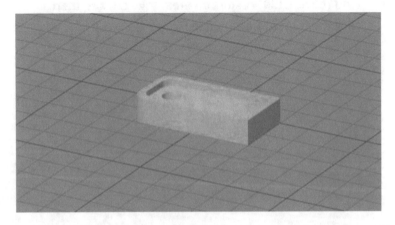

Figure 4-46. *Orient the part in this position using the Ctrl-L quick key*

8. Now select or create a new process. For the first process, use the following settings. I would also recommend searching Google for your printer's profiles as there is a good chance someone has already made a profile for the particular printer you have; remember not all printers are the same, and my settings may not work for your printer. See Figures 4-47 through 4-51.

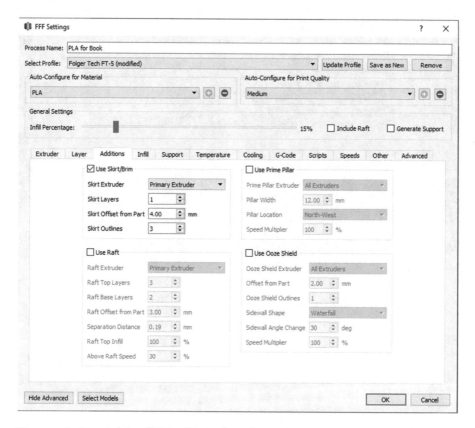

Figure 4-47. *Add a "Skirt/Brim" to the print to purge some plastic*

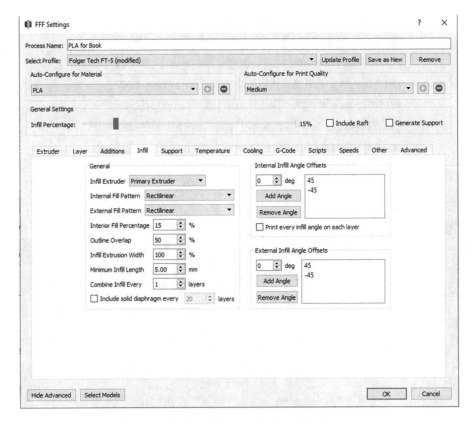

Figure 4-48.   *15% is more than enough for this part*

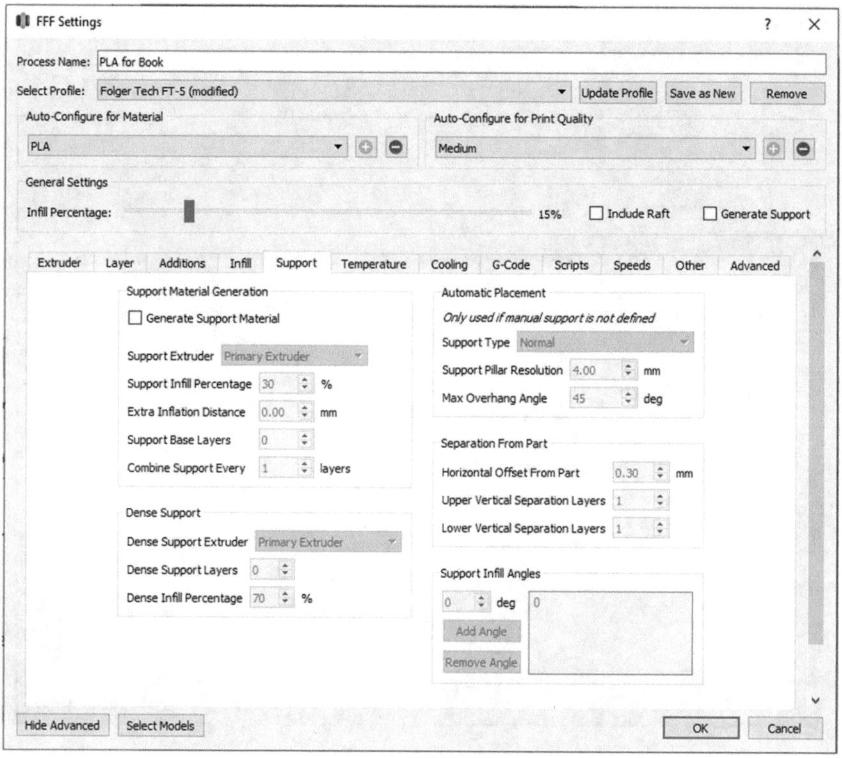

Figure 4-49. *Support tab (just remove the "Generate Support Material" check)*

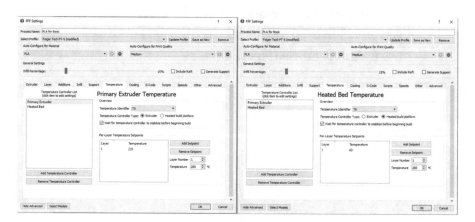

Figure 4-50. *Make sure the temps are correct for your printer*

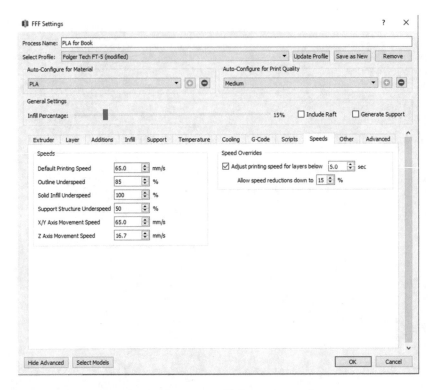

Figure 4-51. *65mm/s work very well for most printers*

9. Now that you have the process sorted out, you will
   need to click the "Prepare to Print!" button which
   you will then need to select the process you want to
   use for this print. See Figure 4-52.

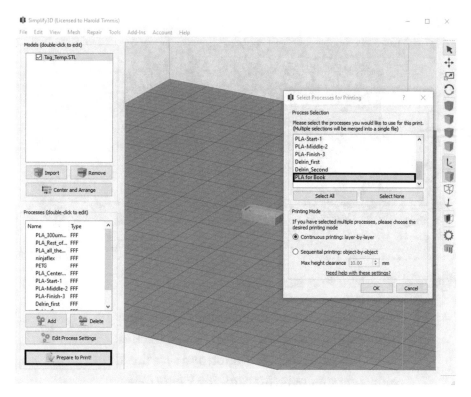

Figure 4-52. *Click the "Prepare to Print!" button and select the process and click OK*

10.   Next will be sent to the Print Preview mode. The Print Preview mode is very important as you can use the Layer Range to Show ➤ Max slider to show you what your print will look like just by sliding it back and forth. You can also use the "Play/Pause" button to run through the print at an accelerated speed. You may also notice small dots on your print; these are retraction points. On the left side of the window, you will notice several checkboxes; these control what you are seeing on the build plate, for example, the retraction points. See Figure 4-53.

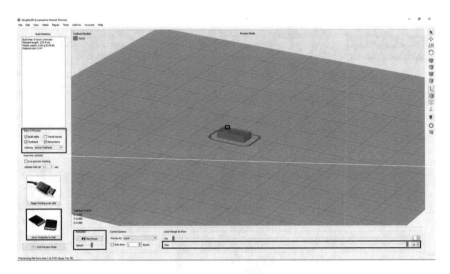

Figure 4-53. *Print Preview functions*

11. Finally, you will need to create the G-code your
printer will use to create the 3D object. Click the
"Save Toolpaths to Disk" button and save the file to
your computer or an SD card. See Figure 4-54.

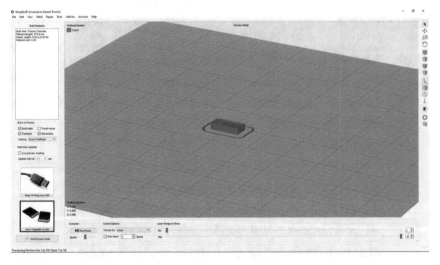

Figure 4-54. *When ready, click the "Save Toolpaths to Disk" button*

12. You will also need to make sure your printer is mechanically configured, meaning the build plate is level, there is plastic loaded into the extruder, and the build plate is ready to have plastic extruded onto it (see the "Parts Do Not Stay on Build Plate" section of this chapter for more information).

13. Then you will need to follow your printer's instructions on how to start the print from an SD card or over Wifi if your printer is wireless. This print should be quick between 2 and 10 minutes; once it is done, use the paint spatula to take the print off the build plate. See Figure 4-55.

Figure 4-55. *Finished print*

Before we get to the summary of this chapter, I just want to say that this chapter had a ton of information, and there is still a lot more about 3D printing that I want to go through before the end of this book. 3D printing has a lot to it, and one chapter would not do 3D printing justice. So, let's review what we have learned in this chapter.

Summary

Alright, another chapter bites the dust. This chapter had a ton of material, so feel free to go over it again. Let's take a look at the summary of this chapter:

- Learned about the different types of 3D printers
- Discovered new tools that will help when 3D printing
- Learned about the different parts of a 3D printer
- Talked about what a slicer is
- Went over a lot of the functions in Simplify3D
- Went over a few troubleshooting tips when 3D printing
- Learned how to create a process in Simplify3D
- Printed our first object

Exercise

1. You may have noticed the print came out a bit smaller than you may want a keychain to be. How could you modify this with either Fusion 360 or Simplify3D to make it larger?

CHAPTER 5

PCB Design

Now that we have taken some time to learn about Fusion 360 and Simplify3D, we need to focus on the electrical aspects of this book. First, we will investigate what a PCB is and briefly describe how it is designed. Then I want to go over PCB Design software that will be used to create PCBs in this book. After that, we will have an in-depth discussion on Eagle and how to make your first PCB, as well as how to load libraries into Eagle. Then we will learn how to export the Gerber files for the final board. Finally, we will review how to get this board manufactured using PCBWay. There is a lot to cover just like the previous chapters, so let's get started.

What Is a PCB

PCB stands for Printed Circuit Board; PCBs are created using PCB Design software. The design software will have both a schematic section and a board section. The schematic section will have a diagram like reference to all connections such as: integrated circuit (IC), passive electrical component, and so on. The board section will have the component layout, wiring, drills, and so on that are needed to create the actual board. Once both sections are completed, the board file will be compiled into a Gerber file which will hold all the information that the PCB manufacturer needs to create the PCB. All of these will be explained in detail in this chapter. Figure 5-1 illustrates some examples of PCBs manufactured by PCBWay.

© Harold Timmis 2021
H. Timmis, *Practical Arduino Engineering*, https://doi.org/10.1007/978-1-4842-6852-0_5

Figure 5-1. *Examples of PCB boards including an Arduino board, battery tester (courtesy of David Segal and Chris Defant), H-bridge, rotary encoder breakout*

PCB Design Software

There are a lot of PCB Design software on the market, such as Altium, KiCAD, and what this book will utilize: Eagle. PCB Design software allows you to create schematics and board layouts. These can then be converted into Gerber files which will then be sent to the board manufacturer. There is a lot to learn with PCB Design software; this chapter will give you a good glimpse and get you ready for the next chapters that will have several board designs.

Eagle

Eagle has a monthly subscription program, so if you only want to use it for this book, you can purchase a monthly license for 15 USD. Eagle is a professional PCB software that can even link to Fusion 360, so you can make sure a PCB fits in its enclosure. It also allows you to connect to various component libraries, so you do have to create every component your board needs. So, let's get started with Eagle.

Eagle's Main Windows

Did I say windows? Yes, Eagle has two main windows that you will be using to create PCBs. The first window we will talk about allows you to create a schematic of the PCB. A schematic is a drawing of all the ICs, resistors, capacitors, headers, and their connections; these connections are called nets. The second window we will discuss focuses on the physical layout of the board; this is important because it will become the Gerber files you send off to the PCB manufacturer.

Schematic Window

As stated earlier, the schematic window will allow you to create a logical diagram of your circuit. This will also connect all the various components using nets that will then become routes when you switch over to the Board Layout window. Let's look at the schematic window and its various menus and controls. See Figure 5-2.

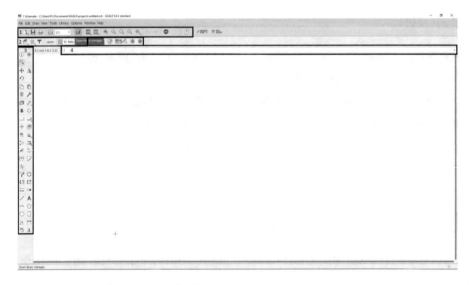

Figure 5-2. *Schematic window*

1. Action bar: This bar has a couple of important
   buttons on it. They are

   a. Open/Save/Print: This is where you can save your
      progress.

   b. Schematic/Board: This button allows you to toggle
      between the board window and the schematic
      window.

2. Parameters bar: This bar holds all the functions for:
   control grid settings and layer control.

   a. Layer settings: Allows you to show or hide layers
      (most of the time, this is used in the board window).

   b. Grid: Allows you to change the resolution of the grid
      and change the units of measurement.

   c. Layer selection box: Select which layer to edit.
      Normally set to "Nets" for the schematic window.

3. Command buttons bar: I will not spend too much time here listing all of the commands (there are a ton), but instead will show you these as we create PCBs throughout the book, but here are a few very common commands:

    a. Info: Allows you to check various properties of a component.

    b. Add Part: Allows you to select the component you want to add to the schematic window.

    c. Delete: Deletes a component from the schematic window and the board window.

    d. Show: Select a net with this option selected, and all nets with that name will be highlighted.

    e. Group: Use this function to select multiple objects.

    f. Net: Nets are used to connect your circuit together; we will be using this function a lot in the coming projects.

4. Command texts bar: In this text box, you can type out commands to quickly move through schematic development. These are typically used when you get a bit more experience in Eagle. If you want to see a list of the commands, go here: `http://web.mit.edu/xavid/arch/i386_rhel4/help/24.htm`.

5. Simulation bar: This bar allows you to evaluate your circuit to make sure it will work as expected.

Board Window

The board window is where you will create the layout of the board with the various layers and routes. Also, you will add any holes or special features that your board may need. See Figure 5-3.

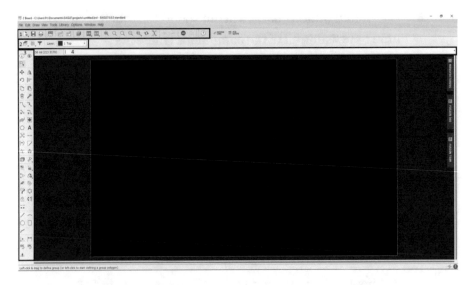

Figure 5-3. *Board window*

1. Actions bar: This bar is just like the one found on the schematics window but has one function I want to mention.

    a. CAM Processor: This is the function that will be used to create the final Gerber file that will be sent to the board manufacturer.

2. Parameters bar: See the "Schematic Window" section.

3. Command buttons: Several of the command buttons are the same, but there are a few that differ.

    a. Route Airwire: These are used to physically connect the circuit from the schematic view together.

    b. Ripup: This will not delete nets; that is to say, this will not remove the connection from component to component; it will just delete the routing of the net and leave a yellow line where the two components terminate.

4. Command texts bar: See the "Schematic Window" section.

Alright, now that we know about the layout of the two main windows in Eagle, we can start to discuss how to add libraries that have already been created to Eagle.

Loading a Library

Now another essential thing you need to know how to do is to have the ability to add libraries to Eagle. This is important because sometimes the components that come with Eagle are not enough, so you have two options: find a library that has the component and add it to Eagle or create the part yourself.

1. Open Eagle. See Figure 5-4.

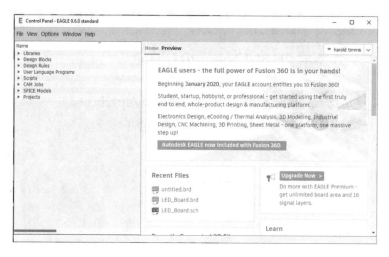

Figure 5-4. *Open Eagle*

2. Open a new File Explorer and navigate to "My Documents."

3. Create a new folder called "Extra Libraries." See Figure 5-5.

Figure 5-5. *Create the Extra Libraries folder*

4. Go to this link: https://github.com/sparkfun/ SparkFun-Eagle-Libraries. See Figure 5-6.

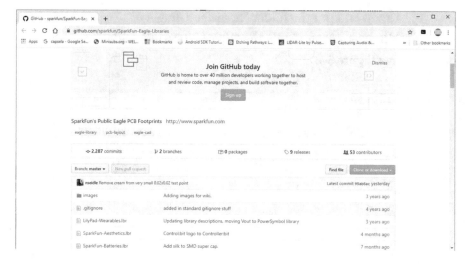

Figure 5-6. *Go to the URL*

5. Download the SparkFun Eagle library. See Figure 5-7.

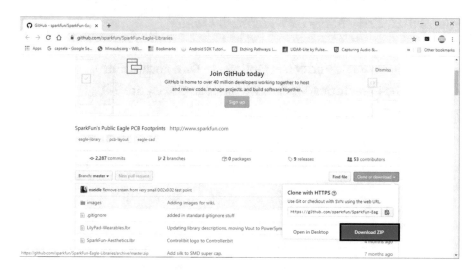

Figure 5-7. *Download the SparkFun Eagle library*

6. Unzip and put the folder "SparkFun-Eagle-Libraries-master" into the "Extra Libraries" folder. See Figure 5-8.

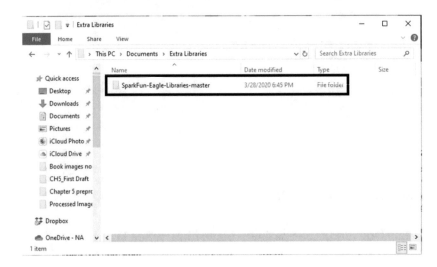

Figure 5-8. *Copy to the Extra Libraries folder*

7. Go to Eagle and select Options ➤ Directories, and the Directories window will appear. See Figure 5-9.

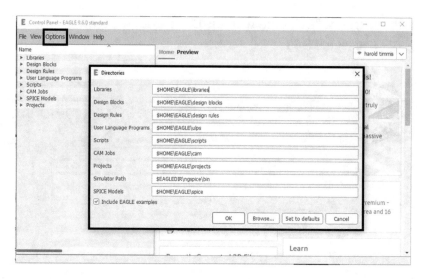

Figure 5-9. *Open Directories*

8. Copy the link address from your File Explorer to the Libraries text box in the Directories window. Remember to add the ";" after the "$HOME\EAGLE\libraries". See Figure 5-10.

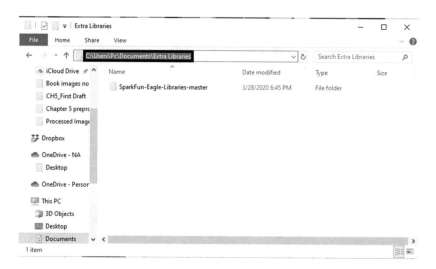

Figure 5-10. *Copy Libraries directory*

9. Click the "OK" button on the Directories window. See Figure 5-11.

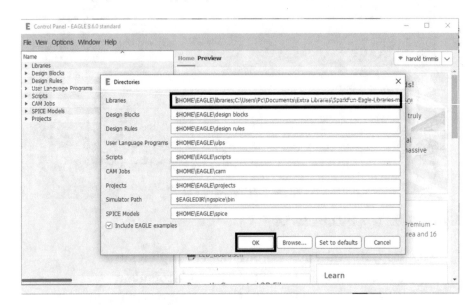

Figure 5-11. *Paste directory*

10. On the front screen of Eagle, go to the Libraries drop-down and click the arrow. See Figure 5-12.

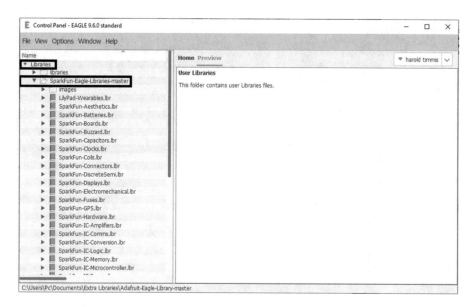

Figure 5-12. *Shows the SparkFun Eagle library loaded*

11. You should now see the SparkFun library. Right-
     click it and click "Use all." One thing to note is that
     you will need to select "Use all" on each library
     when you want to use this for each project. See
     Figure 5-13.

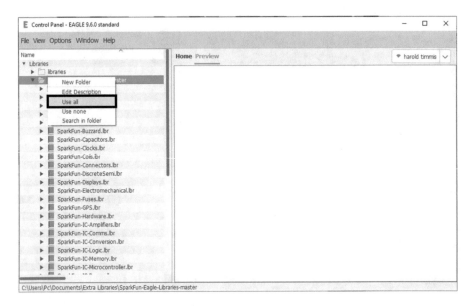

Figure 5-13. *Select "Use all"*

12. The library has now been added and is ready to use.

Alright! Now that we know how to add libraries to Eagle, we can start to create schematics and layouts, but first I would recommend adding the Adafruit library to Eagle. The link for which can be found here: `https://github.com/adafruit/Adafruit-Eagle-Library`.

Creating a Schematic

Finally, we are ready to start creating schematics and board layouts. We will start with the schematic. What we will be making is an LED board with a push button and a terminal block for easy connection to a power supply. So, let's get started.

1. Open Eagle. See Figure 5-14.

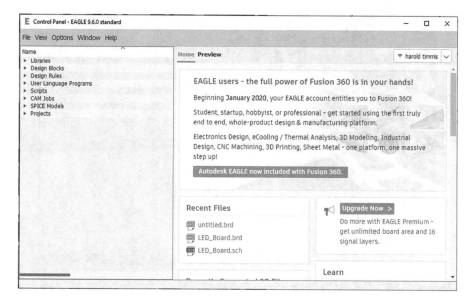

Figure 5-14. *Open Eagle*

2. Go to the Libraries drop-down and right-click the
    SparkFun library we added in the previous section
    and click "Use all." See Figure 5-15.

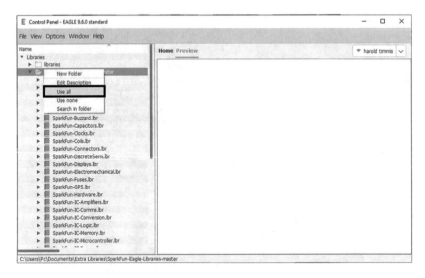

Figure 5-15. *Select "Use all"*

    3.   Select File ➤ New ➤ Schematic; this will open a
schematic window. See Figure 5-16.

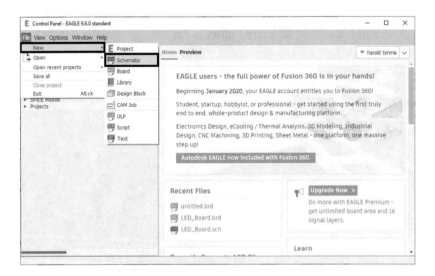

Figure 5-16. *Create a new schematic*

4. Press Ctrl-S and save this schematic as LED_Board.
    See Figure 5-17.

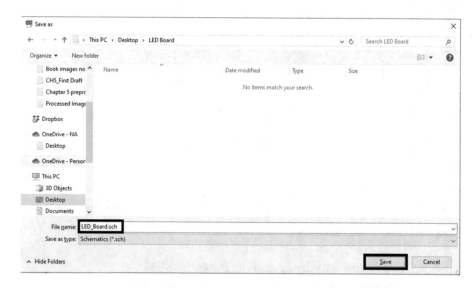

Figure 5-17. *Save the new schematic*

5. Click the Add Part button, and the ADD window will
    appear. See Figure 5-18.

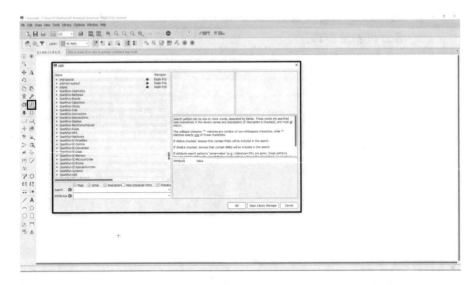

Figure 5-18. *ADD window*

6.   Scroll down to the SparkFun-PowerSymbols
     selection. Then double-click the "5V" text. See
     Figure 5-19.

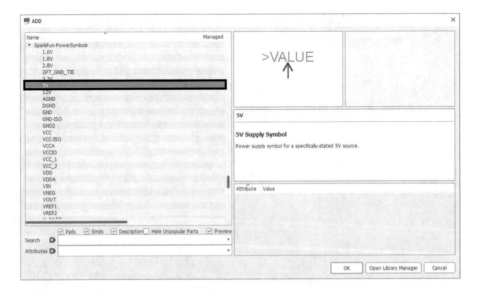

Figure 5-19. *Select 5V symbol*

7.   Add two of the "5V" symbol onto the schematic window by left-clicking the screen. See Figure 5-20.

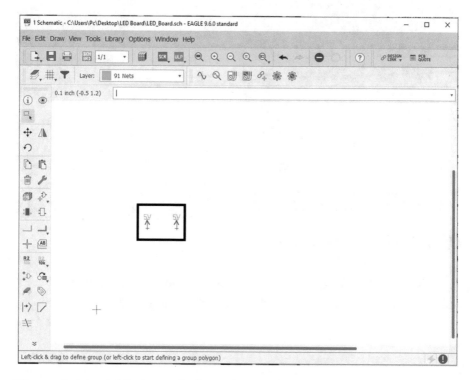

Figure 5-20.   *Add 5V symbols to the schematic window*

8.   Pressing escape will bring you back to the ADD window where you can double-click GND. See Figure 5-21.

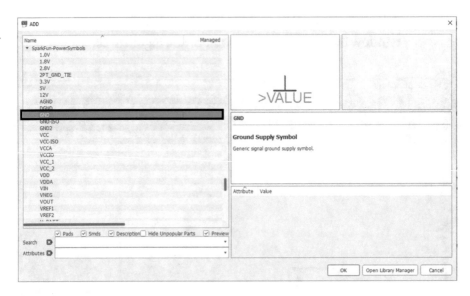

Figure 5-21.   *Select GND symbol*

    9.   Add two "GND" symbols to the schematic window, just
as you did with the "5V" symbol. See Figure 5-22.

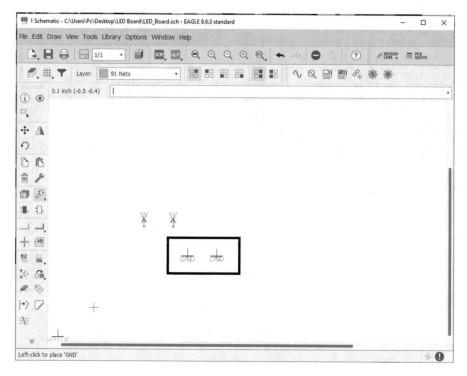

Figure 5-22. *Add GND symbols to the schematic window*

10. Press escape again, which will open the ADD
window again. See Figure 5-23.

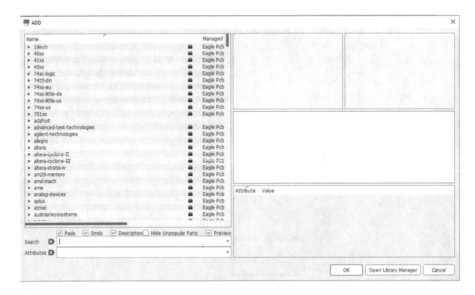

Figure 5-23. *Go to the ADD window again*

11.   In the search bar, type in "LED" and press enter. See
       Figure 5-24.

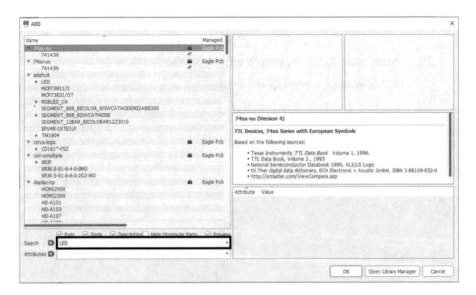

Figure 5-24. *Search for LED*

12.   Scroll down to the SparkFun-LED ➤ LED drop-
down and double-click the "LED3MM." See
Figure 5-25.

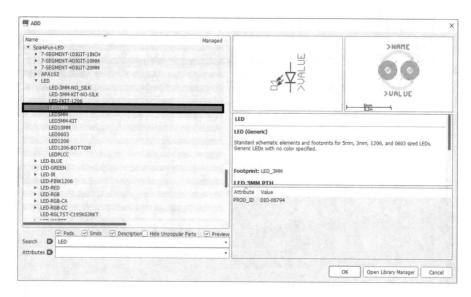

Figure 5-25. *Select LED3MM*

13.   Now if you right-click, you will notice that the LED
symbol will turn 90 degrees. Do this once. See
Figure 5-26.

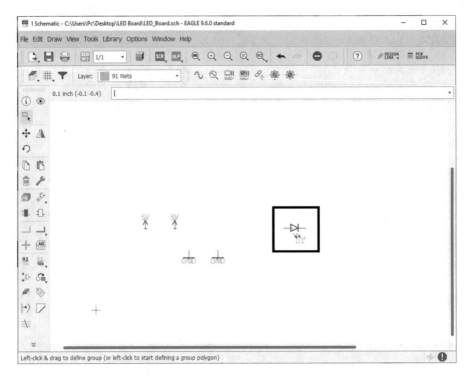

Figure 5-26.   *Add LED3MM symbol to the schematic window*

14.   Press escape again (or click the "ADD" button). In
the search bar, type in "button" and press enter. See
Figure 5-27.

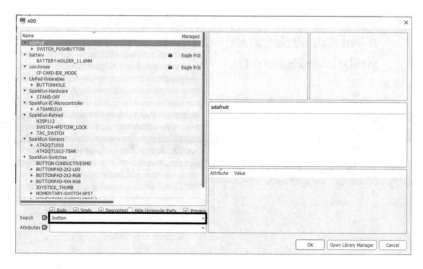

Figure 5-27. *Search for button*

15. Scroll down to SparkFun-Switches and locate MOMENTARY-SWITCH-SPST. Then locate MOMENTARY-SWITCH-SPST-SMD-4.5MM and double-click it. See Figure 5-28.

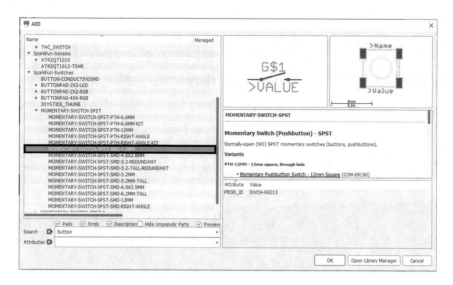

Figure 5-28. *Select the Momentary button*

16. Right-click three times on the schematic window to
     orient the switch correctly and then place the switch
     symbol. See Figure 5-29.

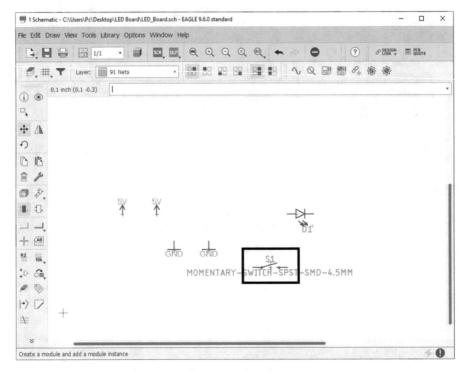

Figure 5-29. *Add the Momentary button to the schematic window*

17.   Click the Info button and then click the switch you
just placed. The info dialog window will open. See
Figure 5-30.

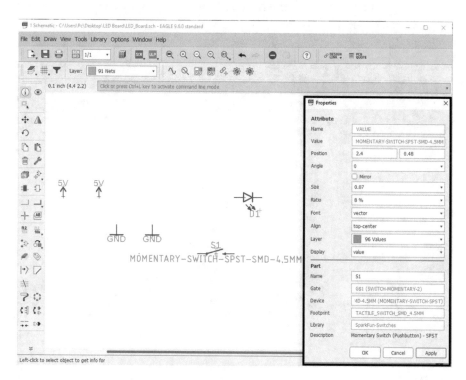

Figure 5-30. *Update the value of the button*

18. If the Properties window you are seeing is not correct, try right-clicking the switch near the "+" symbol; you should see this menu. Make sure you try and right-click the bottommost "+" symbol. See Figure 5-31.

Figure 5-31. *Right-click the "+" next to the button's name*

19.   The Properties menu should have the value of
        "VALUE." See Figure 5-32.

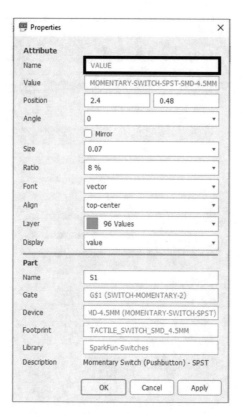

Figure 5-32. *When the proper area of the button is selected, the name will be "VALUE"*

20. Select the "Display" drop-down menu and select "off." See Figure 5-33.

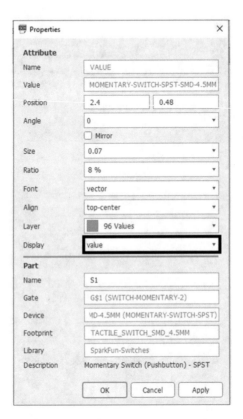

Figure 5-33. *Select "off"*

21. Click the ADD button again. See Figure 5-34.

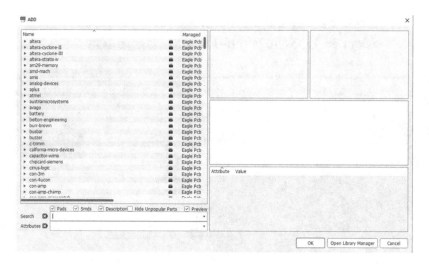

Figure 5-34. *ADD window*

22.   In the search bar, type in "connector" and press
      enter. See Figure 5-35.

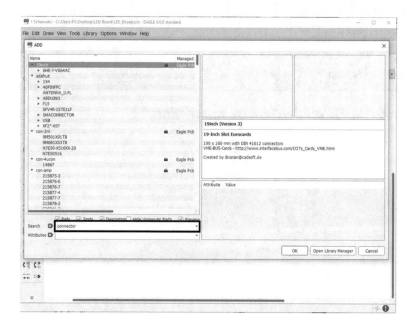

Figure 5-35. *Search connector*

23.   Scroll to the SparkFun-Connectors drop-down; then select the CONN-02 drop-down. See Figure 5-36.

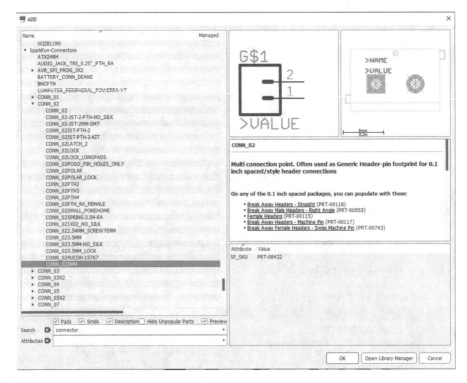

Figure 5-36. *Select the 5mm terminal block*

24. Double-click the "CONN_025MM" and add it to the
     schematic window. See Figure 5-37.

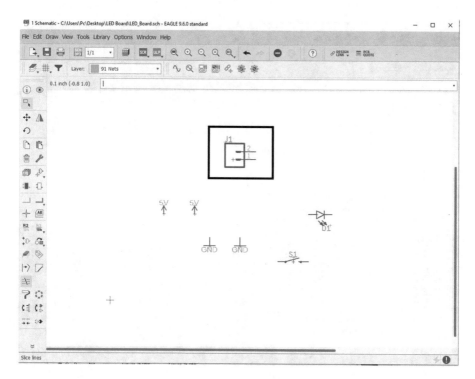

Figure 5-37. *Add the 5mm terminal block to the schematic window*

25.   Click the ADD button again and type in resistor into
        the search box and press enter. See Figure 5-38.

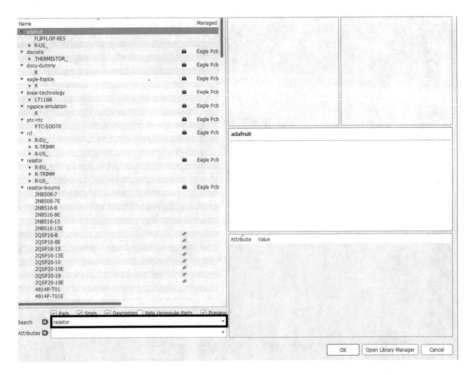

Figure 5-38. *Search resistor*

26.   Go to Resistor ➤ R-US ➤ R-US_R0805 and add it to
the schematic window. See Figure 5-39.

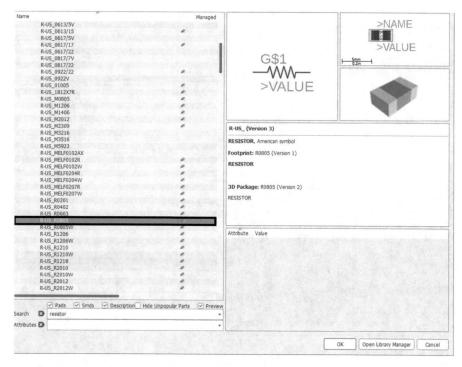

Figure 5-39. *Select the R0805 resistor*

27.   Press escape and click the cancel button. See
       Figure 5-40.

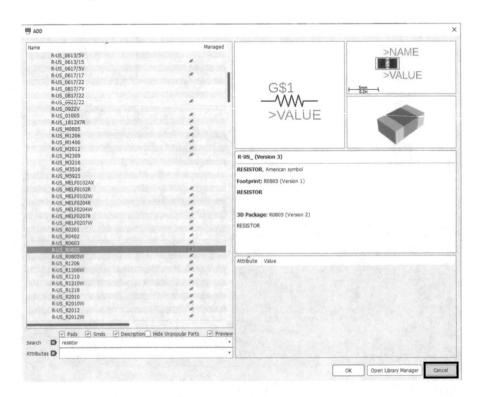

Figure 5-40.   *Get out of the ADD window*

28. Click the "Move" button and configure the symbols like Figure 5-41. Rotate any symbols as needed by selecting the symbol and using a right mouse click.

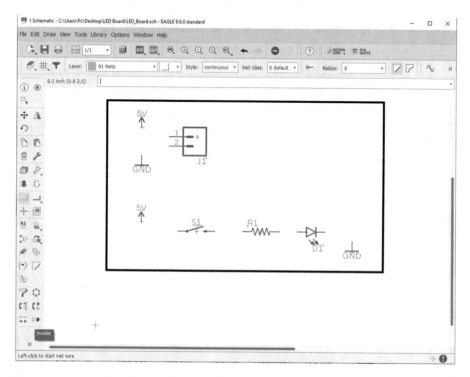

Figure 5-41. *Configure the symbols in these orientations*

29. Click the "Net" button; we are now in the phase where we will be connecting the various components together. Pay special attention to each of these connections as an incorrect connection here means an incorrect connection on the board layout, which can cause serious problems with your board. See Figure 5-42.

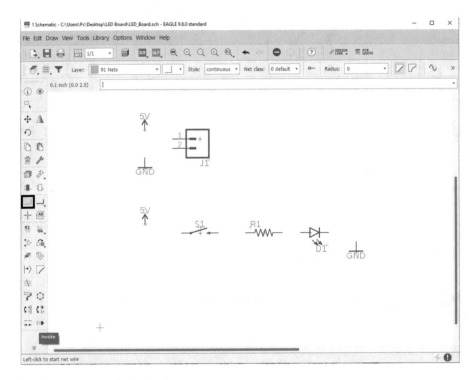

Figure 5-42. Click the "Net" button

30. Connect 5V to the 5mm terminal block. See
    Figure 5-43.

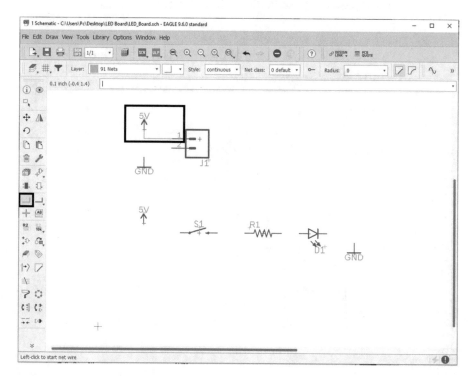

Figure 5-43. *Connect the 5V net to the terminal block*

31.   If you want your schematic to look just like Figure 5-43, you can cycle through the different directions of net shapes by right-clicking while the net button is active.

32.   Connect 5V to the left side of the switch symbol. See Figure 5-44.

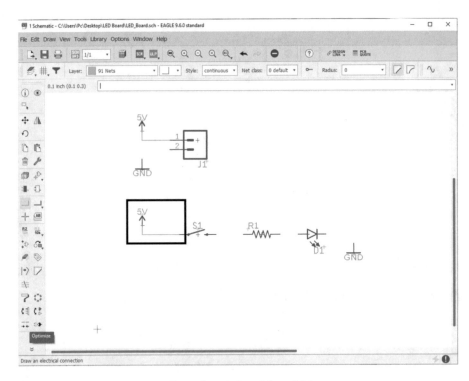

Figure 5-44.   *Connect 5V to the right side of S1*

33. Connect the right side of the switch symbol to the
     left side of the resistor. See Figure 5-45.

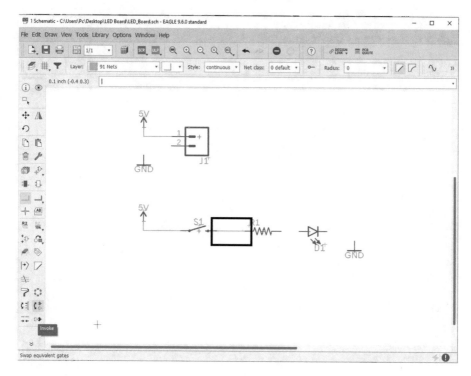

Figure 5-45. *Connect the left side of S1 to the right side of R1*

34. Connect the right side of the resistor symbol to the
     anode (left side) of the LED symbol. See Figure 5-46.

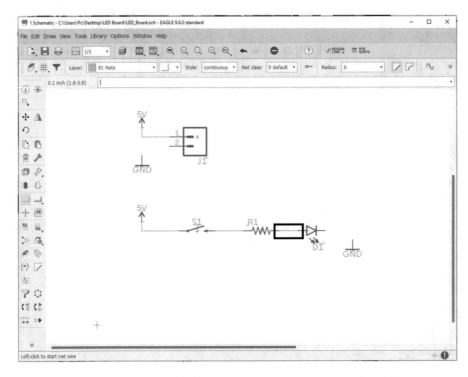

Figure 5-46. *Connect the left side of R1 to the right side of D1*

35. Connect the GND symbol to the 5mm terminal
    block. See Figure 5-47.

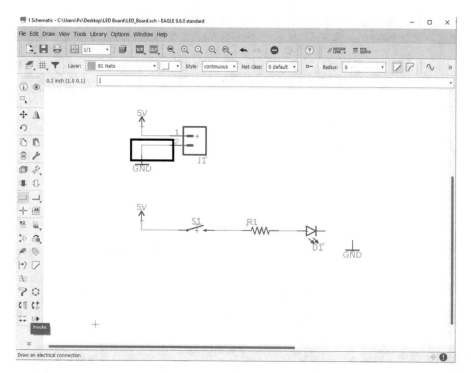

Figure 5-47. Connect GND to the terminal block

36. Connect the GND symbol to the cathode (right side) of the LED. See Figure 5-48.

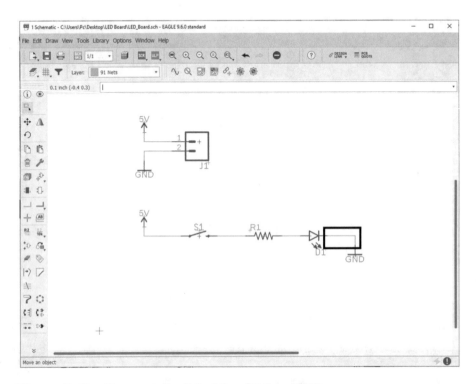

Figure 5-48. *Connect the left side of D1 to GND*

37. In order to add a value to the resistor, right-click the "+" on the resistor and select "Value" on the pop-up menu. Then enter "330ohm" and click "OK." See Figure 5-49.

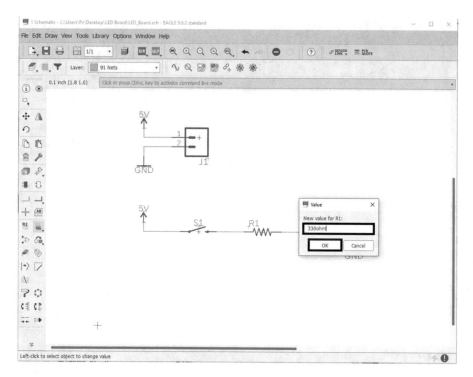

Figure 5-49. *Set the value of R1*

38. The schematic is now done, but in order to create a
    board file for the next section, we need to click the
    "Generate/Switch to Board" button. A dialog will
    come up asking you if you would like to create a
    board file; click the "Yes" button. See Figure 5-50.

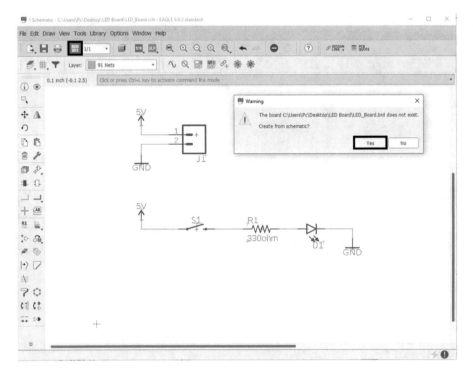

Figure 5-50.   *Create a *.brd file*

39.   This file will automatically be saved as LED_Board.
      brd. See Figure 5-51.

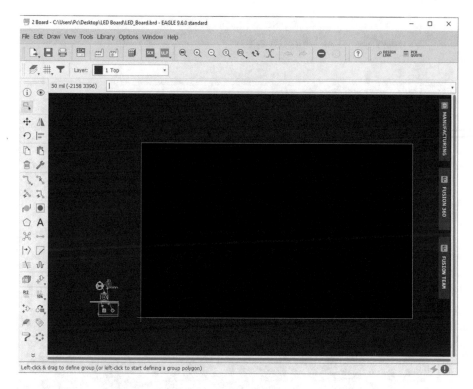

Figure 5-51. *Board window for LED_Board*

Now that the schematic is done and we have a board file, we can focus on the board layout for this project, which is what the next section will cover.

Laying Out a PCB

We have a schematic, but we still need to create a board layout so that a Gerber file can be created and sent off to the board manufacturer. This section will cover several important functions. It is alright if you must do these steps a few times before you get the hang of it; try to follow the layout as best you can.

1. Go to the Board Layout window if you are already
not there. See Figure 5-52.

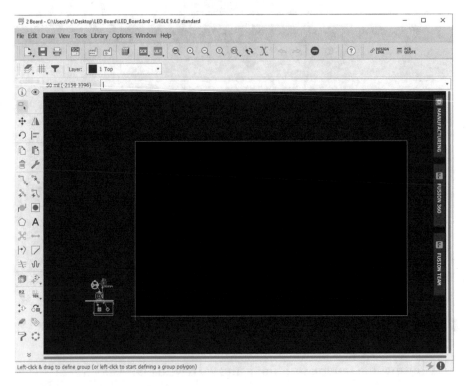

Figure 5-52. Board window

2. Click the Grid button and make sure it looks like
    Figure 5-53.

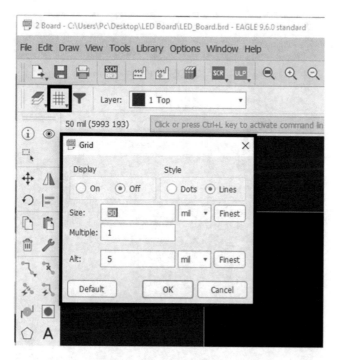

Figure 5-53. *Make sure the grid is the same*

3.   Once the Board Layout window is open, click the
      "Info" button. See Figure 5-54.

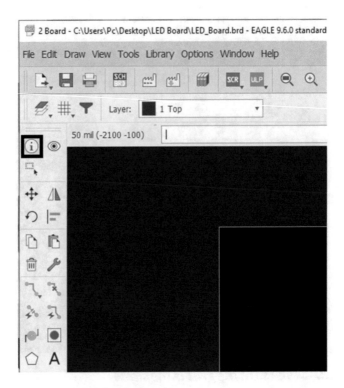

Figure 5-54. *Select the "Info" button*

4. Click the left vertical line, and a menu should
   appear. See Figure 5-55.

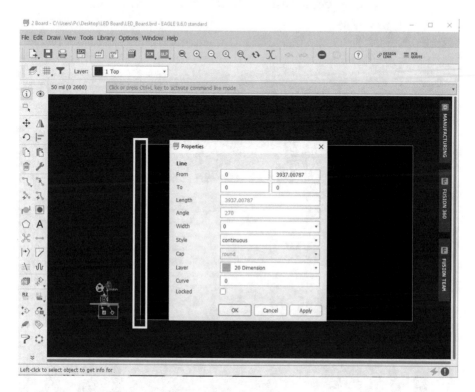

Figure 5-55. *Select the left vertical line*

5. In the second text box next to "From," type in 542 (if this value makes your board huge, please make sure you change your "Grid" to "mil") and click "OK." See Figure 5-56.

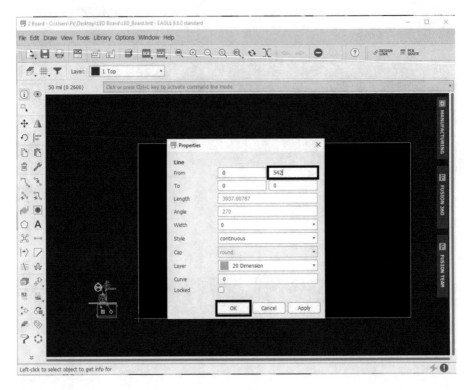

Figure 5-56. *Update vertical line value*

6. Now click the bottom horizontal line, and the same box should appear. See Figure 5-57.

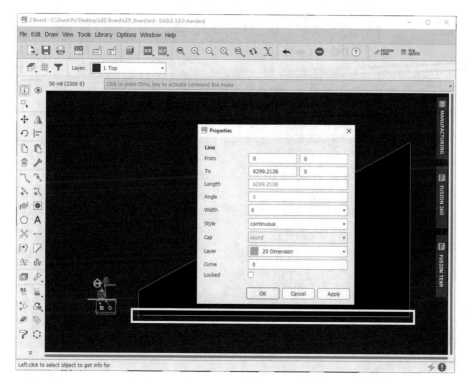

Figure 5-57. *Select bottom horizontal line*

7. Type 1294 into the box right next to the "to" and click "OK." See Figure 5-58.

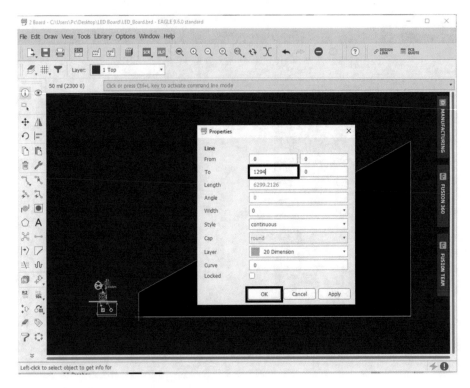

Figure 5-58. *Update horizontal line value*

8. Now click the top horizontal line (or what would be horizontal had we not updated the other lines). See Figure 5-59.

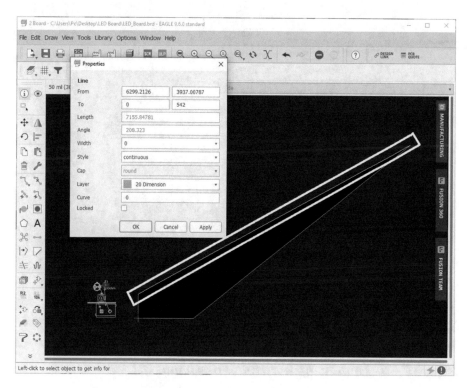

Figure 5-59. *Select top horizontal line*

9. Type 1294 into the box right next to "From" and click "OK." See Figure 5-60.

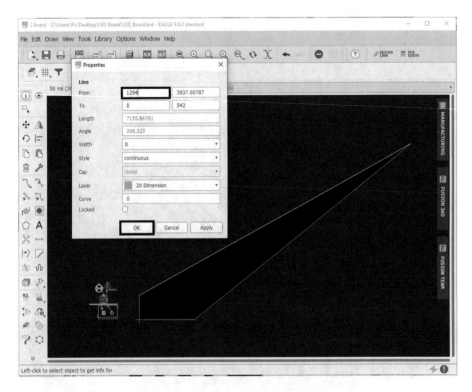

Figure 5-60. *Update top horizontal line value*

10.   Click the right-side vertical line. See Figure 5-61.

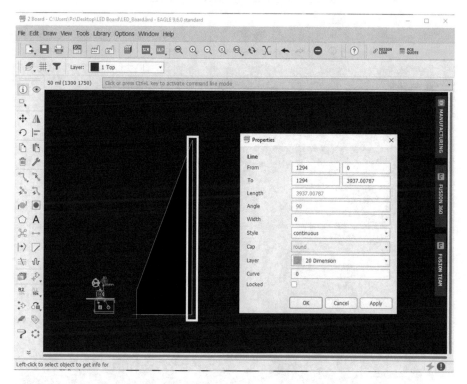

Figure 5-61. *Select right vertical line*

11. Type 542 into the second box next to "To," and you now have the dimensions for the PCB. See Figure 5-62.

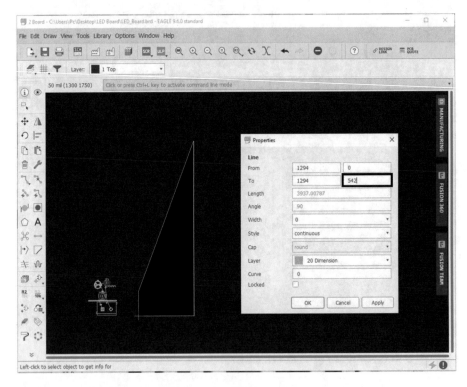

Figure 5-62. *Update right vertical line value*

12.   Click the "Move" button and select the terminal
      block. See Figure 5-63.

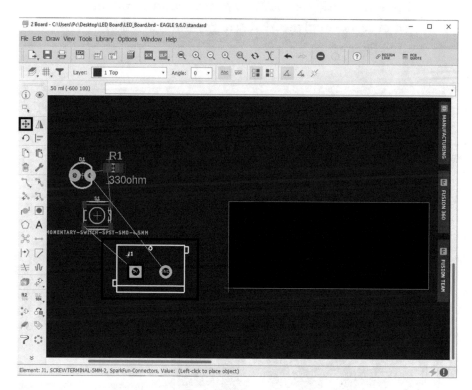

Figure 5-63.   *Select the "Move" button*

13.   Rotate the terminal block and move it onto the
       PCB. You can use the "Info" button and type in the
       position "155" and "365," or you can move it with the
       mouse and hold the Alt Key to get more precision.
       See Figure 5-64.

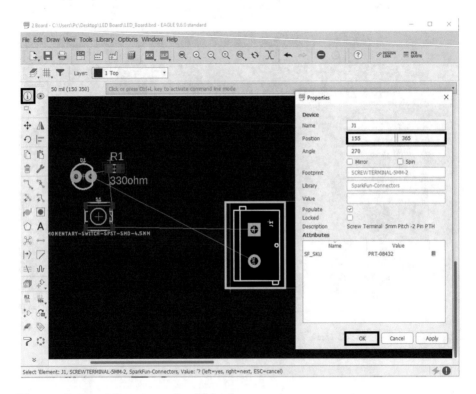

Figure 5-64. *Move terminal block*

14.   Next, move the push button onto the PCB. Pay
attention to the yellow lines going from one
component to the next. These lines are the nets you
created in the schematic. The position for the button
should be "540" and "265." See Figure 5-65.

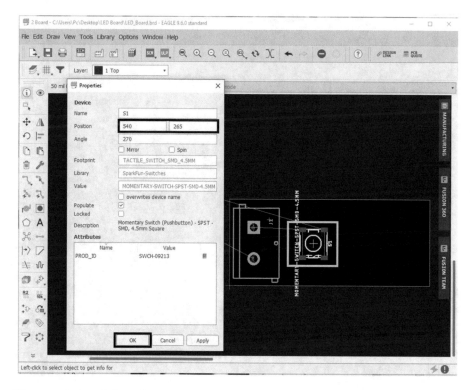

Figure 5-65. *Move button*

15. You may notice that the push button's device name is very long and not necessary to put on the PCB. If you zoom in to the PCB and right-click the "+" right next to the name, you can select "Delete," and this will remove the name from the PCB. See Figure 5-66.

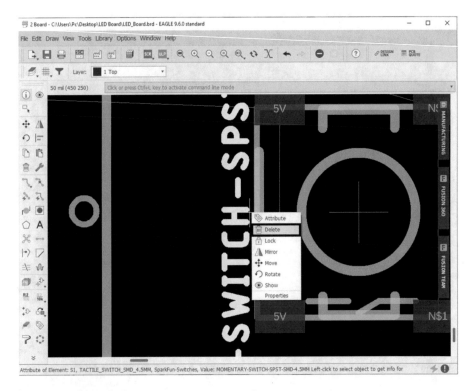

Figure 5-66. *Delete button name value*

16. Now add the resistor to the PCB, positioned at "860" and "270." See Figure 5-67.

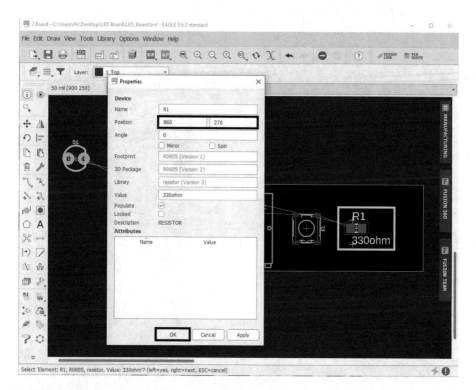

Figure 5-67. *Move resistor*

17.   Now add the LED to the PCB, positioned at "1135" and "280." You have now finished arranging the parts onto the PCB. See Figure 5-68.

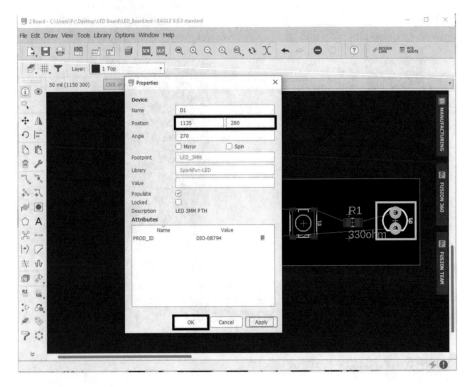

Figure 5-68.   *Move LED*

18.   Select the "Route Airwire" button. See Figure 5-69.

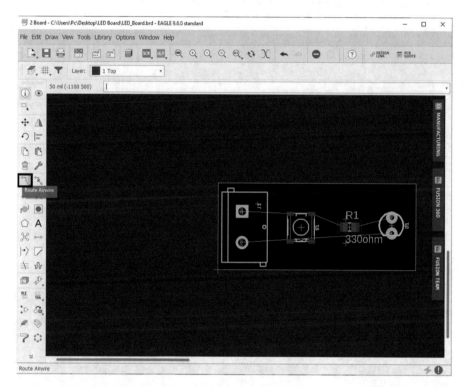

Figure 5-69. *Select the Route Airwire button*

19.   At the top, select 12 from the "Width:" drop-down
menu, or you can just enter "12." See Figure 5-70.

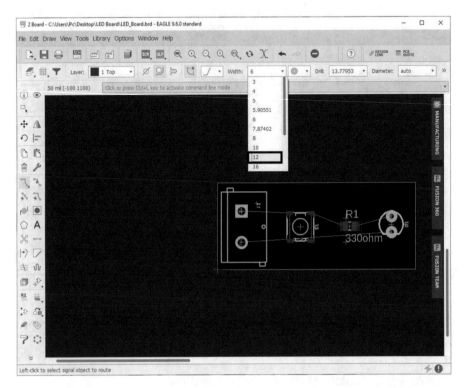

Figure 5-70. *Select 12mil route*

20.   Left-click the 5V contact on the terminal block (J1),
       then move your mouse over to the top-left contact of
       the push button (S1), and left-click that contact. See
       Figure 5-71.

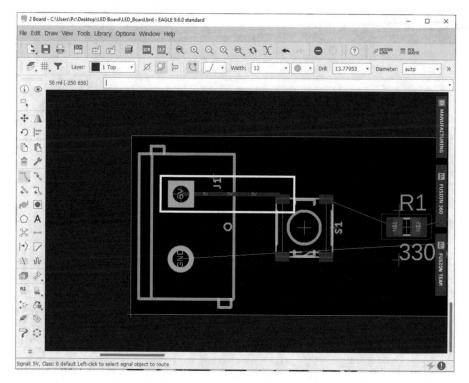

Figure 5-71.   *Connect terminal block to 5V*

21. Left-click from the 5V contact on the push button
     (S1) and drag your mouse to connect the route to
     the other 5V contact on the push button (S1). See
     Figure 5-72.

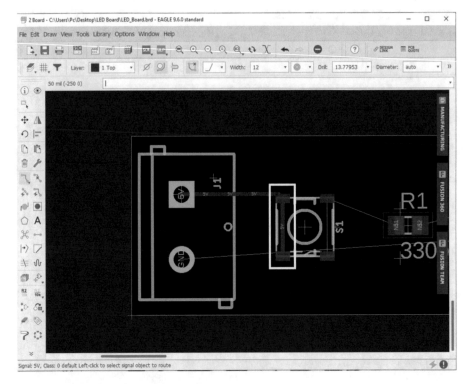

Figure 5-72. *Connect 5V lines*

22. Left-click the top-right contact on the push button and connect it to the left contact of the resistor (R1). See Figure 5-73.

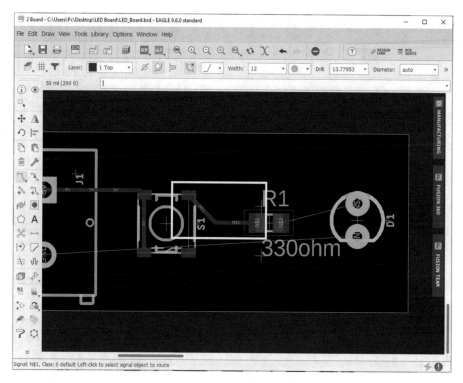

Figure 5-73. *Connect button to resistor*

23.   Left-click the top-right contact on the push button
      again and connect it to the right-bottom contact
      "N$1." See Figure 5-74.

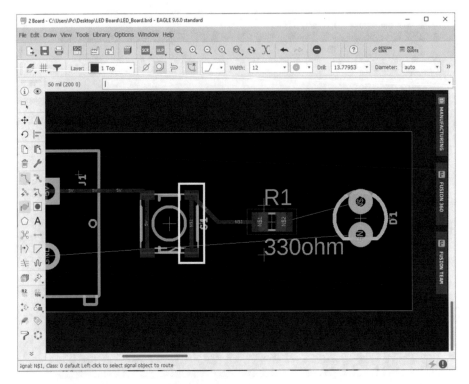

Figure 5-74. Connect buttons right side

24. Next, left-click the right contact of the resistor and connect the other end to the top contact of the LED (D1). See Figure 5-75.

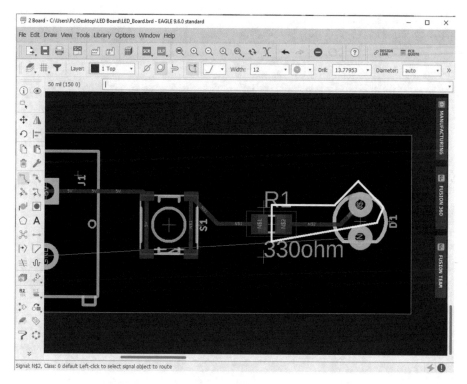

Figure 5-75. *Connect resistor to LED*

25.   To select the bottom layer, go to the top and
       change the "Layer:" drop-down to "16 Bottom." See
       Figure 5-76.

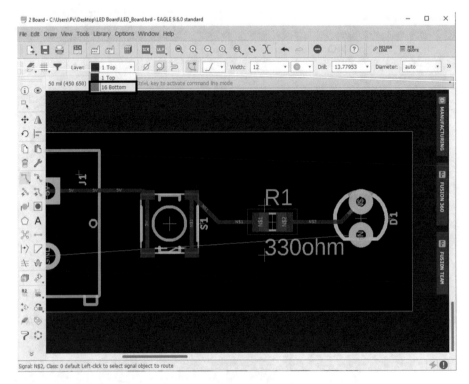

Figure 5-76. *Select the bottom layer*

26.   Select the bottom contact on the terminal block (J1) and connect the other end to the bottom contact of the LED (D1). Because this is on the bottom layer of the board, you can pass right through top layer contacts and routes as long as the contacts are not on the bottom layer as well. A good example of this is that when you pass underneath an SMT (surface mount) part which is only on the top layer, but if there is a through-hole contact, you will have to go around that part. See Figure 5-77.

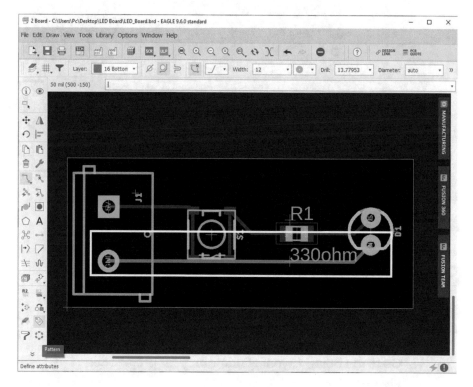

Figure 5-77. *Connect the terminal block to GND*

27.   The board is now ready to be made into a Gerber file. See Figure 5-78.

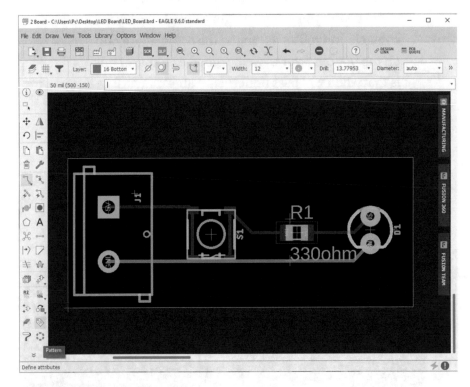

Figure 5-78. *Final board*

Exporting Gerber Files

Creating a Gerber file is very simple in Eagle and is also a very important step as it is the file that you will eventually send to the board manufacturer.

1.   Go to the Board Layout window for your project. See Figure 5-79.

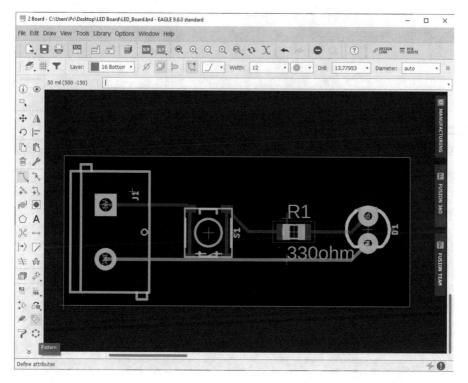

Figure 5-79. *Final board*

2. Go to File ➤ CAM Processor. Make sure your current
    project is saved. See Figure 5-80.

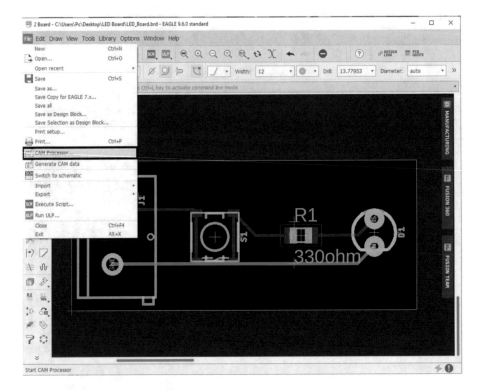

Figure 5-80. *Select CAM Processor...*

3. At the top, you will see the "Job" file that is currently being utilized, "template_2_layer.cam." This job will work for the current PCB we have created, but if we say had a four-layer board, this job would need to be modified to include those layers, as well as any other layers, such as soldermask or silkscreens those layers may also employ. See Figure 5-81.

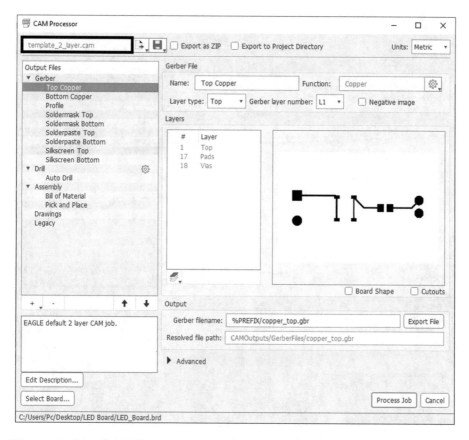

Figure 5-81. *CAM Processor window with "Job" name highlighted*

4. If you select the "Top Copper" layer, you will see a
   preview of that layer. Same thing goes for any of the
   other selections that the CAM Processor shows. See
   Figure 5-82.

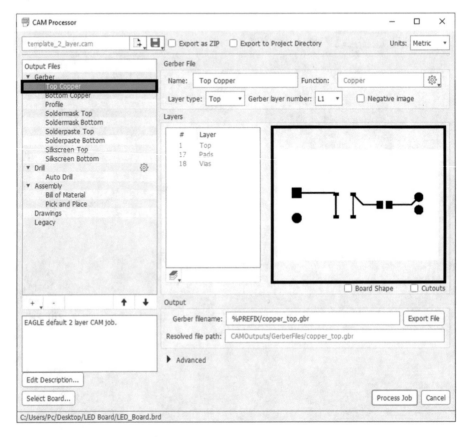

Figure 5-82. *Preview of the Top Copper of the PCB*

5. Click the "Process Job" button, and Gerber files will be generated after you select where you want them to be stored and what name you want to give them. See Figure 5-83.

Figure 5-83. *Save Gerber files*

6. When done, just exit out of the CAM Processor window and close out Eagle.

PCB Manufacturers

There is a plethora of board manufacturers in the United States and in China. I personally use PCBWay for both professional and personal projects, but there are 100s of board manufacturers ready to make your board. Figure 5-84 illustrates what I used to create this board.

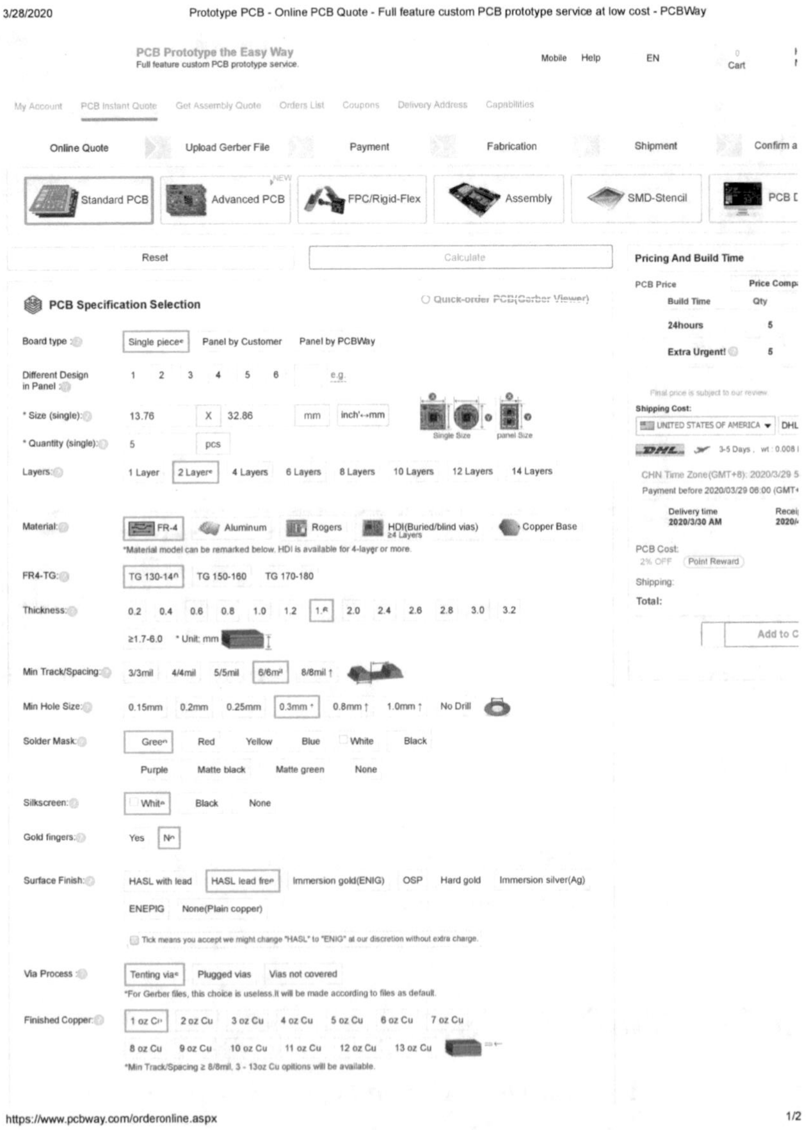

CHAPTER 5   PCB DESIGN

Figure 5-84. *Common settings for board manufacturing*

Summary

Well, you have made it through all of the first five chapters which I know contained a ton of information, and I am sure not all of it has been retained, which is fine because in the next five chapters we will be focusing on using and reinforcing these new skills to do some pretty cool project, but first let's take a look at some of the highlights of this chapter:

- Looked at what a PCB is and what kind of software is needed in order to make a PCB

- Took a tour of Eagle and some of the most important functions

- Learned how to load a third-party library into Eagle

- Learned the basics on how to create a schematic

- Learned the basics on how to create a board layout

- Learned how to export Gerber files

- Took a look at PCBWay as a board manufacturing company

CHAPTER 6

Robot Engineering Requirements: Controlling Motion

Alright, we have made it through several chapters of basic knowledge to continue through this book. From now on, I will be explaining only new concepts; for everything else, I would suggest looking at the previous five chapters for assistance. In this chapter, we will be using all the knowledge we gained in those previous chapters to work on a project for a company named Naticom. Naticom is a robotics company, and they want you to develop several prototypes and updates of a robot; for this chapter, that robot will be the first prototype and will require you to create a PCB, design a robot chassis, write some Arduino code, and physically make the prototype with a 3D printer. So, let's get started with this chapter as we have a lot to cover.

Hardware Explained: The H-Bridge

An H-bridge gets its name from the configuration of the npn and pnp transistors that make it. See Figure 6-1.

© Harold Timmis 2021
H. Timmis, *Practical Arduino Engineering*, https://doi.org/10.1007/978-1-4842-6852-0_6

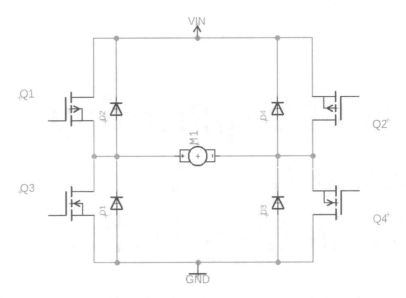

Figure 6-1. *Simple H-bridge circuit*

Note   If you search Google for "TB6612FNG," the first item should be Digi-Key; from this website, you can view the datasheet.

This is a very cool and important circuit to know how to use because it allows you to control DC motors, and it is even possible to control a stepper motor. The H-bridge we will use for this project will be the TB6612FNG. This is a very good and easy-to-use H-bridge. Let's look at the datasheet to see what this H-bridge is capable of (see Figures 6-2 through 6-8).

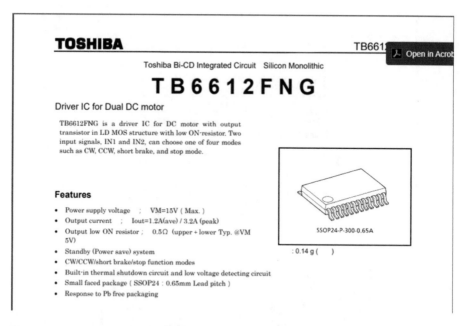

Figure 6-2. *First page of datasheet*

The first thing that is important to note is on page 2 which shows the pinout of the TB6612FNG, which is very useful when you are trying to figure out what signals need to be connected and what signals can be left floating or set to GND (0V) or +5V.

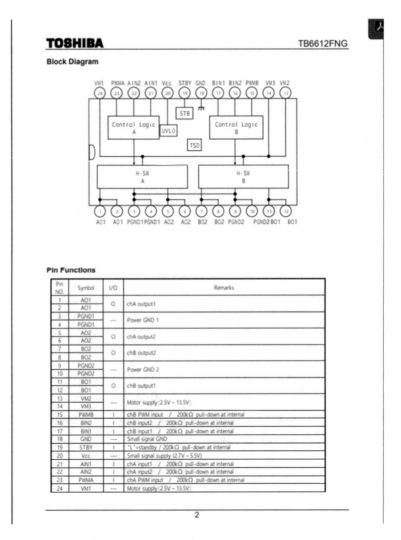

Figure 6-3. *Second page of datasheet*

The third page is also very important because it explains what operating voltages will work with the TB6612FNG. For example, the supply voltage for this H-bridge can be between 6 and 15V, which means VM1 must be connected to a supply voltage of 6V to 15V. The rest of the pins that will be connected to power can have a value of –0.2 to 6V, which is fine because the Arduino we are using will use 0 to 5V to control these pins. AIN1, AIN2, BIN1, and BIN2 are used to control the direction of the motor and will eventually be connected to a logical NOT circuit that will turn a bit from 1 (+5V) to 0 (GND) or 0 (GND) to 1 (+5V), creating a motor that will go clockwise (CW) or counterclockwise (CCW). The PWM pins will control the amount of power the motor will have using a duty cycle of 0 to 100% which will be represented by the Arduino program as a value from 0 to 255. Also, on this page is the "operating range." The values to pay attention to here are the supply voltages both VCC and VM. Then the most important value in this datasheet is the output current which is set to 1A for each channel of this H-bridge, which means each motor can draw 1A continuously without hurting this driver.

TOSHIBA
TB6612FNG

Absolute Maximum Ratings (Ta = 25°C)

Characteristics	Symbol	Rating	Unit	Remarks
Supply voltage	VM	15	V	
	Vcc	6		
Input voltage	VIN	-0.2 ~ 6	V	IN1, IN2, STBY, PWM pins
Output voltage	Vout	15	V	O1, O2 pins
Output current	Iout	1.2	A	Per 1ch
	Iout	2		tw=20ms Continuous pulse, Duty 20%
	(peak)	3.2		tw=10ms Single pulse
Power dissipation	PD	0.78	W	IC only
		0.89		50 × 50 t=1.6(mm) Cu 40% in PCB mounting
		1.36		76.2 × 114.3 t=1.6(mm) Cu 30% in PCB mounting
Operating temperature	Topr	-20 ~ 85	°C	
Storage temperature	Tstg	-55 ~ 150	°C	

Operating Range   (Ta=-20 ~ 85°C)

Characteristics	Symbol	Min	Typ.	Max	Unit	Remarks
Supply voltage	Vcc	2.7	3	5.5	V	
	VM	4.5	5	13.5	V	
Output current (H-SW)	Iout	---	---	1.0	A	VM 5V
		---	---	0.4		5V > VM 4.5V
Switching frequency	fPWM	---	---	100	kHz	

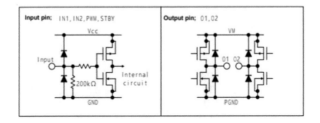

3

Figure 6-4. *Third page of datasheet*

The fourth page shows us how to use the H-bridge; for example, in order to turn the motor CCW, AIN1 needs to be low (GND), AIN2 needs to be high (+5V), PWM needs to be some voltage from 0.1V (motor low power) to 5V (motor full power), AO1 is LOW (GND), and AO2 is HIGH

(+6V to +13V). Finally, there are some nice diagrams to show you what the circuit looks like in the various states of this H-bridge.

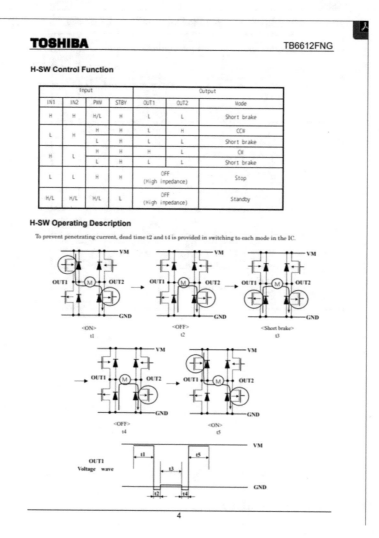

TOSHIBA   TB6612FNG

H-SW Control Function

Input				Output		
IN1	IN2	PWM	STBY	OUT1	OUT2	Mode
H	H	H/L	H	L	L	Short brake
L	H	H	H	L	H	CCW
		L	H	L	L	Short brake
H	L	H	H	H	L	CW
		L	H	L	L	Short brake
L	L	H	H	OFF (High impedance)		Stop
H/L	H/L	H/L	L	OFF (High impedance)		Standby

H-SW Operating Description

To prevent penetrating current, dead time t2 and t4 is provided in switching to each mode in the IC.

4

Figure 6-5. *Fourth page of datasheet*

271

The fifth page will show you the various characteristics of the H-bridge.

TOSHIBA   TB6612FNG

Electrical Characteristics (unless otherwise specified, Ta = 25°C, V$_{cc}$=3V, VM=5V)

Characteristics	Symbol		Test Condition	Min	Typ.	Max	Unit
Supply current	Icc(3V)		STBY=Vcc=3V, VM=5V	---	1.1	(1.8)	nA
	Icc(5.5V)		STBY=Vcc=5.5V, VM=5V	---	1.5	2.2	
	Icc(STB)		STBY=0V	---	---	1	μA
	IM(STB)			---	---	1	
Control input voltage	VIH			Vcc×0.7	---	Vcc+0.2	V
	VIL			-0.2	---	Vcc×0.3	
Control input current	IIH		VIN=3V	5	15	25	μA
	IIL		VIN=0V	---	---	1	
Standby input voltage	VIH(STB)			Vcc×0.7	---	Vcc+0.2	V
	VIL(STB)			-0.2	---	Vcc×0.3	
Standby input current	IIH(STB)		VIN=3V	5	15	25	μA
	IIL(STB)		VIN=0V	---	---	1	
Output saturating voltage	Vsat(U+L)1		Io=1A,Vcc=VM=5V	---	0.5	(0.7)	V
	Vsat(U+L)2		Io=0.3A,Vcc=VM=5V	---	0.15	(0.21)	
Output leakage current	IL(U)		VM=Vout=15V	---	---	1	μA
	IL(L)		VM=15V,Vout=0V	-1	---	---	
Regenerative diode VF	VF(U)		IF=1A	---	1	1.1	V
	VF(L)			---	1	1.1	
Low voltage detecting voltage	UVLD		(Designed value)	---	1.9	---	V
Recovering voltage	UVLC			---	2.2	---	
Response speed	tr		(Designed value)	---	24	---	ns
	tf			---	41	---	
	Dead time	H to L	Penetration protect time	---	(50)	---	
		L to H	(Designed value)	---	(230)	---	
Thermal shutdown circuit operating temperature	TSD		(Designed value)	---	175	---	°C
Thermal shutdown hysteresis	Δ TSD			---	20	---	

5

Figure 6-6. *Fifth page of datasheet*

Skipping to the seventh page, we can see a typical application for this H-bridge, which can be very useful when you are creating a PCB for this H-bridge.

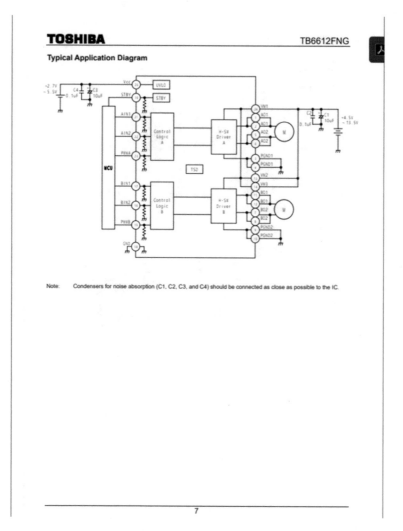

Figure 6-7. *Seventh page of datasheet*

Lastly, we get to page 8 which has the measurements of the H-bridge, which is very useful when you need to make a footprint for a component. Luckily, this H-bridge has several devices already created for us in Eagle, so we will not have to recreate this footprint or symbol for this H-bridge.

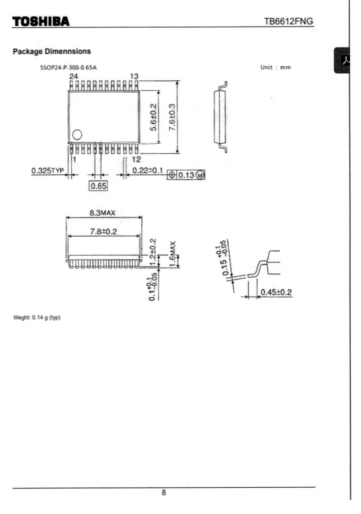

Figure 6-8. *Eighth page of datasheet*

Well, now that we know a bit more about this H-bridge, we can move on to the fun part and create a motor driver board that we can use to create the robot for Naticom.

Chapter Project: Creating the First Prototype

Here, we are now at the start of a project; the first thing we will work on is gathering the requirements for this project; then we will start to work on the various parts to complete this project such as designing the H-bridge, designing the chassis, printing the chassis, assembling the chassis, and finally troubleshooting the first prototype.

Controlling Motors with Serial Commands

Now that you understand what an H-bridge is, we can visit our Naticom to see if it has any projects for us to complete that require using the Arduino to control motors. It does! So, our first steps are gathering the requirements and creating the requirements document.

Requirements Gathering

Now, the customer has set up a meeting and has several requirements for a robot controlled by the Arduino using serial communication; the Arduino will drive two motors with the help of a custom H-bridge PCB. The client's project also requires that the user send the motor's parameters in a comma-separated format to the serial monitor (shown in Figure 6-9) as follows:

```
1,255,1,255
```

In this format, the first parameter is the direction of motor A, the second parameter is the speed of motor A, the third is the direction of motor B, and the fourth is the speed of motor B. The serial monitor displays the information in this format:

```
Motor A
1
255
```

Motor B

1

255

Note   Comma-separated format is a very common way for data to be passed and collected from the Arduino and many other peripherals.

Naticom wants each of the comma-separated parameters to go to these specific pins. The pins are 12, 3, 13, and 11. Another requirement is that the final prototype needs to be configured on a custom chassis once the hardware and software have been tested.

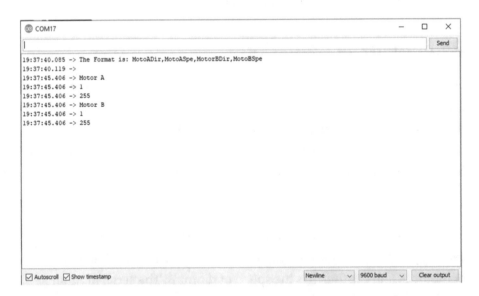

Figure 6-9. *The user will type values for the direction and speed of the motors into the serial monitor shown here*

Note   When using the serial monitor, make sure that newline is selected in the line ending parameter.

Now that you have notes for this project, we can configure them into a requirements document.

Outlining the Software Requirements

The following are the software requirements:

- Create a program that sends comma-separated data to the Arduino to control the speed and direction of two motors. The user should enter the data in this format:

  `1,255,1,255`

- The first and third parameters in the comma-separated values are the direction of motors A and B, and the second and fourth parameters are the speeds of motors A and B.

- The serial monitor should output the data in this format:

  ```
  Motor A
  1
  255
  Motor B
  1
  255
  ```

- The overall purpose of this program is to control the speed and direction of two 6V motors.

Now that we have the hardware and software requirements, we can create the software's flowchart. Figure 6-10 shows the flowchart for this project.

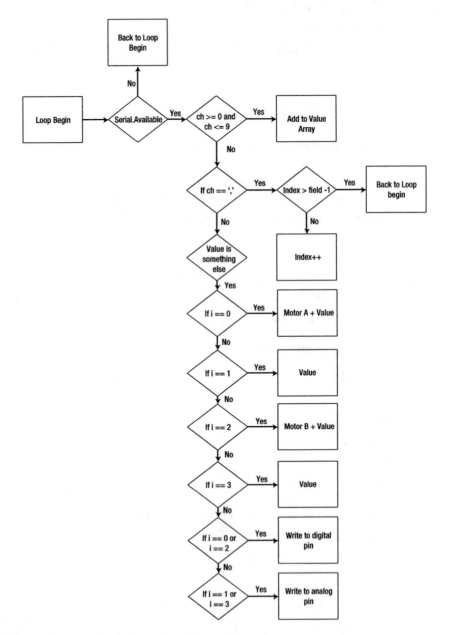

Figure 6-10. *Flowchart for this project*

Alright, the next section will cover designing the H-bridge for this project.

Creating an H-Bridge PCB

First, let's get all the circuits we will need for this PCB on the schematic by using the "ADD" button. Configure it in the orientations seen in Figure 6-11. For the parts used on this PCB, look at the Bill of Materials found in this chapter's source and look up each part using the "Found" column.

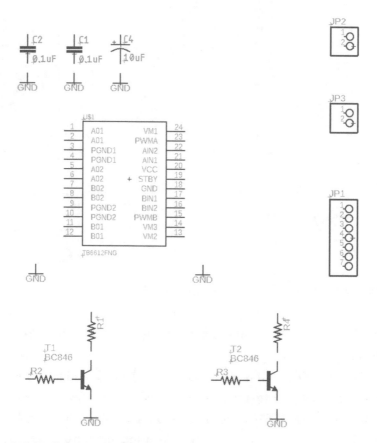

Figure 6-11. *Schematic layout*

Next, let's add the nets to each of these components. See Figure 6-12.

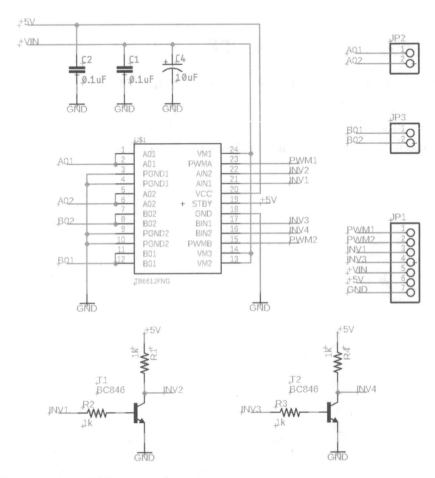

Figure 6-12. *Add nets to the components*

Now I want to explain what is happening in this circuit, mainly the inverters for AIN1 and AIN2 (BIN1 and BIN2 have identical circuitry). If AIN1 is HIGH (+5V), then AIN2 is LOW (GND); this is a logical not or an inverter due to the pull-up resistor R9. When AIN1 is LOW, AIN2 will be pulled to +5V, and if AIN1 is HIGH, the transistor will activate and force AIN2 to GND. This allows us to control the direction of the motor with only the use of one pin per motor instead of using two pins; this can be very useful if you do not have a ton of GPIO (general-purpose input/output) pins. You may also notice some capacitors on the +5V and VIN nets. These are here to filter electrical noise as we do not want the H-bridge to act in an unexpected way.

Next, go ahead and click the "Value" button for both of the two-pin headers and update its value to "609-1317-ND." Do this also for the seven-pin header, but update its value to "WM4205-ND." This will be used later when you need to get the parts for this board, or you need to tell the PCB manufacturer what parts to buy.

Now that the schematic is done, we can move on to laying out the PCB. Here are the coordinates of each component and the size of the current PCB. It is also very important to get the correct orientations of the components, so make sure all the components are in the right orientation and that all the yellow wires look the same as well. See Figure 6-13 for the component orientations.

Table 6-1.

Component	X	Y	Unit
U$1	400	500	Mil
C1	450	300	Mil
C2	325	300	Mil
C4	400	200	Mil
JP2	100	611.81	Mil
JP3	100	392.913	Mil
JP1	920	480	Mil
R1	650	600	Mil
R2	775	750	Mil

(continued)

Table 6-1. (*continued*)

Component	X	Y	Unit
R3	750	375	Mil
R4	775	250	Mil
T1	650	750	Mil
T2	650	250	Mil
PCB	1000	1000	Mil

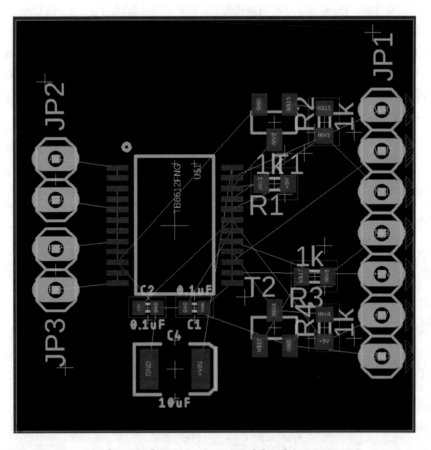

Figure 6-13. *Configure the components like this*

Let's move on to the routing of this board as it has a few very important elements to it. You will notice there are two pins for each of the motor pins (A01, A02, B01, B02). This is not on accident; this is to ensure that when the motors are encountering a load, the traces do not burn up, so it is important to give these pins larger traces to allow more current to be drawn (remember that the max current draw for each channel is 1A). Let's go ahead and add 24mil traces to A01 of JP2 to the A01 of the H-bridge (connect A02 of JP2 to A02 on the H-bridge), and do the same for the B01 and B02 signals; only they attached to JP3. See Figure 6-14.

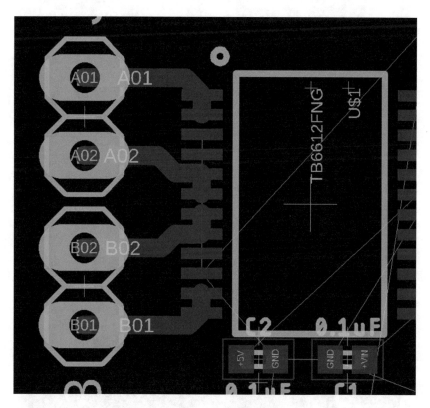

Figure 6-14. *Connect A01, A02, B01, and B02*

Now we can route those filter caps we talked about during the schematic portion of this project. Connect +VIN of the 10uF capacitor to +VIN of the 0.1uF filter cap. This will finally be connected to the +VIN pin on the H-bridge (all of this using the 24mil trace). Switching to a 16mil wire for the +5V routes. Let's connect the 0.1uF cap's +5V pad to the +5V pins of the H-bridge (just remember you do not have to follow my routing perfectly; just be sure not to short any of the traces). Next, connect the +5V pad from the 1kohm resistor of the INV4 to the +5V pad of the 0.1uF filter cap we just connected to the H-bridge. See Figures 6-15 and 6-16.

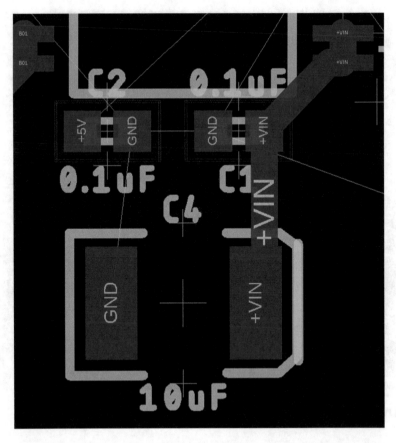

Figure 6-15. *Connect VIN to the filter caps*

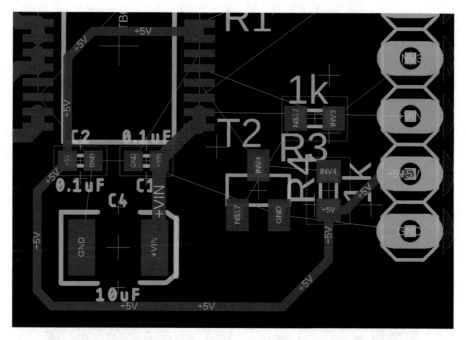

Figure 6-16. *Connect +5V*

Now we are going to do something a little different. We are going to use a "via" to pass a signal from the top of the PCB to the bottom of the PCB; this will allow us to get under other routes that would otherwise cause a short which would cause the H-bridge circuit not to work. See Figure 6-17 if you want to see what a short would look like. We will start with the resistor for the INV4 that we hooked up in the previous paragraph. First, connect the +5V pad to the +5V header. See Figure 6-16. Switch to a 12mil route. Connect the INV4 from the 1k resistor to the collector of the transistor. This is the pull-up resistor we discussed earlier. Now select the collector of the transistor, move the route close to the +VIN route then place the route, next press the wheel button on your mouse; this will automatically create a via (don't worry if it is large or a square shape); place the via on top of the route you just placed (you are now on the bottom side of the PCB) and drag the route toward the INV4 pad of the

H-bridge. Press the wheel of your mouse again, and you will move back to the top layer of the PCB, and you can connect to the INV4 pad of the H-bridge. Now to make these vias smaller and of the correct shape, click the "Info" button and select the via next to the transistor. For shape, select "round." For drill, select 13.77; if 13.77 is not an option, you can just type 13.77 into the drill text box. Do the same for the other via next to the INV4 pad of the H-bridge. See Figures 6-18 and 6-19.

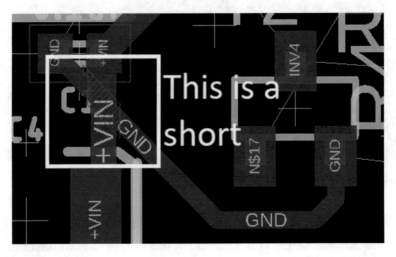

Figure 6-17. *This is a short and should always be avoided*

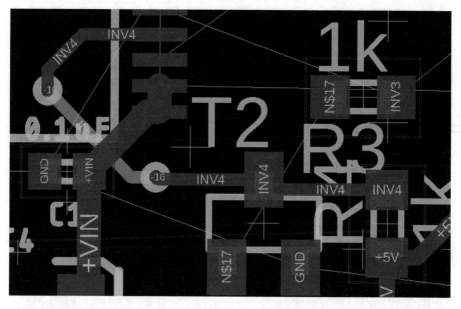

Figure 6-18. Connect INV4

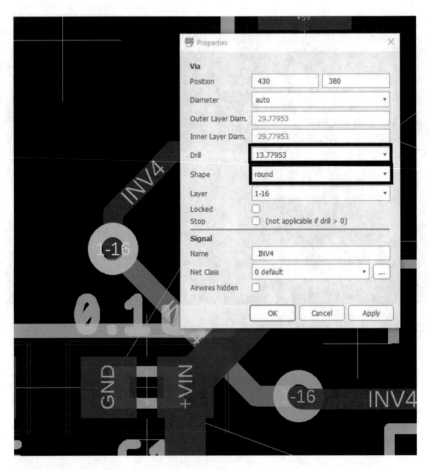

Figure 6-19.   *Update the vias for INV4*

Note   You may find it difficult to select a via to get the Properties menu. If you find yourself selecting the trace instead of the via, you can cycle through the various components by right-clicking until the via is highlighted and then selecting it with a left-click.

Now let's connect the base of the transistor (N$17) to the base resistor's N$17 pad. Again, a via will be needed in order to avoid other routes. You can use the same 12mil vias. Next, connect the INV3 pad of the resistor to the INV3 header pin and then connect to the INV3 of the H-bridge. See Figures 6-20 and 6-21.

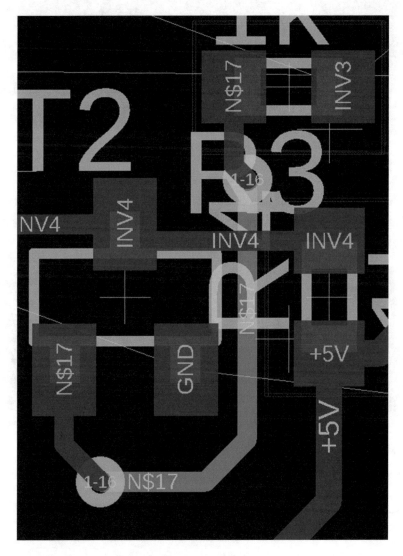

Figure 6-20. *Connect the N$17 using vias*

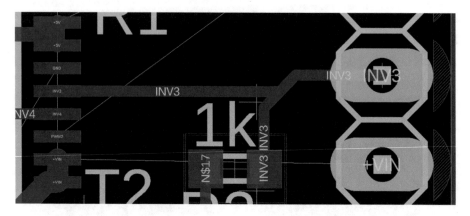

Figure 6-21. *Connect INV3*

When you place a route, you may have to remove it because it interferes with another signal or it is not in the most optimal position. This is when the "Ripup" button comes into use, and trust me you will use it a lot during the routing process of a PCB. See Figures 6-22a and 6-22b.

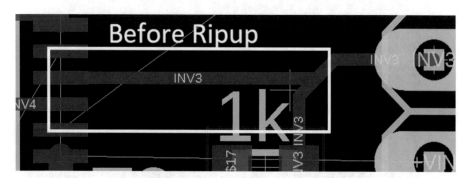

Figure 6-22a. *Before the Ripup tool is used*

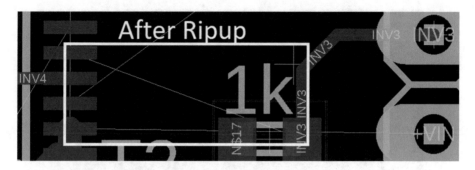

Figure 6-22b. After the Ripup tool is used

Let's move on to the other inverter circuit. Switch to a 16mil trace. Then route the +5V pad of the resistor in front of the transistor to the +5V pad of the H-bridge. Switch to a 12mil trace. Then take the INV2 pad of that same resistor and connect it to the INV2 of the H-bridge and the INV2 of the transistor. Next, connect the PWM1 signal from the header pin to the PWM1 pad of the H-bridge. See Figures 6-23, 6-24, and 6-25.

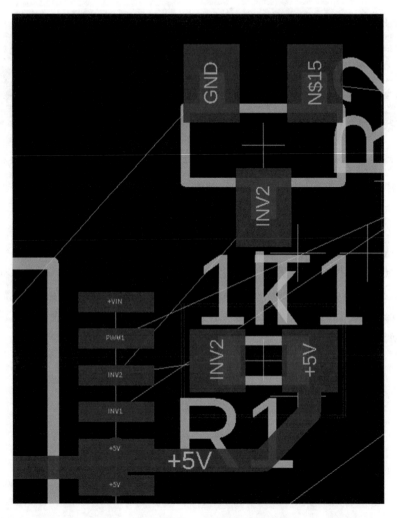

Figure 6-23. *Route +5V from R1 to the H-bridge*

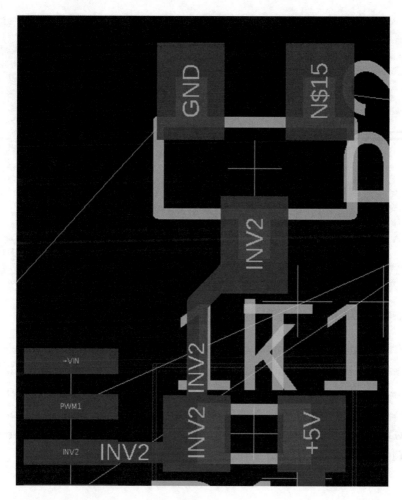

Figure 6-24. *Connect INV2 from R1 to T1*

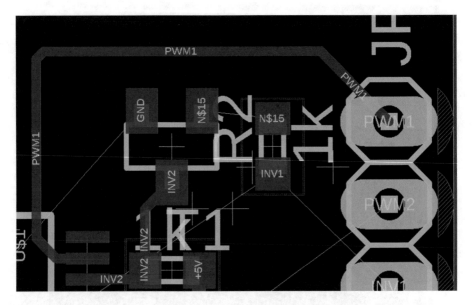

Figure 6-25. *Connect PWM1 from JP1 to the H-bridge*

Stay on the 12mil trace and connect the N$15 signal of the transistor to the N$15 of the resistor next to the transistor. Connect INV1 to the INV1 header pin. Then connect the INV1 pad of the resistor to the INV1 pad of the H-bridge; this will require you to use a couple of vias to get past the PWM1 signal. Use the same specs for the vias as the other inverter circuit. See Figures 6-26, 6-27, and 6-28.

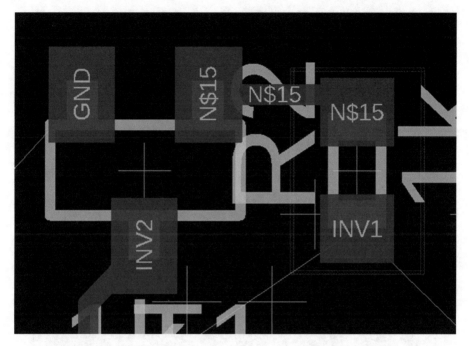

Figure 6-26. *Route N$15*

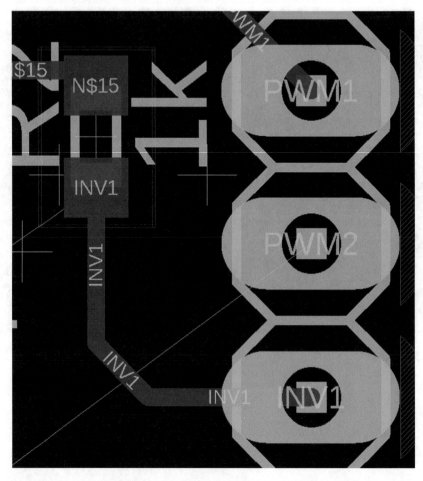

Figure 6-27. *Route INV1 to JP1*

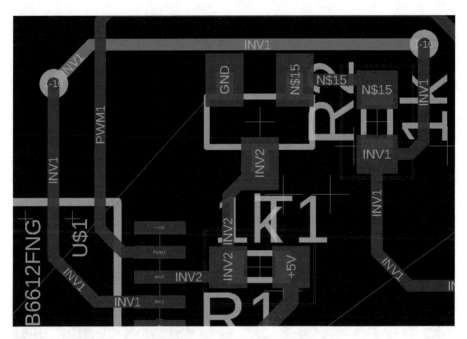

Figure 6-28. *Route the rest of INV1 to the H-bridge*

Note   While you have been routing, you may have noticed there is a
new menu bar at the top; this menu has a lot of cool features such as
routing avoidance settings, route shape, route width, via shape, and
via drill.

Now let's connect PWM2 from the H-bridge to the PWM2 header using
a 12mil trace; again you will need to use a via, but this time you will not
need to switch back from the bottom because the header is on both sides
of the PCB. See Figure 6-29.

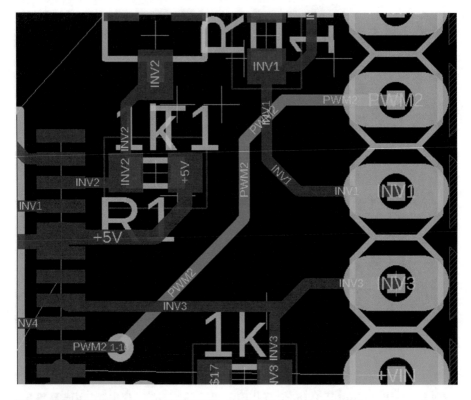

Figure 6-29. *Connect PWM2 from the H-bridge to JP1*

Now we need to connect all the +VIN signals together; to do this, switch to a 24mil trace and select the +VIN pad at the top of the PCB (pin 24 of the H-bridge). Using a via, go from the top to the bottom of the PCB, move through the center of the H-bridge, and use another via to get back to the top of the PCB and connect to the other +VIN pads on the H-bridge. Finally, connect the +VIN pad (pads 13 and 14 of the H-bridge) to the header pin marked +VIN; you may have to use a via. These vias will be much larger than the 12mil vias that we previously used; they will be 25.59mil vias. See Figures 6-30, 6-31, and 6-32.

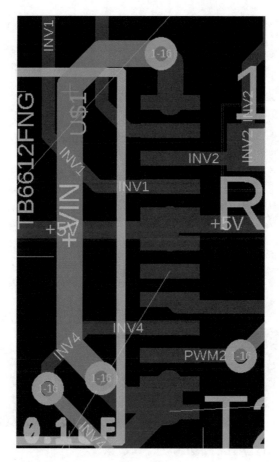

Figure 6-30. *Connect +VIN pins together*

Figure 6-31. *Connect the +VIN pin of the H-bridge to the header pin (+VIN)*

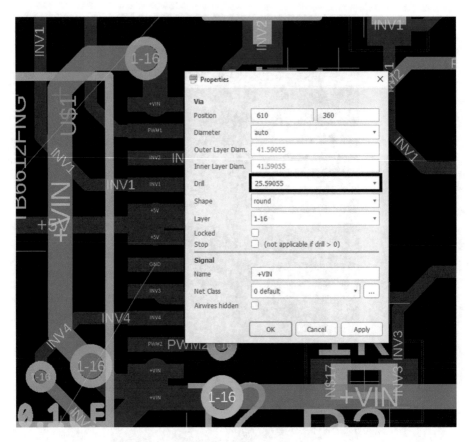

Figure 6-32. *Make the routes 25.59055mils*

That should do it for the routing, but there are a few more things to do before we move on. It is always a good idea to make sure all your routes have been made. To do this, click the "Layer Settings"; this will open a menu that will allow you to hide layers of the PCB. See Figure 6-33. Go ahead and select the "Hide Layers" button. You will notice that all your hard work has disappeared; well not really, it is just hidden. See Figure 6-34. Go ahead and click the "19 Unrouted" layer. If you see any yellow, this means that you have a trace that needs to be routed; otherwise, your circuit will not work correctly. See Figure 6-35. We have several traces that need to be connected, and they are all GND. In order to make sure all GNDs are connected, we need to create vias that will connect the GNDs together.

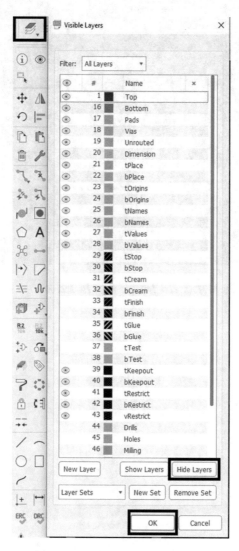

Figure 6-33. *Hide all of the layers*

Figure 6-34. *Screen after all layers are hidden*

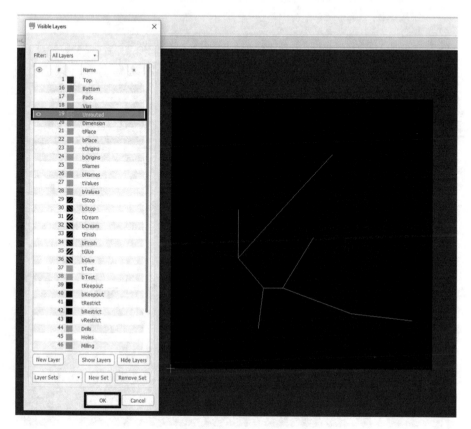

Figure 6-35. *Shows all of the unrouted traces*

Go ahead and show all the layers by going to the "Layer Settings" window and clicking "Show Layers," then click "OK." See Figure 6-36. Now go ahead and click the "Via" button; add vias near the unrouted areas of the PCB. See Figure 6-37. Now click the "Name" button and select one of the new vias and name it "GND"; do this for each of the vias. See Figure 6-38.

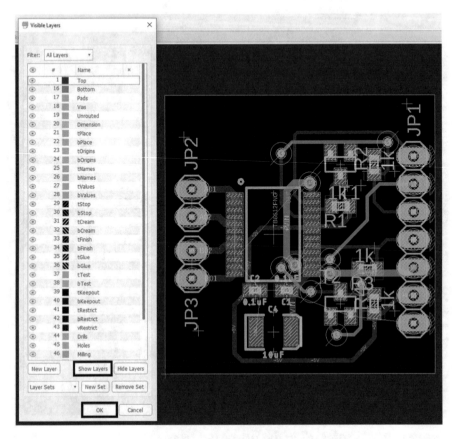

Figure 6-36. *Select "Show Layers" and click "OK"*

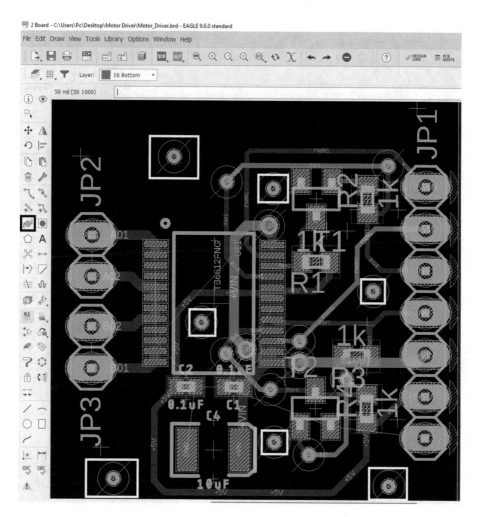

Figure 6-37. *Add some vias to the layout*

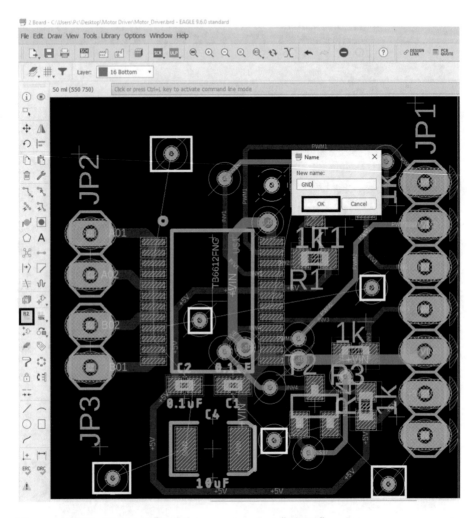

Figure 6-38. *Name all of those new vias "GND"*

We need to add holes at these coordinates: y-axis: 100mil x-axis: 900mil and y-axis: 100mil x-axis: 100mil. To do this, click the "Hole" button and place it in an open area on the PCB. Click the "Info" button and select the hole. See Figure 6-39. For position, type 100 for the first value and 900 for the second value. Then put the drill size 118.11024 and click "OK." See Figure 6-40. Do this for the second hole except the values will be 100mil and 100mil. See Figure 6-41. You may also have to move a via out of the way.

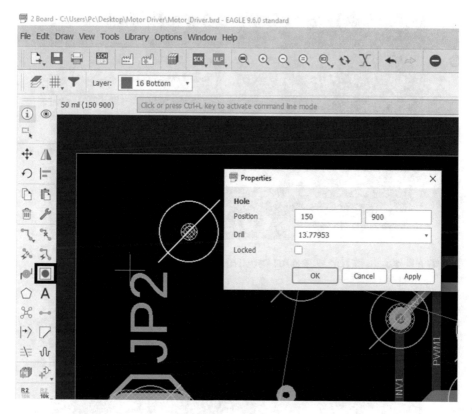

Figure 6-39. *Add holes to the layout*

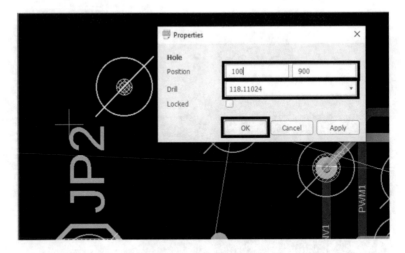

Figure 6-40. *Set the size and location of the via*

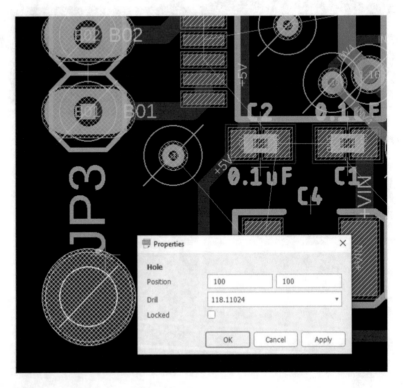

Figure 6-41. *Create a second hole*

Now if you see any text on the outside of the PCB, go ahead and move it onto the PCB; just make sure it is close to the component it represents. See Figure 6-42.

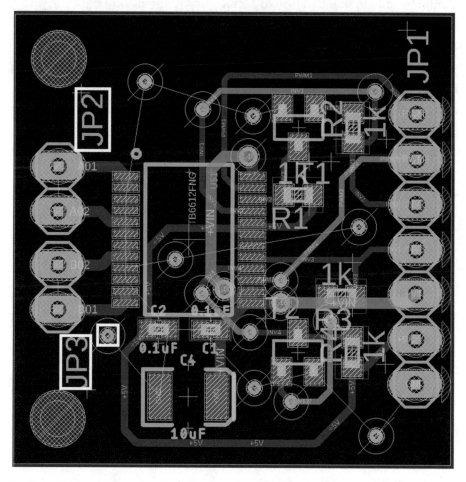

Figure 6-42. *Move the header labels and the via that is interfering with the second hole*

Finally, the last thing we need to do is create some ground planes for the PCB; this is very important as it will connect those GND vias together so that we do not have any floating grounds. First, select the "Polygon" button and select the origin of the PCB. See Figure 6-43. Now go ahead and place a square along the perimeter of the PCB. If you need more precision while you are placing this outline, you can hold the "Alt" key and you should be able to make a close to perfect perimeter around the PCB; just make sure you close the square where the PCB's origin is. See Figure 6-44. You will know that the polygon has been closed because a window will pop up asking you to name the polygon. Name it GND. See Figure 6-45. Do this for the bottom layer as well; just make sure you select the bottom layer in the Layers selection box. See Figure 6-46. Finally, click the "Ratsnest" button, and you will see that a top and bottom ground plane has been added to your PCB. See Figure 6-47. You should check that you have no unrouted traces.

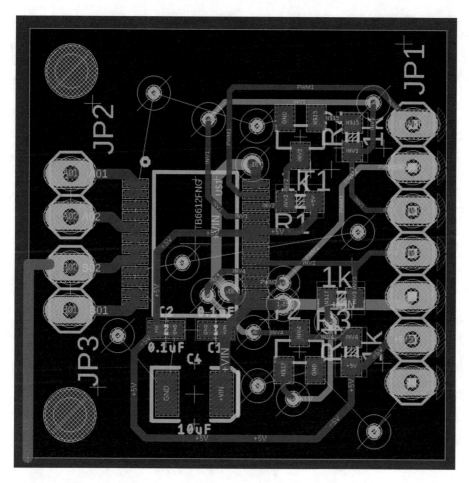

Figure 6-43. *Start to make the polygon on the top layer*

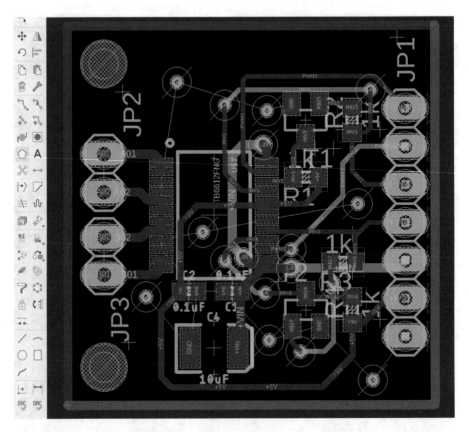

Figure 6-44. *Make sure the polygon ends at the origin*

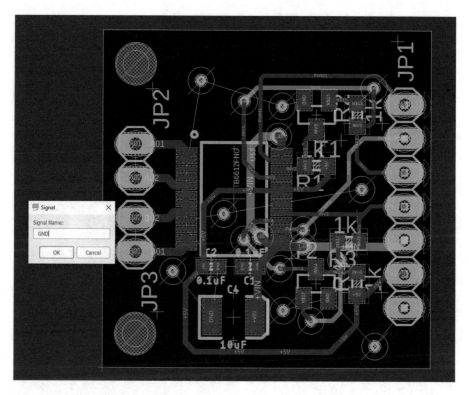

Figure 6-45. *Name the plane GND*

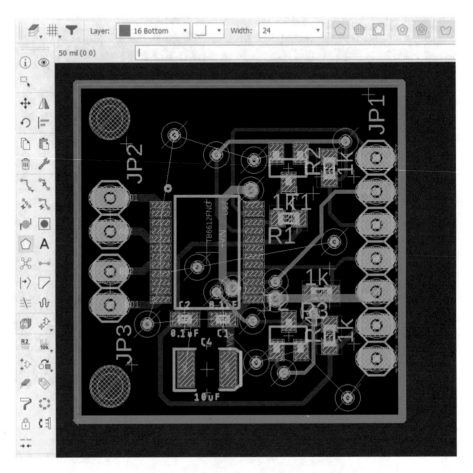

Figure 6-46. *Create a GND plane for the bottom layer*

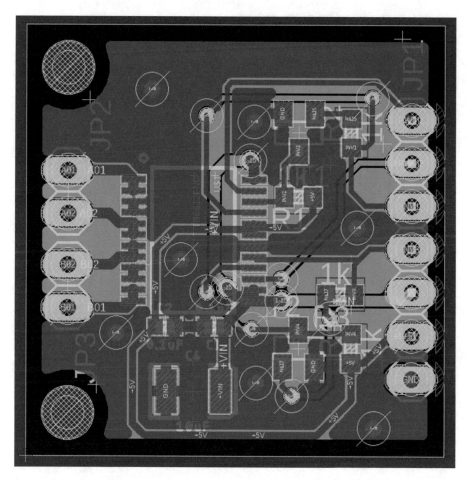

Figure 6-47. *Click the "Ratsnest" button*

You will notice that there is indeed some unrouted traces for GND; to fix these, we need to reconfigure the traces for A01, A02, B01, and B02. See Figure 6-48. Then add two vias between the two sets of signals and click the "Ratsnest" button. See Figure 6-49. If you need to use a 12mil trace to connect the new vias to the GND pads on the H-bridge. See Figure 6-50.

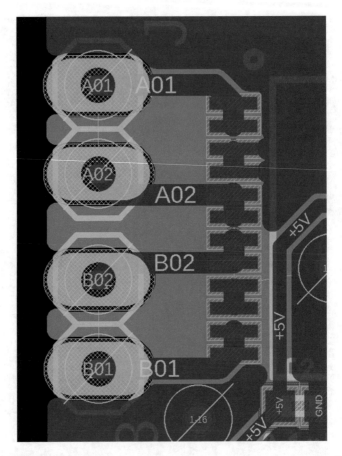

Figure 6-48. *Redo the A01, A02, B01, and B02 routes using the ripup tool and the route tool*

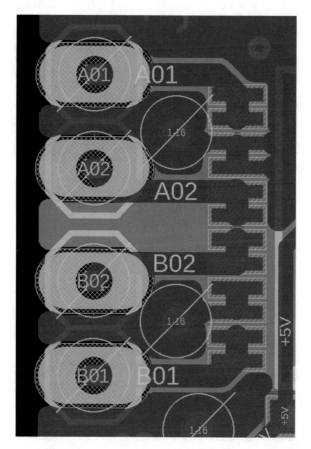

Figure 6-49. *Add vias in between A01 and A02 and B01 and B02*

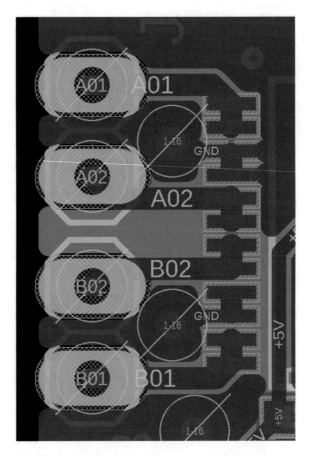

Figure 6-50. *Add 12mil traces to connect the GNDs*

Now you will need to send this board to be made; as I have stated before, I use PCBWay quite often, and they work very well for me. You can also get this board assembled by them which I recommend if you are a novice at soldering surface mount hardware (SMT). Also, you will need to extract the Bill of Materials. To do this, go to CAM Processor again, select "Bill of Material," then select your name and location for the file, and click the "Export File" button. This will be a text document. If you are unsure, you can download the content for this book and look under:

Chapter 6\CH6_PCBs\driver with TB6621FNG\Gerber\CAMOutputs\ Assembly. When purchasing the connectors for this motor driver, make sure you purchase these connectors:

> 2 x 609-1317-ND: This is the FCI two-pin header.

> 1 x WM4205-ND: This is the main connector for the motor driver.

Both are Digi-Key part numbers.

Wow! That was a lot of work well done, but the job is not over yet; we still need to create the first prototype of the robot chassis, which is the subject of the next section.

Designing a Robot Chassis

Well, the wait is over; we need to make the 3D model that will be the chassis we develop through the entire book. This is just the first version of the chassis, but we still want to get it as right as we can. For this chassis, the customer wants a three-wheeled robot controlled by an Arduino. Let's go ahead and get started on the 3D model.

1. Go ahead and open Fusion 360 and create a new project; name it Chassis_v1.

2. Create a new component by right-clicking the main component at the top of the browser. See Figure 6-51. You can name that component "Chassis."

Figure 6-51.   Create a new component

3.   Start a new sketch and create a rectangle 160mm by
      140mm. See Figure 6-52.

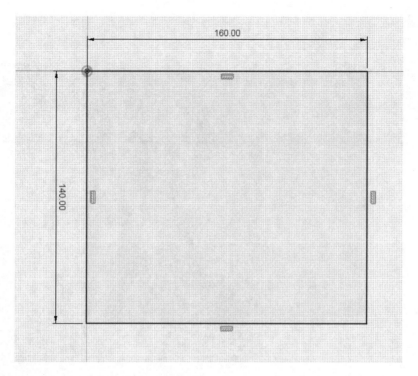

Figure 6-52. *Create a rectangle*

4. Extrude that rectangle out 5.08mm.

5. Create two 4mm holes for the caster wheel. They should be 39.45mm apart and 15mm away from the front edge of the chassis. See Figure 6-53. Remember to use the distancing tool (press the "d" key) to create the constraints in Figure 6-53. Also, convert all non-essential lines to construction lines by selecting the line and pressing the "x" key.

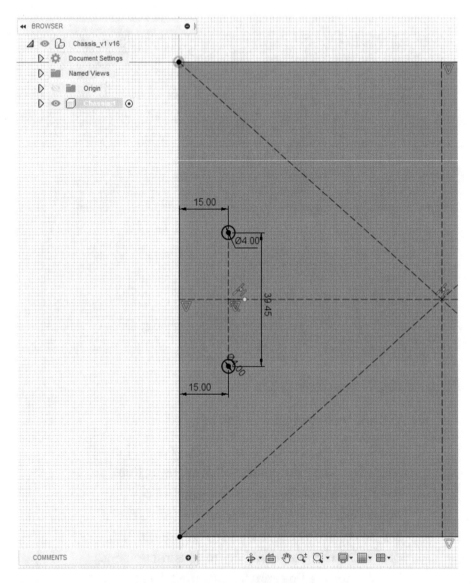

Figure 6-53. *Add the holes for the caster wheel*

6.   Extrude to the bottom surface of the chassis. This
     will make two 4mm holes.

7. Let's make a spot for the Arduino to go. We need
    two holes again. Follow Figure 6-54. Remember
    you want to make sure the rectangle and holes are
    constrained. You can tell this sketch is constrained
    because all lines are black.

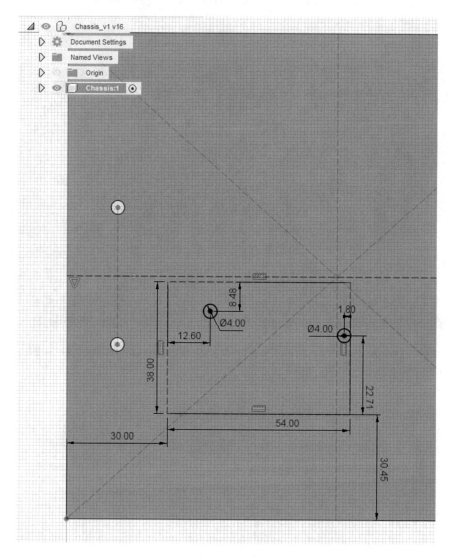

Figure 6-54. Add the holes for the MEGA 2560 Pro

8. Extrude the two 4mm holes again to the bottom of the chassis.

9. Flip to the bottom of the chassis and start a new sketch. Draw two 10mm circles around the two Arduino holes you already made. See Figure 6-55.

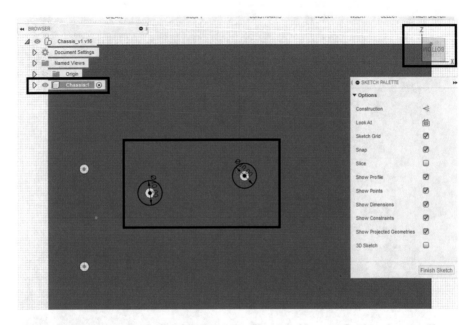

Figure 6-55. *Move to the bottom and create some circles that will hide the screws from view*

10. Extrude these 3mm into the chassis.

11. Make a 50mm chamfer ⬟ Chamfer at the front of the chassis. See Figure 6-56.

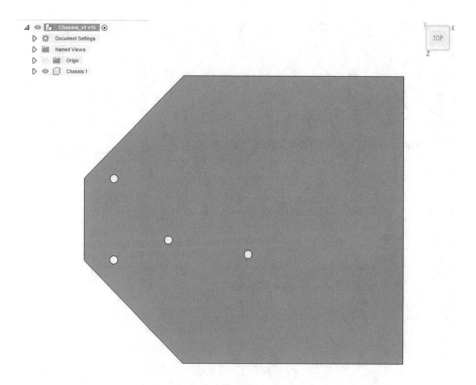

Figure 6-56. *Add two 50mil chamfers*

12. Go back to the top of the chassis and create a
rectangle to represent the battery holder and then
two more rectangles that will be holes for a zip tie.
See Figure 6-57 for the measurements.

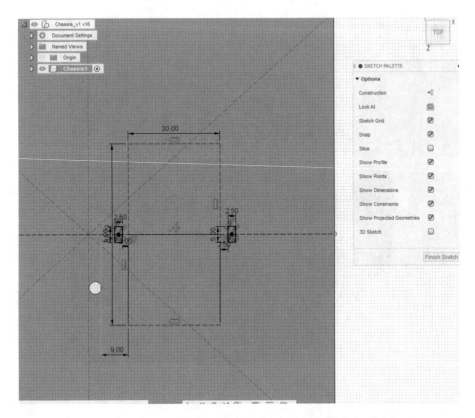

Figure 6-57. *Add the holes for zip tie that will hold the battery pack*

13. Extrude the two small rectangles to the bottom of the chassis.

14. Now let's make the holes and the stand for the H-bridge we created in the previous section. It is easy to get these measurements as we created the board. Use Eagle to get these distances if you want some practice. See Figure 6-58. The platform is used to make sure the PCB is stable.

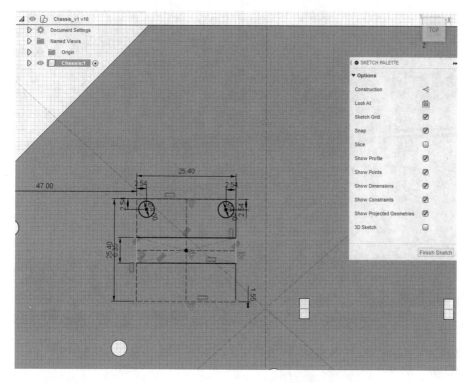

Figure 6-58. *Add the holes and support for the motor driver*

15. Extrude the holes to the bottom of the chassis and extrude the rectangle up 14.45mm. If you have different standoffs, you should measure them and use that value here instead.

16. Switch to the bottom of the chassis and create a sketch around the holes you just extruded for the H-bridge. 10mm holes will work. See Figure 6-59.

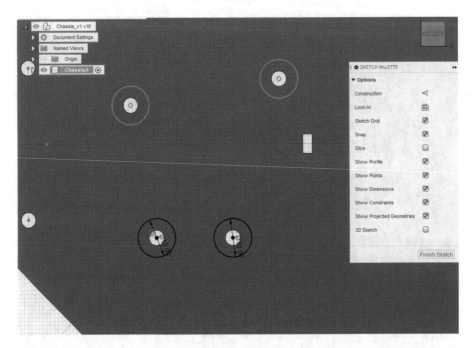

Figure 6-59. *Add two more holes that will hide the screws from view*

17. Extrude the circles 3mm into the chassis.

18. Create a few more components named Motor_
     Bracket_Left, Motor_Bracket_Right, Motor_Right,
     and Motor_Left. See Figure 6-60.

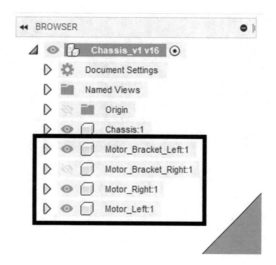

Figure 6-60. *Create four more components*

19. Select the Motor_Right component.

20. Create a rectangle 49mm from the back of the chassis. See Figure 6-61 for all the measurements of the motor. Where did I get these measurements? I went to the distributer and looked at the datasheet of the motor. Later, in this book, I will show you how to import 3D models that have already been created. Making this representation of the motor is nice because it allows us to create a model around it.

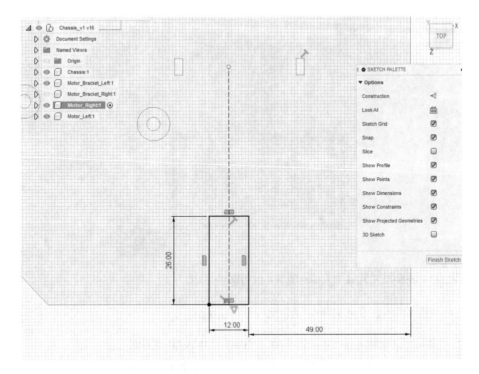

Figure 6-61. *Create a rectangle for the right motor*

21. Extrude the rectangle out 10mm.

22. Switch to the Motor_Left component.

23. Make the same drawing on the other side of the chassis. Use the mirror tool, or you can just draw it out again. See Figure 6-62.

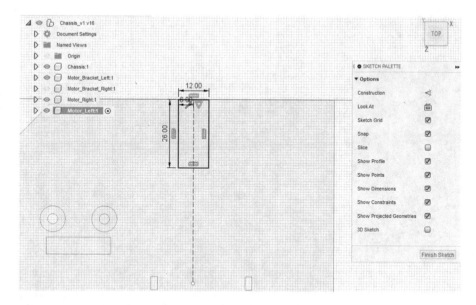

Figure 6-62. *Create the rectangle for the left motor*

24. Extrude the Motor_Left out 10mm.

25. Select the Motor_Bracket_Left component.

26. Create a sketch on the front face of the Motor_Left.

27. Use the outline tool to create a 0.03mm outline of the front of the motor.

28. Use the trim tool to remove the bottom and top pieces of the outline.

29. Use the line tool to create half of the bracket, and then use the mirror tool to create the second half of the bracket. Make sure it is fully enclosed. See Figure 6-63. Extrude this –16mm.

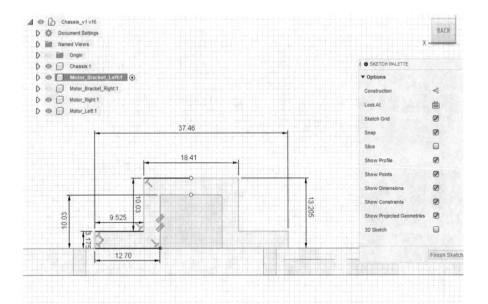

Figure 6-63. *Create the outline of the left motor bracket*

30.   We need something to hold the motor in the bracket from the front, so make a rectangle on the front of the bracket. See Figure 6-64.

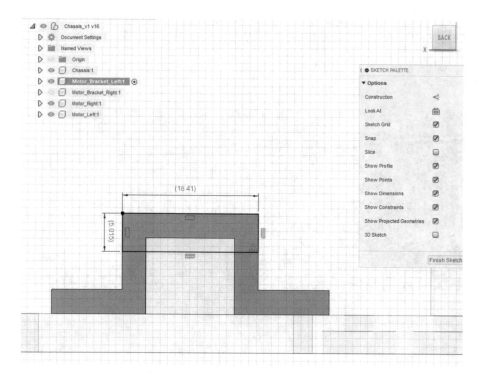

Figure 6-64. *Create the front stop rectangle for the motor bracket*

31. Extrude out 2.5mm.

32. Make a small rectangle on the bottom of the bracket that will allow full access to the shaft of the motor for the wheel couple. See Figure 6-65.

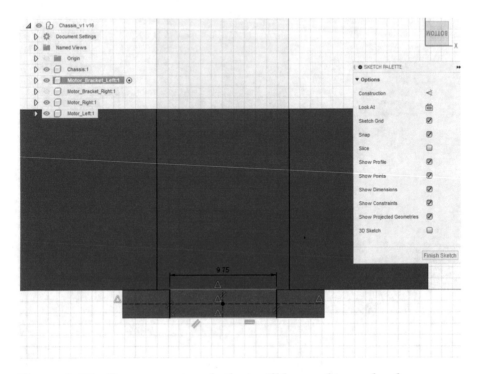

Figure 6-65. *Create a rectangle that will be used to make clearance for the motor axle*

33. Extrude it up –1.84mm.

34. Make two 3mm holes in the center of each of the wings of the bracket. See Figure 6-66.

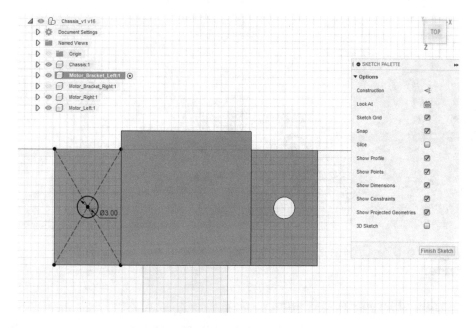

Figure 6-66.   *Create the holes for the motor bracket*

35. Extrude them to the bottom of the bracket. If you must make the chassis invisible, that is fine.

36. Extend the back of the bracket by 10.03mm. Use the extrude tool to do this.

37. Create another brace for the back of the bracket; this will make sure the motor does not slip out the back of the bracket. See Figure 6-67.

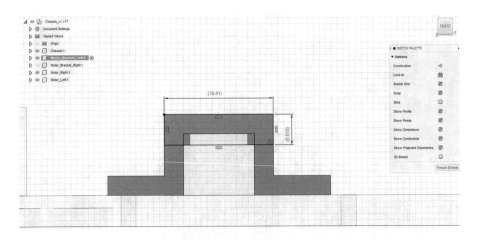

Figure 6-67. *Create a rectangle that will hold in the back of the motor*

38. Extrude it out 2.5mm.

39. Extrude 0.03mm of plastic from the back of the two braces at the front of the motor bracket. See Figure 6-68. If you need to hide the motor and chassis, that is fine.

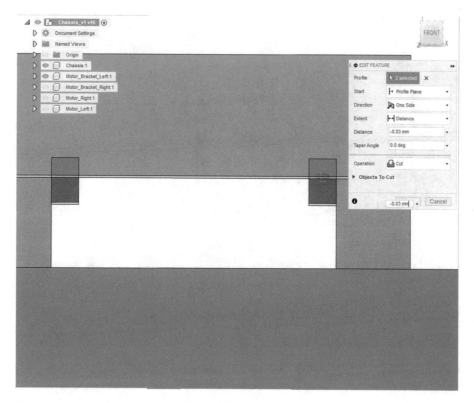

Figure 6-68. *Cut 0.03mm from the front brace of the motor bracket*

40. Go back to the chassis component.

41. On the top of the chassis, create two 4.3mm holes where the motor bracket wing holes are. You can use the sketch of the motor bracket; just make sure you select the top of the chassis as your plane; otherwise, you may be drawing on the top of the motor bracket which will not work. See Figure 6-69.

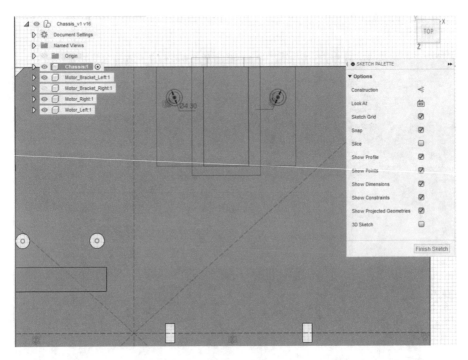

Figure 6-69. *Create the holes for the chassis that will hold the motor bracket*

42.   Mirror these two holes to the other side of the
       chassis. See Figure 6-70.

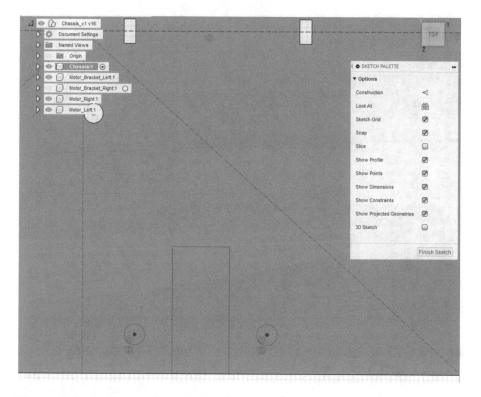

Figure 6-70. *Mirror these holes for the other motor bracket*

43. Select these circles on the top of the chassis and extrude into the chassis 3.43mm.

44. Select the Motor_Bracket_Left component and sketch on the frontmost rectangle.

45. Sketch a small rectangle. See Figure 6-71.

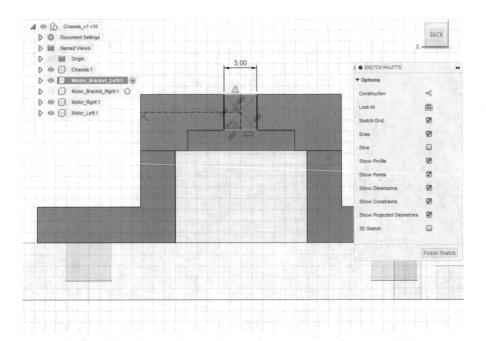

Figure 6-71. *Make a small rectangle that will allow you to tighten the set screw of the wheels*

46. Cut (opposite of extrude) into the bracket –2.5mm.

47. Select the chassis component.

48. Create a center rectangle next to the Arduino holes. See Figure 6-72 for the measurements.

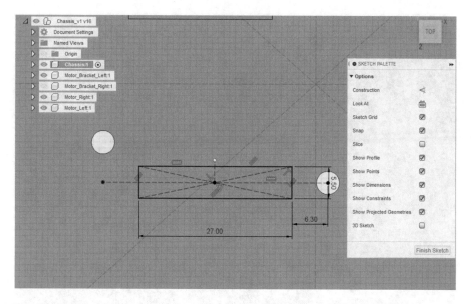

Figure 6-72. *Create a rectangle that will be the support of the MEGA 2560 Pro*

49.   Extrude the rectangle out 14.45mm.

That was a lot of steps, and I have a few more things for you in this section. I don't just want to give you the measurements, I also want you to learn how to take measurements. So here are a few examples of how I was able to get the measurements of hole locations and object sizes.

Caster wheel:

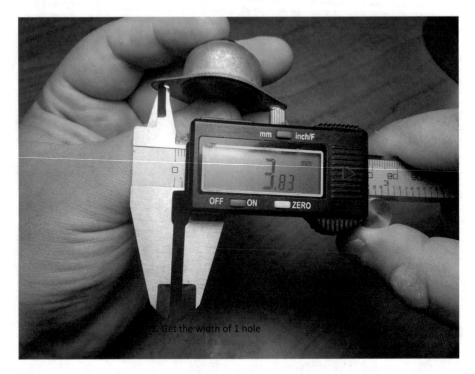

Figure 6-73. *Get the width of one hole*

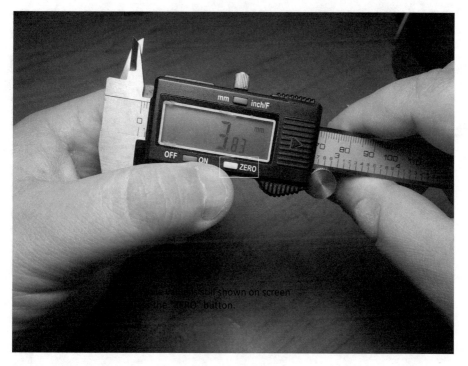

Figure 6-74. *Press the zero button without moving the calipers*

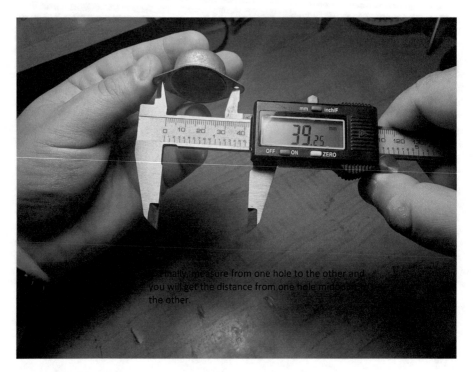

Figure 6-75. *Measure from one hole to the other*

MEGA 2560 Pro:

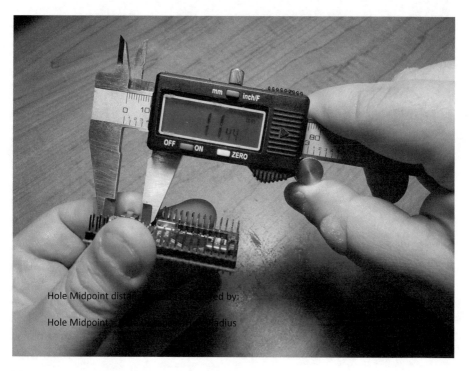

Figure 6-76. *Measuring the Arduino 1*

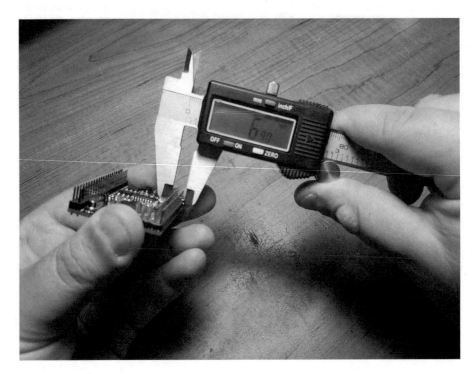

Figure 6-77. *Measuring the Arduino 2*

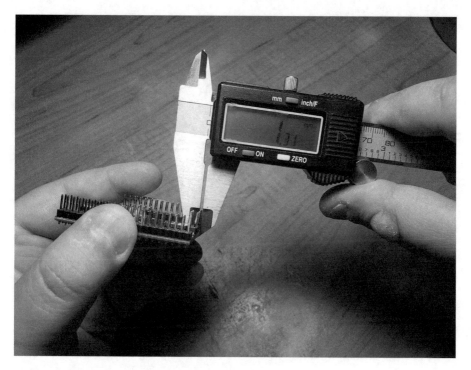

Figure 6-78. *Measuring the Arduino 3*

Figure 6-79. *Measuring the Arduino 4*

Micro motor:

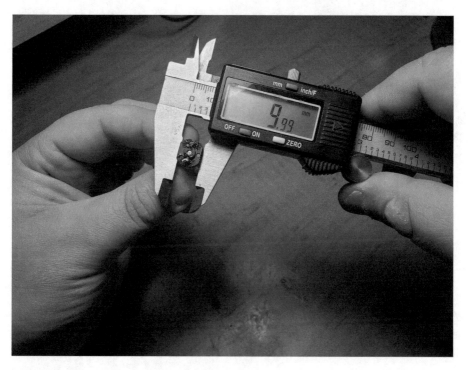

Figure 6-80. *Micro motor measurement 1*

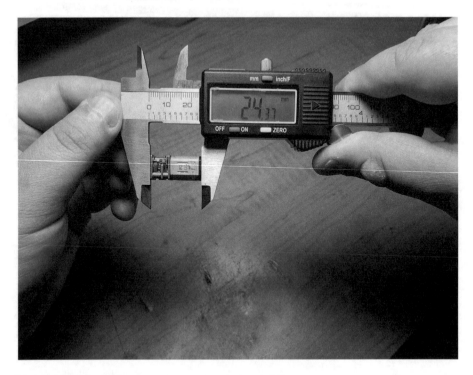

Figure 6-81. *Micro motor measurement 2*

Now that you understand how some of these parts were measured, you can measure other objects and get good at it. The next section will focus on 3D printing the chassis and motor brackets.

Assembly

Before we get started with the assembly of the chassis, please look at the Bill of Materials for this chapter and make sure you have all the components needed.

Now on to the assembly, gently take the 3D printed hardware off your build plate. Use a painter's spatula this will save you time and will be less likely to break your build plate. Clean off any glue that may be on your print before you try to assemble.

The first thing we are going to add onto the chassis is the M2.5 brass inserts; this can be done with a hammer or with a vise. See Figure 6-82.

Press brass insert into plastic using vise.

Figure 6-82. *Press the four brass inserts into the chassis*

Next, solder the wires (wires should be no more than 10" long) onto the micro motor; make sure you try to avoid melting the plastic housing on the back of the motor. See Figure 6-83. Do this for both motors.

Figure 6-83. *Solder the motors*

Now take one of the female to female wire and cut two 2″ pieces and solder one side to the power side (red wire) of the 9V connector, and the other will be soldered to the GND (black wire). See Figure 6-84. Use some heat shrink to make sure there is no exposed wire.

Figure 6-84. *Create the power cable*

Now crimp the other side of the 28 AWG wire with the FCI female sockets. See Figure 6-85. Do this for all four wires.

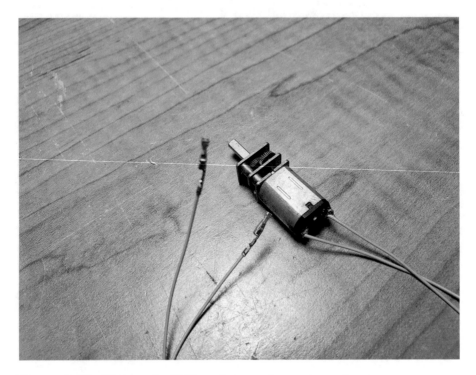

Figure 6-85. *Crimp the FCI sockets to the motor wire*

Now insert these sockets into the blue FCI housing. Make sure the "+" wire in the second hole (right side) of the FCI housing.

Go ahead and do this for the second wire as well, except put it in the first hole (left side) of the FCI housing. See Figure 6-86.

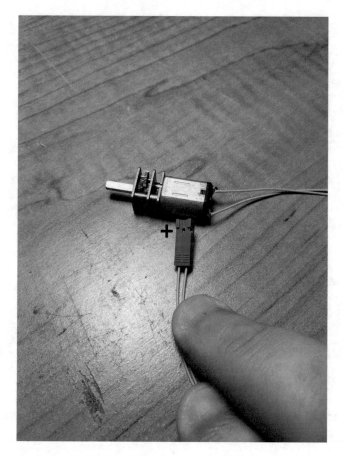

Figure 6-86. *Put the FCI sockets into the FCI housing*

Now go ahead and put the motor into the motor bracket. Be careful with the wires as you don't want to shear them off the motor. It is a snug fit, but that is what we want. See Figure 6-87.

Figure 6-87. *Put the micro motors into the motor brackets*

Attach the motor brackets to the chassis, with the 2.5mm x 8mm screws. See Figure 6-88.

Figure 6-88. *Attach the motor brackets to the chassis*

Attach the motor driver and the MEGA 2560 Pro to the chassis, with the standoffs. It is easier to add the standoffs to the chassis first and then attach the components to them. See Figure 6-89.

Figure 6-89. *Attach the motor driver and the MEGA 2560 Pro to the chassis*

Next, let's attach the battery pack to the chassis. Use a zip tie to secure it to the chassis. Make sure the 9V connector on the battery pack is on the right side of the chassis and that the batteries are in the holder. See Figure 6-90.

Figure 6-90. *Attach the 6V battery pack*

Now attach the caster wheel to the chassis, using the M3 x 10mm screws and 25mm standoffs. See Figure 6-91.

Figure 6-91. *Attach the caster wheel*

Next, attach the two wheels to the two motors, using the wheel couples and wheel set. See Figure 6-92.

Figure 6-92. *Attach the two 4" disk wheels; make sure you tighten the set screws!*

Connect the FCI connectors from the motors to the motor driver. See Figure 6-93.

Figure 6-93. *Attach the two motors to the two motor channels on the motor driver*

Now it is time to connect the wires from the motor driver to the MEGA 2560 Pro. Connect GND from the motor driver to the GND on the MEGA 2560 Pro. See Figure 6-94.

Figure 6-94. *Attach GND from the motor driver to the GND of the MEGA 2560 Pro*

Next, wire the motor controller in this configuration.

Table 6-2. *Motor Driver Pinout*

Motor Driver Pin	MEGA 2560 Pro
GND	GND
+5V	+5V
+VIN	+VIN
INV3	Digital Pin 12
INV1	Digital Pin 13
PWM2	Digital Pin 3
PWM1	Digital Pin 11

Now connect the positive side of the 9V connector to the +VIN of the MEGA 2560 Pro, and finally connect the negative side of the 9V connector to the GND of the MEGA 2560 Pro. See Figure 6-95.

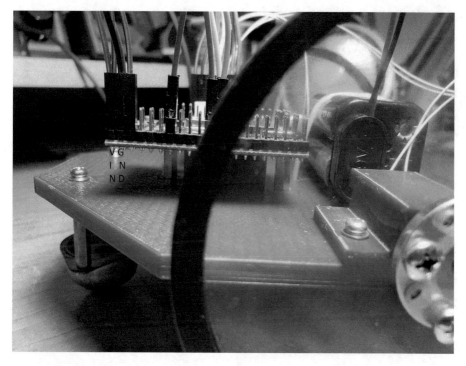

Figure 6-95. *Connect the 6V power from the battery pack to the VIN on the Arduino and then connect GND from the 6V battery pack to GND on the Arduino*

And that is it! The first prototype chassis is finished as far as the hardware is concerned; now it is time to tackle the software portion of this chapter.

Writing the Software

Now, we will move on to the software for this project. We need to communicate with both digital and analog pins. For this project, we will be interfacing data by means of serial communication, so we must send in multiple sets of data, specifically the direction of motor A, speed of motor A, direction of motor B, and speed of motor B. We need to use comma-separated format to parse the data to their respective digital or analog pins. After that, we need to display the data on the serial monitor in this format:

```
Motor A
1
255
Motor B
1
255
```

Listing 6-1 shows the code.

Listing 6-1. Code for the client's project

```
const int fields = 4; // amount of values excluding the commas
int motorPins[] = {12,13,3,11}; // Motor Pins
int index = 0; // the current field being received
int values[fields]; // array holding values for all the fields

void setup()
{
  Serial.begin(9600); // Initialize serial port to send and
  receive at 9600 baud

  for (int i; i <= 3; i++)           // set LED pinMode to output
  {
    pinMode(motorPins[i], OUTPUT);
  }

  Serial.println("The Format is: MotoADir,MotoASpe,MotorBDir,Mo
  toBSpe\n");  // \n is a new
                    // line constant that will output a new line
}

void loop()
```

```
{
if( Serial.available())
  {
    char ch = Serial.read();
  if(ch >= '0' && ch <= '9') // If it is a number 0 to 9
    {
      // add to the value array and convert the character to an
         integer
      values[index] = (values[index] * 10) + (ch - '0');
    }
  else if (ch == ',') // if it is a comma increment index
    {
      if(index < fields -1)
      index++; // increment index
    }
  else
    {

      for(int i=0; i <= index; i++)
        {
            if (i == 0)
            {
              Serial.println("Motor A");
              Serial.println(values[i]);
            }
            else if (i == 1)
            {
              Serial.println(values[i]);
            }
            if (i == 2)
            {
```

```
      Serial.println("Motor B");
      Serial.println(values[i]);
    }
    else if (i == 3)
    {
      Serial.println(values[i]);
    }

    if (i == 0 || i == 1)  // If the index is equal to 0 or 2
    {
        digitalWrite(motorPins[i], values[i]);
                        // Here we see a logical error
    }
    if (i == 2 || i == 3) // If the index is equal to 1 or 3
    {
        analogWrite(motorPins[i], values[i]);
                        // Here we see a logical error
    }

  values[i] = 0; // set values equal to 0
  }
    index = 0;
  }
}
}
```

Notice that the code will run—with unexpected results. Look at the initialization of motorPins, and you'll see that the array is out of order with the format we were given: motor A direction, motor A speed, motor B direction, motor B speed. This is one of those pesky logical errors, and it brings us to the next section, debugging the Arduino software.

Debugging the Arduino Software

Now that we have discovered the logical error, we need to fix it. Listing 6-2 contains the corrected array in bold.

Listing 6-2. Corrected code for project 1

```
const int fields = 4; // amount of values excluding the commas.
int motorPins[] = {12,3,13,11}; // Motor Pins
int index = 0; // the current field being received
int values[fields]; // array holding values for all the fields

void setup()
{
  Serial.begin(9600); // Initialize serial port to send and
                         receive at 9600 baud

  for (int i; i <= 3; i++)          // set LED pinMode to output
  {
    pinMode(motorPins[i], OUTPUT);
  }

  Serial.println("The Format is:
MotoADir,MotoASpe,MotorBDir,MotoBSpe\n");
}

void loop()
{
if( Serial.available())
  {
    char ch = Serial.read();
  if(ch >= '0' && ch <= '9') // If the value is a number 0 to 9
    {
      // add to the value array
```

```
    values[index] = (values[index] * 10) + (ch - '0');
  }
else if (ch == ',') // if it is a comma
  {
    if(index < fields -1) // If index is less than 4 - 1
    index++; // increment index
  }
else
  {

    for(int i=0; i <= index; i++)
      {
        if (i == 0)
        {
          Serial.println("Motor A");
          Serial.println(values[i]);
        }
        else if (i == 1)
        {
          Serial.println(values[i]);
        }
        if (i == 2)
        {
          Serial.println("Motor B");
          Serial.println(values[i]);
        }
        else if (i == 3)
        {
          Serial.println(values[i]);
        }

        if (i == 0 || i == 2)  // If the index is equal to 0
                                               or 2
```

```
    {
       digitalWrite(motorPins[i], values[i]);
                // Write to the digital pin 1 or 0
                // depending what is sent to the Arduino.
    }
    if (i == 1 || i == 3) // If the index is equal to 1
                                 or 3
    {
       analogWrite(motorPins[i], values[i]);
                // Write to the PWM pins a number between
                // 0 and 255 or what the person entered
                // in the serial monitor.
    }

  values[i] = 0; // set values equal to 0
  }
  index = 0;
  }
}
}
```

At this point, I want to discuss the finer details of this code. The first thing I want to point out is where we parse the data to be sent to the correct pins:

```
if(ch >= '0' && ch <= '9') // If the value is a number 0 to 9
  {
    // add to the value array
    values[index] = (values[index] * 10) + (ch - '0');
  }
else if (ch == ',') // if it is a comma
  {
    if(index < fields -1) // If index is less than 4 - 1
    index++; // increment index
  }
```

```
else
            // This is where the data is passed to the digital
            and analog pins
```

This part of the code first checks to see if an input character from 0 to 9 exists. If so, it converts the character type to an integer type by subtracting by 0, which has an integer value of 48, and tells the microcontroller to see this value as an integer instead of a character. Next, it checks to see if the character is a comma. If so, it will check to see if the index is greater than or equal to 3. If the value is less than 3, it will increment the index value. The if-elseif statement handles any other values such as numerical values, which is what the characters are converted to.

Next, I would like to discuss the parsing of the data to the digital and analog pins and how we formatted the data on the serial monitor. The code looks like this:

```
for(int i=0; i <= index; i++)
        {
          if (i == 0)
          {
            Serial.println("Motor A");
            Serial.println(values[i]);
          }
          else if (i == 1)
          {
            Serial.println(values[i]);
          }
          if (i == 2)
          {
            Serial.println("Motor B");
            Serial.println(values[i]);
          }
```

```
else if (i == 3)
{
  Serial.println(values[i]);
}

if (i == 0 || i == 2)   // If the index is equal to 0
                           or 2
{
   digitalWrite(motorPins[i], values[i]);
           // Write to the digital pin 1 or 0
           // depending what is sent to the Arduino.
}
if (i == 1 || i == 3)
           // If the index is equale to 1 or 3
{
   analogWrite(motorPins[i], values[i]);  // Write
   to the PWM pins a number between
           // 0 and 255 or what the person entered
           // in the serial monitor.
}
```

The for loop iterates through all the indexes (in this case, 0–3). The first and second if statements and if-elseif statements are printing the data to the serial monitor, which is where we get the format:

```
Motor A
1
255
Motor B
1
255
```

Do you see an easier way of programming this format? (Hint: Use switch.) After those if statements, we come to the code that separates the data to its appropriate pin, which is what the company asked for, so the format this code accepts is motor A direction (0 or 1), motor A speed (0 to 255), motor B direction (0 or 1), and motor B speed (0 to 255). Now that we have the software sorted out, we can focus on testing the hardware.

Troubleshooting the Hardware

When debugging, first start with the software unless there is an obvious issue with the hardware. For example, a wire is not connected to the correct pin. If you copied the code straight from this book, chances are it is not a software issue. Next, we need to make sure we are entering data into the serial monitor correctly. Type 1,255,1,255 into the serial monitor and press the "Enter" key. Also, make sure the serial monitor is in "Newline" configuration at the bottom right of the serial monitor. Now if none of that resolves your issues, we need to move on to checking the hardware.

The first thing to check with the hardware is that the power and ground are not shorted. There is an easy way to check this. Disconnect all power from the Arduino and motor driver by disconnecting the 6V connector on the battery pack. Configure your multimeter to check for continuity. Continuity will check to see if a signal is connected to another signal. Check your multimeter's user manual to see which setting you need to be in to check for continuity; normally, it is a secondary test to resistance or sometimes the diode test. Now take the positive lead of the multimeter and put it on the positive side of the 6V connector (the connector that should now be disconnected from the battery pack). Go ahead and put the negative lead of the multimeter to the GND side of the 6V connector. If you see 0ohms or hear a beeping, you have a short somewhere between the 6V battery pack and the Arduino or even the motor controller. See Figure 6-96. Now if you want to check to see if the Arduino has the short, disconnect VIN and GND from the motor controller to the Arduino. See Figure 6-97.

Connect the two leads from the multimeter to the 6V power connector. See Figure 6-98. If you get a short still, then chances are the Arduino you have is defective, or you have a wire connected incorrectly (this has a higher probability of being the problem than the first case). If you find that the short is not on the Arduino, then it must be on the H-bridge itself. Check the H-bridge orientation on the PCB and make sure the first pin is where it is supposed to be. See Figure 6-99. Next, check the soldering of the IC and make sure there are no shorts between pins that should not be connected to each other. See Figure 6-100. You can use the large connector and make sure none of these are shorted as well. I hope this helped to isolate the problem if your problem was a short between +VIN and GND. If you don't find a short between +VIN and GND but instead have a short from +5V to GND, do the same exact steps, just instead of connecting the multimeter to +VIN, connect it to +5V on the Arduino.

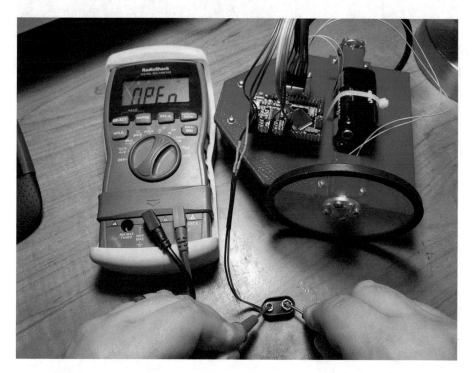

Figure 6-96. *Check if there is a short between VIN and GND*

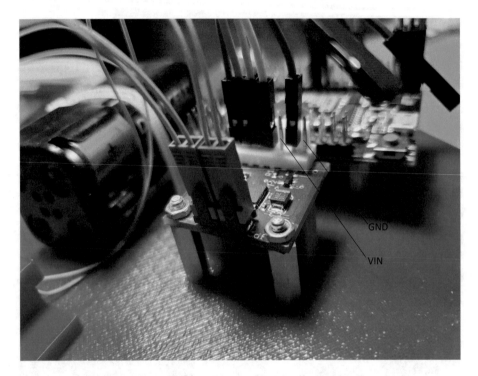

Figure 6-97. *Disconnect the VIN and GND from the motor driver*

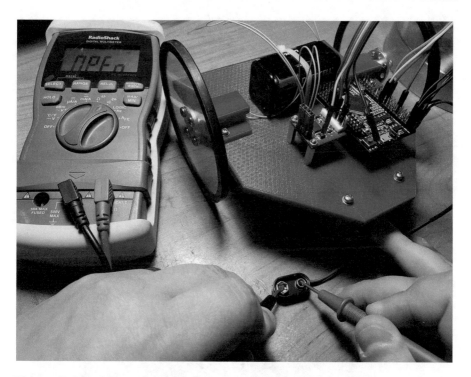

Figure 6-98.   *Then check if there is a short between VIN and GND*

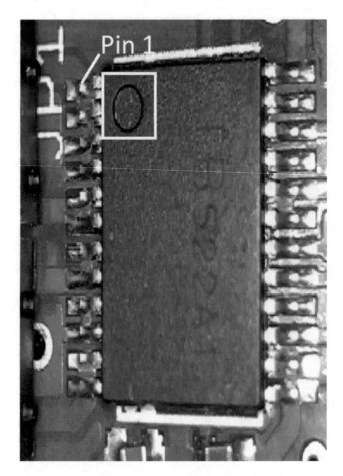

Figure 6-99. *Make sure the chip is oriented in the correct manner*

Figure 6-100. *Check for any shorts on the H-bridge*

Now if you do not have a short at all, chances are you just have something wired incorrectly; make sure your wiring matches Table 6-1 found in the "Assembly" section of this chapter.

If all wires are correctly in place, make sure they are connected by using a continuity test from each of the wire's destination. For example, make sure you are getting a short when you connect +VIN from the motor controller (pins 13 and 14 of the H-bridge) to the +VIN of the MEGA 2560 Pro. See Figure 6-101.

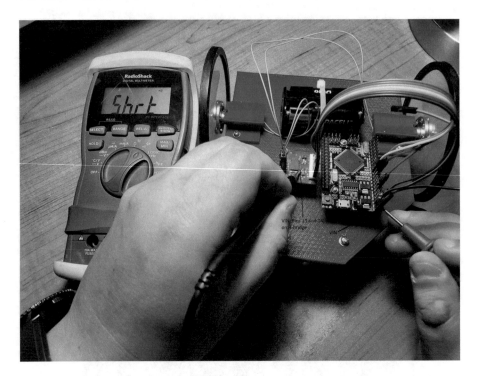

Figure 6-101. *Make sure all the pins are connected where they should be. VIN is just one example*

Finally, you may need to make sure your motor controller is manufactured correctly. If you did the soldering, then you can fix this on your own, but if you had PCBWay or another board manufacturer assemble your boards, you may want to make sure all the components are on the board correctly and are the right parts.

Note   If you need to, copy and paste the code from the "Debugging the Arduino Software" section to the Arduino IDE to make sure everything is correct.

Finished Prototype

Naticom should be very happy with the first prototype as it has all the features that Naticom wanted. Figure 6-102 shows the final first prototype.

Figure 6-102. *Final prototype*

Summary

This was a very large chapter and covered a lot of old and new material. Let's review what we learned:

- Learned about what an H-bridge was and how it is used

- Learned about gathering requirements from a company

- Learned how to create a schematic and reinforced skills learned in Chapter 5

- Learned how to create a multicomponent 3D model

- Learned how to take measurements of various pieces of hardware

- 3D printed and assembled a 100% custom chassis

- Learned how to control motors over the serial monitor

- Learned how to troubleshoot hardware and how to find continuity issues within a circuit

Exercise

1. Create your own 3D printed wheel that will still connect to the aluminum motor couple. Be creative as really you can make almost any kind of wheel you want.

CHAPTER 7

Final Project PCB

Moving into the major project for this book will not be easy as it will involve a lot of different pieces, the first of which is the PCB for the MEGA 2560 Pro Arduino board. In this chapter, we will explore what it takes to go from a requirements document to a finished PCB. Do not get discouraged and always know that the final PCB can be downloaded, so that you can review it and compare it to what you are currently doing. Like before, not everything will be shown in this chapter for creating the schematic or laying out the PCB, but anything that is new will be explained, so that you don't get lost in the schematic or layout because compared to the other schematics in this book, it is the largest and most complex, which will lead me to the next item on the agenda, creating different schematic pages.

Creating Schematic Sheets

We have not covered sheets yet; they are very easy to use. All you need to do is turn on the sheets window (if it is not already on); to do this, right-click anywhere on the menus of the schematic page, and a window will pop up. Select the "Sheets" option, and the Sheets window will appear. See Figure 7-1. Now to make a new sheet, all you must do is right-click a sheet and select "New" from the pop-up window. See Figure 7-2. That about does it for Sheets; let us get into the project and see what we will be making.

© Harold Timmis 2021
H. Timmis, *Practical Arduino Engineering*, https://doi.org/10.1007/978-1-4842-6852-0_7

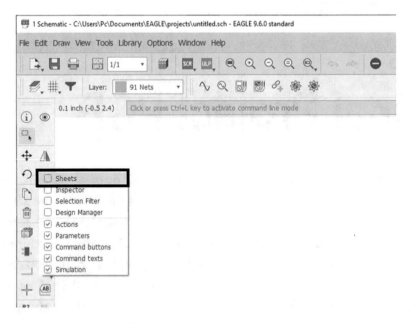

Figure 7-1. *Select the "Sheets" checkbox*

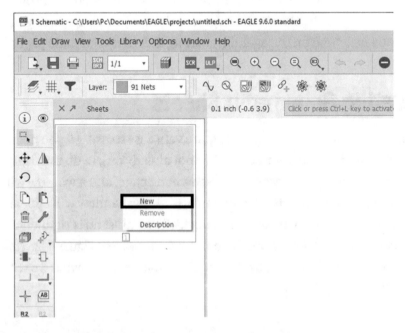

Figure 7-2. *Right-click a sheet and select "New"*

Final Project: NatBot

The NatBot product is an open source robot that will allow students or professionals to gain experience with robots. Naticom wants you to design and build this product to their specifications.

The NatBot is a complex robot that will require a PCB to be developed, 3D hardware to be designed and printed, and lastly software needs to be created to control and receive information from the NatBot. Let us take a deeper look at the requirements in the sections that follow.

Requirements Gathering (PCB)

Naticom has put together a requirements document for each phase of the NatBot. They are PCB, 3D model, software, and finally hardware/software integration. For this chapter, we will be focusing on the requirements for the PCB which are the following:

- Needs to run on four independent wheels that can be controlled individually.

- Needs to be able to sense acceleration in X, Y, and Z directions.

- Must use a rechargeable battery, preferably a single-cell Li-Poly battery, and the battery must be able to be charged on the NatBot via USB.

- Must be able to send and receive information over Bluetooth.

- Must be able to detect objects in front of it at a range of 1.5in to 25in and must be able to work in sunlight.

- The robot must be able to run for 20mins.

- The robot must have a temperature sensor with a temperature sensing range of 0 to 100C with a +/- 5C accuracy.

- The robot needs an OLED display to give some feedback as to what the robot is doing. Must be around a 1in screen.

- Receive GPS information and store it on an onboard SD card.

- The robot may need to have some breakouts for future hardware/software updates.

Alright, those are not all very specific requirements, but they are enough for us to start imagining what this PCB would need to fulfill these requirements. In the next section, we will dive into the requirements and lay out a plan to meet each of them.

Outlining the Hardware Requirements

Alright, so we have several requirements; let us go through each bullet point and put together a road map that will lead us to success:

- Needs to run on four independent wheels that can be controlled individually.

  This one is relatively straightforward; the NatBot requires four wheels that will steer independently. This can be accomplished using some geared DC motors and maybe some Servos to turn the wheels.

- Needs to be able to sense acceleration in X, Y, and Z directions.

  Another straightforward request! We can use an accelerometer to meet these requirements; there are plenty of good accelerometers that are inexpensive and effective.

- Must use a rechargeable battery, preferably a single-cell Li-Poly battery, and the battery must be able to be charged on the NatBot via USB.

  This is also straightforward but will still be difficult because we have so much hardware to power, and a 3.7V 2Ahr battery is still limited. We will need to use a couple of boost regulators to power the various systems of the NatBot. For example, we will need a separate regulator for the microcontroller, the motors, and the servos as they will run on different voltages. The charging circuit is very straightforward as there are several circuits we can use.

- Must be able to send and receive information over Bluetooth.

  Again, this is a pretty simple request; we can use an RN-42 Bluetooth module that will connect to the Arduino via UART and fulfill this requirement.

- Must be able to detect objects in front of it at a range of 1.5in to 25in and must be able to work in sunlight.

  Alright, this one could have multiple answers, but because the product owner wants the device to work in the sunlight, an ultrasonic sensor would probably work the best as it does not require any light to determine distance and is also affordable.

- The robot must be able to run for 10 to 20mins.

  This is more of a power requirement than anything else. We just need to calculate the current draw of each device we choose and make sure it falls into the threshold 10 to 20mins.

- The robot must have a temperature sensor with a temperature sensing range of 0 to 100C with a +/– 5C accuracy.

  Okay, here is another sensor for the robot that will be easy to furnish. There are many temperature sensors we can choose from, and many of them check all the boxes of this requirement.

- The robot needs an OLED display to give some feedback as to what the robot is doing. Must be around a 1in screen.

  This can be tricky to find, but there are a lot of drop-in LCDs that we can use to fulfill this requirement.

- Receive GPS information and store it on an onboard SD card.

  This requirement is straightforward as well; we will probably use a drop-in GPS module that will only require us to route a single connector.

- The robot may need to have some breakouts for future hardware/software updates.

  We will need to make sure we add some duplicate headers to the PCB so that the users can add their own hardware if needed.

  Okay, now that we have a good idea as to what we will need to do in order to fulfill these requirements, we can start to talk about the actual hardware we are going to implement and how we will implement each piece of hardware.

Creating the NatBot PCB

In this section, I want to go over creating the PCB's dimensions because there are a few new things that need to be explained. Figure 7-3 shows the dimension layer of the NatBot; you will notice the additional holes that are used to pass wires from the servo motors and the DC motors to the main board.

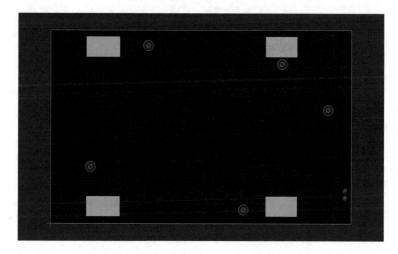

Figure 7-3. *Final board dimensions*

Let us look at how to make these four rectangles into the PCB dimensions.

1. Create a new schematic and board file and name it NatBot v1.0.

2. Open the board file in Eagle.

3. The size of the NatBot will be 160mm by 100mm, which is the initial board size that Eagle starts with, so you should not have to change these dimensions. See Figures 7-4 and 7-5.

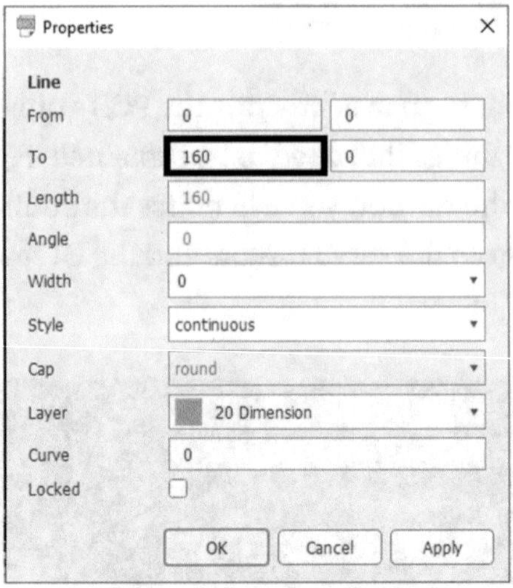

Figure 7-4. *Horizontal length*

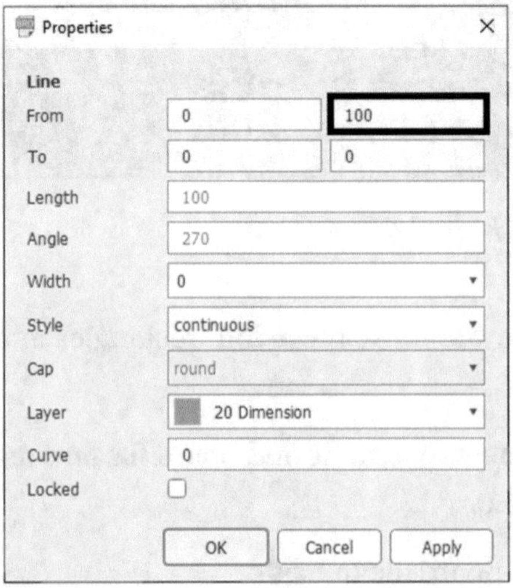

Figure 7-5. *Vertical length*

4. Select the "Rect" function. See Figure 7-6.

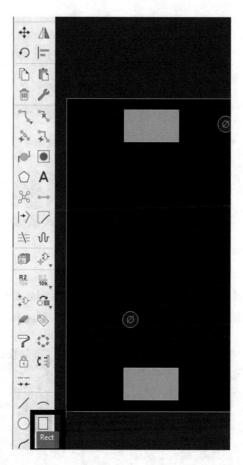

Figure 7-6. *Select Rect from the functions menu*

5.   Select the Holes layer. See Figure 7-7.

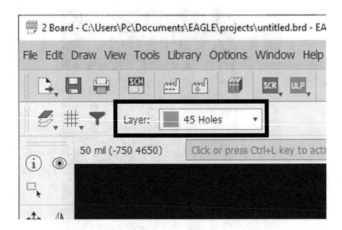

Figure 7-7. *Select the "Holes" layer*

6.   Left-click within the board perimeter and create a
rectangle. Do not make it too large. See Figure 7-8.

Figure 7-8. *Add a rectangle to the layout*

7. Create three more of these rectangles. See Figure 7-9.

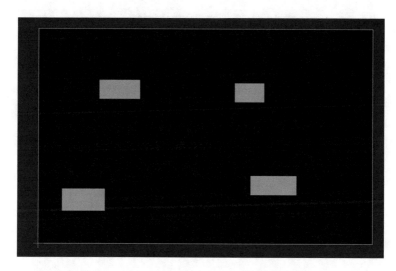

Figure 7-9. *Add the rest of rectangles to the layout*

8. Click "Info" and select the bottom-left rectangle. Enter in these values. See Figure 7-10.

Properties			×
Rectangle			
From	19.05	3.81	
To	36.83	13.97	
Width	17.78		
Height	10.16		
Angle	0		
	☐ Mirror		
Layer	▮ 45 Holes		▼
Locked	☐		
	OK	Cancel	Apply

Figure 7-10. *Dimensions of the bottom-left rectangle*

9.   Here are the top-left rectangle values. See Figure 7-11.

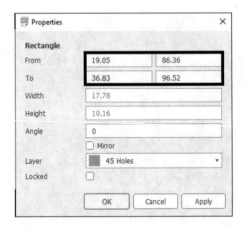

Figure 7-11. *Dimensions of the top-left rectangle*

10.   Here are the top-right rectangle values. See Figure 7-12.

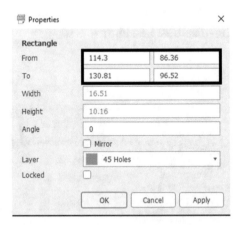

Figure 7-12. *Dimensions of the top-right rectangle*

11.   Here are the bottom-right rectangle values.
      See Figure 7-13.

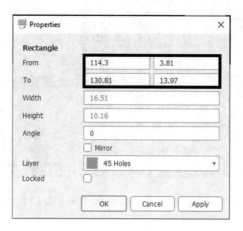

Figure 7-13. *Dimensions of the bottom-right rectangle*

12.   Now we just need to add dimension lines to each
      of the rectangles. To do this, select the "Line"
      function and trace around each of the rectangles.
      See Figures 7-14 and 7-15.

Figure 7-14. *Select the Line function*

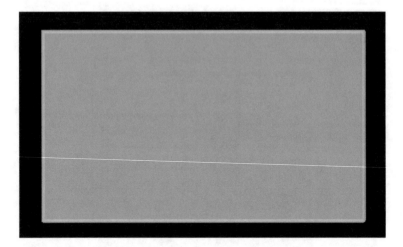

Figure 7-15. *Add the outline to each of the four rectangles*

13.   That should do it; the final product should look
       something like this. See Figure 7-16.

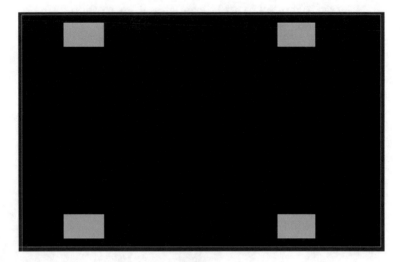

Figure 7-16. *Final dimension layout*

Alright, now that that part is squared away, we can take a look at the ground planes for the NatBot. This will be a little different as we have an antenna that cannot have anything under it; this is so there is no distortion in the signal. Let us take a look on how to accomplish this.

1. Select the "Polygon" function, select the tKeepout layer, select the right-angle trace, and select a 0.254mm as the trace width. See Figure 7-17.

Figure 7-17. *Select the Polygon function and use these perimeters*

2. Create a polygon like the one shown in Figure 7-18.

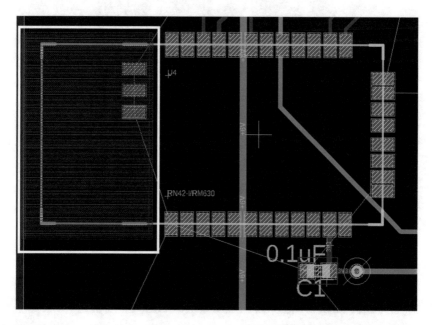

Figure 7-18. *Add a top layer keepout zone under the Bluetooth antenna*

3. Do the same for the bKeepout layer.

4. Now select the "Polygon" function again, and start
    to make the top GND plane, but once you get to the
    keepout zone, go around it. See Figure 7-19.

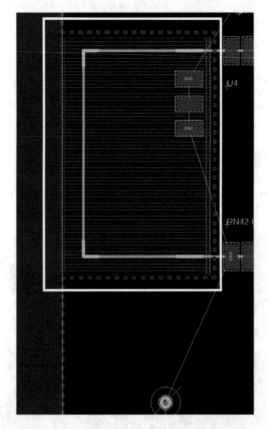

Figure 7-19. *Route the ground plane around the keepout zones*

5. Do the same for the bottom ground plane.

6. That will do it for the ground plane. One thing to
    make sure is that you do not clip out any used pins
    with the keepout zone.

That sums up all the new techniques we need in order to create the NatBot. The next section will cover the new hardware for this project, what the schematic should look like, and finally how each of the components should be routed.

Hardware Explained: The NatBot PCB

In this section, we are going to explore the hardware that we will use to fulfill all the requirements of the NatBot project. This will also include the schematic and routing of the various pieces of hardware. All the knowledge you learned in the previous chapters will be used here; if there is anything new to explain, it will be in the next section of this chapter. If you find that you are stuck, you may want to look at Chapters 5 and 6.

DC Motor

Description:

We will be using a geared micro motor at 180 rpm that has a no-load current of 20mA; these motors will meet all requirements by the product owner. The following link will direct you to the seller of this product:

Micro DC Motors

Schematic:

There are four of these motors, so we will need to use two H-bridges to control all four motors. We will also need four PWM outputs and four regular digital outputs. Figure 7-20 illustrates the schematic for the H-bridges.

Motor Drivers/Servos

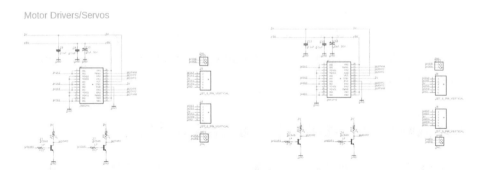

Figure 7-20. *H-bridge and motor header schematic*

Layout:

The layout for the H-bridges is much like the layout of the previous chapters' H-bridge. One thing to be concerned about is if you have other signal wires under the H-bridge because it can spike and cause noise on signal lines that can cause problems with other circuits. Figures 7-21A through 7-21F illustrate the layout of both H-bridges and motor connectors.

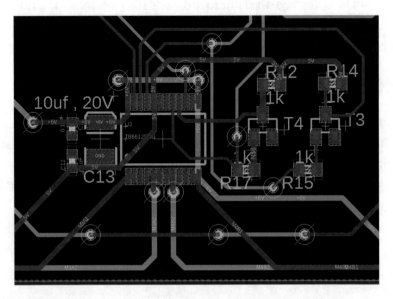

Figure 7-21A. *Bottom H-bridge configuration*

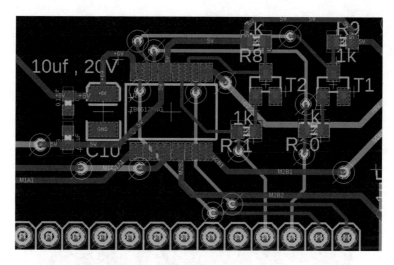

Figure 7-21B. *Top H-bridge configuration*

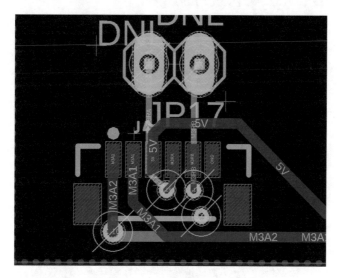

Figure 7-21C. *Bottom-left motor header*

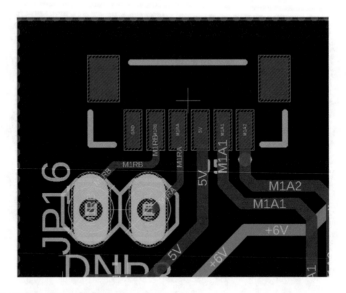

Figure 7-21D. *Top-left motor header*

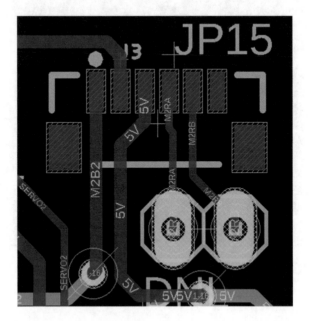

Figure 7-21E. *Top-right motor header*

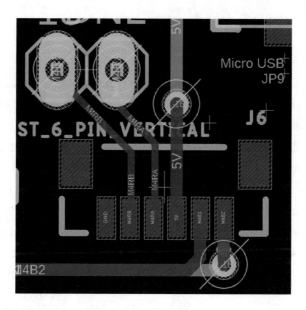

Figure 7-21F. *Bottom-right motor header*

IO on MEGA 2560:

    M1PWM D44

    M1DIR1 D42

    M2PWM D46

    M2DIR1 D40

    M3PWM D12

    M3DIR1 D25

    M4PWM D13

    M4DIR1 D26

Servo

Description:

We will be using a micro servo for our robot because we need it to be able to power four of these at the same time, and larger servos require a lot of power; a simple hobby servo can draw 1 to 2 amps which is quite a bit for our tiny robot. The GH-S37D micro servo is perfect for our applications as they are small and require a lot less power >300mA to start and to run around 40mA with no load. One thing to also be careful with is the torque and strength of the servo motor. We cannot make the apparatus that holds these servos too heavy, and the robot itself must not be too heavy as the servo motors will have a hard time turning the wheels of the robot. A lot of design will need to go into figuring out a suitable mount for these servos.

Micro Servos

Schematic:

The schematic for the four servos is very simple, just a header with GND, +6V, and signal; also, adding a 0.1uF capacitor to lower the noise is a good practice. See Figure 7-22.

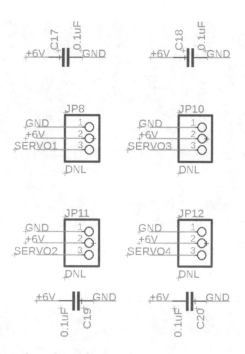

Figure 7-22. *Servo header schematic*

Layout:

The layout for the servos needs to be a bit strategic because both the DC motors and the Servos need to be in the same area, and we need an area for the servo motor wires to come up through the PCB and the chassis. We also need to make sure we do not put any Servo signal wires under any high noise hardware such as the H-bridges. Figures 7-23A through 7-23E illustrate the layout of the Servo headers and the connection to the MEGA 2560 Pro.

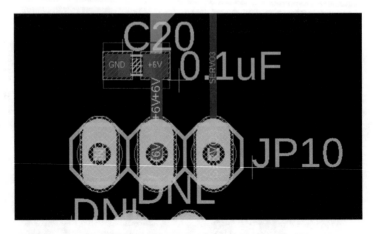

Figure 7-23A. *Bottom-left Servo header (Servo3)*

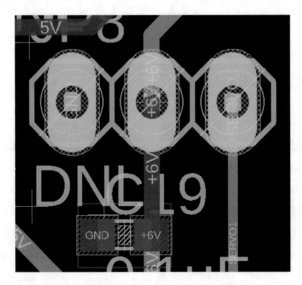

Figure 7-23B. *Top-left Servo header (Servo1)*

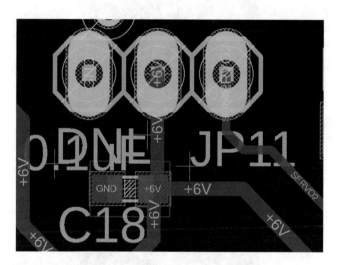

Figure 7-23C. *Top-right Servo header (Servo2)*

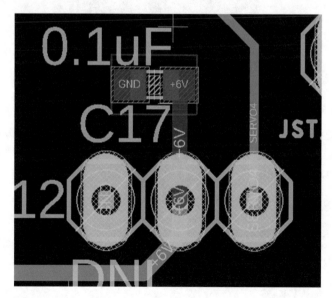

Figure 7-23D. *Bottom-right Servo header (Servo4)*

Figure 7-23E. *Servo headers connected to the MEGA 2560 Pro*

IO on MEGA 2560:

SERVO1 D4

SERVO2 D5

SERVO3 D6

SERVO4 D7

Accelerometer

Description:

The accelerometer is a very cool piece of hardware that allows you to detect acceleration in the X, Y, and Z plane. The particular accelerometer we will be using is an ADXL362; this accelerometer will allow us to detect certain acceleration, for example, if the robot flips over or if the robot crashes. The ADXL362 works with 3.3V microcontrollers, so since the MEGA 2560 Pro is a 5V device, we will need to use a level shifter to make sure we do not fry the ADXL362. The ADXL362 uses SPI, which means we will need to connect it to the MEGA 2560 Pro's SPI pins and a CS pin.

ADXL362

Schematic:

There are a few things to consider for the schematic. One is that there is a level shifter that connects to MOSI, SCK, and CS. You may notice that MISO is not connected to the level shifter; this is on purpose as the MEGA 2560 is the master device, and the ADXL362 is the slave device, hence the name Master In Slave Out (MISO). A filter cap is added to remove any noise from the 3V3 power bus. See Figure 7-24.

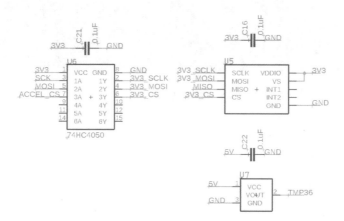

Figure 7-24. *Accelerometer schematic with level shifter*

Layout:

The layout is pretty uneventful other than the fact that the pads of the ADXL362 are very small, which means we need to use smaller traces, so we don't short any pins together. For that, we will be using 12mil traces for the signal wires and 16mil traces for the 3V3 power bus. The level shifter is much easier to route as it has larger pads and has plenty of room in between the pads. See Figure 7-25.

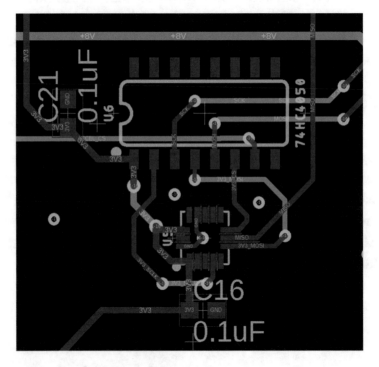

Figure 7-25. *Accelerometer layout*

IO on MEGA 2560:

      MOSI D51

      MISO D50

      SCK D52

      CS D27

Charging Circuit

Description:

The charging circuit is actually the same circuit found on the SparkFun LiPo Charger Basic; the only difference is how it is connected to the boost regulators. The IC we are using to charge the 2000mAh battery is a MCP73831 which is a single-cell charger for Li-Ion and Li-Poly batteries. Since we are going to use a single-cell Li-Poly battery, this is the perfect charge management controller. We will keep it set at a charge rate of 500mAh, which means if the 2000mAh battery is completely depleted, it will take 4 hours to charge. It is also important to note that you should look at the datasheet of each of these ICs for layout guidelines.

MCP73831T

Schematic:

The schematic is pretty simple; you charge the battery over USB at 500mAh, which is set by the 2.0k resistor on the programming line (Pad 5). Also, S1 is used to send the VCC line to the VCCP which is connected to the two boost regulators, or it will disconnect power from the boost regulators for charging purposes. See Figure 7-26.

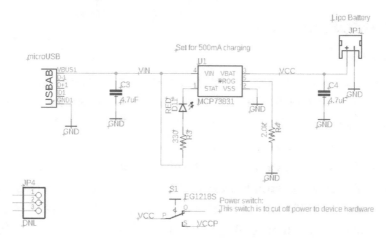

Figure 7-26. *Charge circuit schematic*

Layout:

The layout is very similar to the recommended layout in the datasheet minus the vias for heat dissipation. See Figure 7-27.

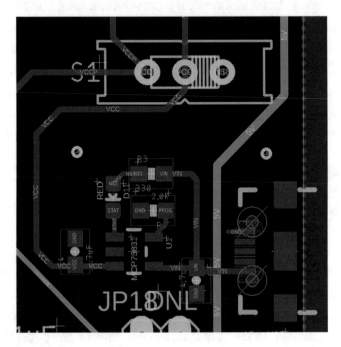

Figure 7-27. *Charge circuit layout*

Buck/Boost Regulator

Description:

There are two boost regulators on the NatBot; one is for stepping up the 3.7V single-cell Li-Poly battery to 6V for the DC motors and the servo motors, and the other is used to power the MEGA 2560 Pro. The first boost regulator is the S18V20F6 regulator which will boost our 3.7V to 6V for the DC motors and the servo motors and will allow for up to 2A to be drawn. The second boost regulator is a S9V11MA and can be adjusted using a small screwdriver. The input for this will be the batteries' voltage, and the output will be 8V at about 1.5A. Setting this should be done on a solderless breadboard with a meter reading the output voltage.

8V Boost Regulator
6V Boost Regulator

Schematic:

This is a very simple schematic for the 8V regulator as it is just a five-pin header with a 0.1in pitch. The 6V regulator requires a special footprint, which can be found in the course materials for this book and was supplied by SnapEDA. Both enables for the regulators are broken out, and the PG (Power Good indicator) is also broken out and is very useful to test brownout conditions for the 8V regulator. See Figure 7-28.

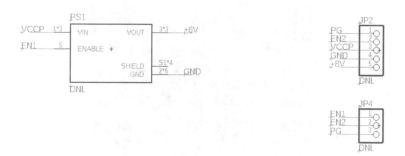

Figure 7-28. *Buck/boost schematic*

Layout:

The layout for the 8V regulator will require us to route VCCP to VIN, and VOUT is connected to the VIN of the MEGA 2560 Pro. GND is connected to the ground, and EN and PG are broken out on a header. For the 6V regulator, VIN is connected to VCCP, and VOUT is connected to each of the micro motor 6V pins and each of the 6V Servo pins. GND is connected to the ground, and the EN is broken out to a header. See Figures 7-29A and 7-29B.

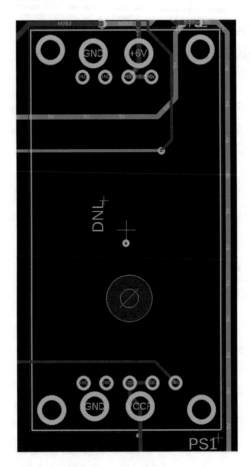

Figure 7-29A. *6V boost regulator layout*

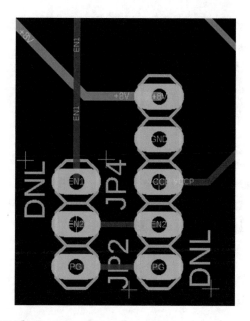

Figure 7-29B. *8V boost regulator layout*

IO on MEGA 2560:

8V regulator VOUT VIN

Bluetooth

Description:

We will be using the RN-42 for our Bluetooth communication module. It will allow us to control the robot with another application. The RN-42 is a UART Bluetooth module that has four connections to the MEGA 2560 Pro. The first line is 3.3V; this is power from the linear regulator on the MEGA 2560 Pro. The second is an RX which will receive messages from our program and then relay those messages to the MEGA 2560 Pro, for example, when we want to tell the robot to turn. The TX will transmit data back to our program, for example, sending GPS data back to the program. There is a level shifter on the TX; this is so when we send data to the RN-42, we don't damage it as it cannot handle the 5V signal from the MEGA 2560 Pro. The reset line for the Bluetooth module is also broken out for

415

debugging purposes. The Bluetooth module will use Serial1. You may wonder why this is connected to Serial1 and not Serial0; this is so we can program the MEGA 2560 Pro without having to disconnect anything from the TX and RX lines.

RN-42

Schematic:

This is a pretty easy schematic because the RN-42 can be found in the SparkFun library. Remember to flip the TX and RX signals at the microcontroller's headers. See Figure 7-30.

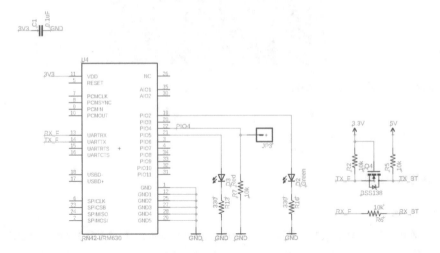

Figure 7-30. *Bluetooth schematic*

Layout:

The footprint for the RN-42 is a bit different than the actual footprint we will use; this can be changed, or if you are like me, you can ask the board manufacturer to put Kapton tape over the pads to make sure they don't short to anything, and also make sure you do not route these pads as the GND will then be right under the antenna and may cause intermittent issues. Also, you will notice a keepout zone around the antenna; this just means no routes can go under the antenna. See Figure 7-31.

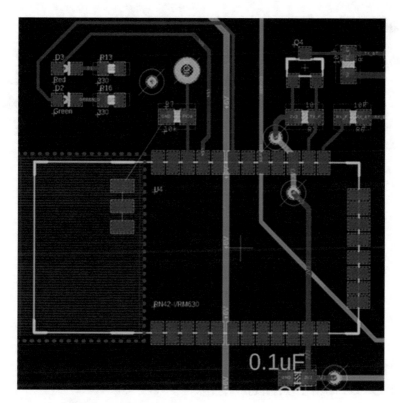

Figure 7-31. *Bluetooth layout*

IO on MEGA 2560:

RX_BT D18

TX_BT D19

Ultrasonic Sensor

Description:

This sensor will allow us to detect items in front of the robot; the sensor we will be using is the Parallax PING Ultrasonic sensor. This sensor uses a digital line to pulse out a high-frequency sound that sound bounces back and based on the amount of time it takes for the sound to get back is the distance of the object in front of the robot. The PING can sense objects from 2cm to 3m.

417

Parallax Ping Ultrasonic Sensor

Schematic:

The header will have three pins; they are 5V, GND, and U_SIG. The only thing extra is a filter capacitor for noise reduction. See Figure 7-32.

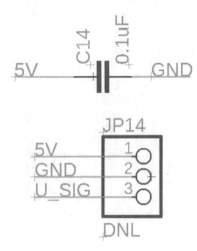

Figure 7-32. *Ultrasonic schematic*

Layout:

This device needs to sit at the front of the robot and not too close to the RN-42 as we do not want to interfere with the antenna. Other than that, it is a pretty easy layout. See Figure 7-33.

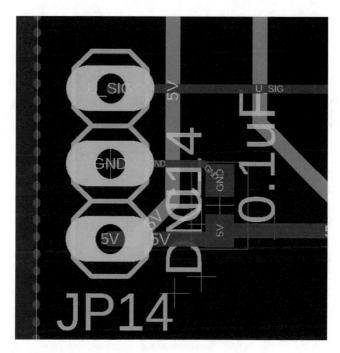

Figure 7-33. *Ultrasonic layout*

IO on MEGA 2560:

U_SIG D22

Temperature Sensor

Description:

We will be using a TMP36 for our temperature sensor, which can read a range of temperatures from –40C to 125C; it uses an analog input, which means we will scale this range from 0 to 1023 and should get a good accuracy +/–2C. With a simple equation, you can calculate the temperature: C = 100 * (Voltage) – 50.

419

TMP36

Schematic:

It is a very simple circuit; all it requires is the TMP36 and a filter cap. The TMP36 has three pins; they are 5V, GND, and signal. The signal line will go into the A0 pin of the MEGA 2560 Pro. See Figure 7-34.

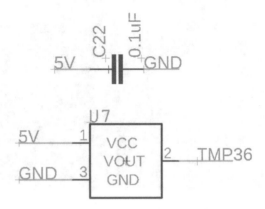

Figure 7-34. *Temperature sensor schematic*

Layout:

The TMP36 is a pretty small package, so it does not take up too much board space; also, its routing is very easy as it only has three pins. See Figure 7-35.

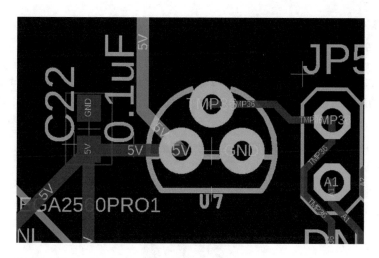

Figure 7-35. *Temperature sensor layout*

IO on MEGA 2560:

TMP36 A0

OLED Display

Description:

The OLED display that will be used is a combination OLED SD card read/write which will allow us to do some data logging as well as display data on the OLED. The OLED we will use is a 16-bit color OLED from Adafruit, which also includes a nice library for adding text and shapes to the OLED. This is an SPI device, so it will use MOSI, MISO, SCK, and two CS pins, one for the OLED and the other for the SD card. This breakout board also already has on board level shifting, so there is no need for extra components on the main board. DC (Data/Command) when this pin is high, it interprets data as a command, and when this pin is low, it interprets that data as data; more on this later when we get into the software. The Res pin is also broken out; this is a reset pin for the OLED— when it is held low, the chip is reset. A normal operation for the reset pin is held high.

421

OLED

Schematic:

This device will connect to SPI and will have two CS pins, one for the OLED and the other for the onboard SD card read/write. See Figure 7-36.

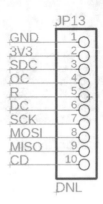

Figure 7-36. *OLED schematic*

Layout:

The layout is just as easy as it is a ten-pin header. See Figure 7-37.

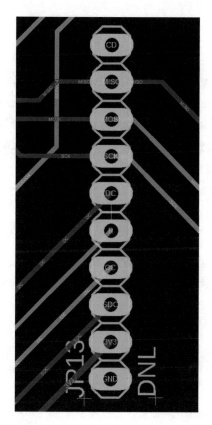

Figure 7-37. *OLED layout*

IO on MEGA 2560:

  SDC D30

  OC D31

  DC D28

  R D29

GPS

Description:

The GPS we are using is a UART GPS, which means it will again use a serial line just like the Bluetooth module. TX_GPS and RX_GPS are used to send and receive information from the GPS module. Hardware wise, this device is very simple to connect to. The software on the other hand may be a bit more challenging.

UART GPS

Schematic:

We are going to use a six-pin JST header that will connect the GPS module directly to the Serial2 and is powered by 5V from the MEGA 2560 Pro. See Figure 7-38.

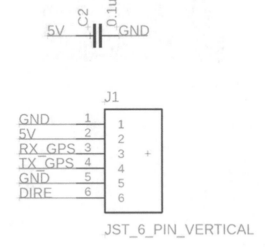

Figure 7-38. *GPS schematic*

Layout:

The layout is also nice as it is just a 90-degree JST six-pin header with a filter capacitor. We must make sure we watch out for electrical noise on the RX and TX lines. See Figure 7-39.

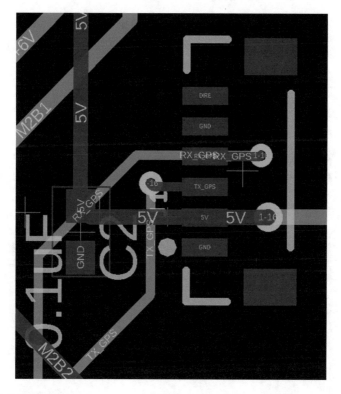

Figure 7-39. *GPS layout*

IO on MEGA 2560:

TX_GPS D17

RX_GPS D16

Headers

Description:

The headers for the MEGA 2560 Pro are Samtec connectors that can be ordered with these part numbers:

SSW-121-02-T-D   42   pin header   2 x 21

SSW-103-02-T-D   6   pin header   2 x 3

SSW-116-02-T-D   32   pin header   2 x 16

Schematic:

This is where we tie everything together to communicate with the NatBot. It may look complex, but it is very simple. Normally, this is the last page that is finished because it has all the signal lines going to and from in. See Figure 7-40.

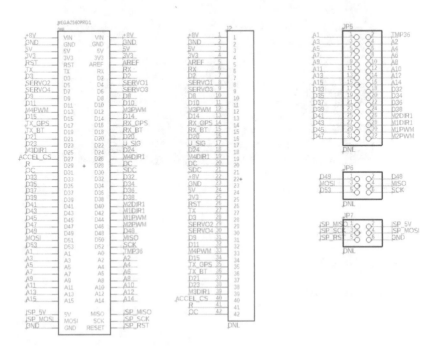

Figure 7-40. *Header schematic*

Layout:

The layout is very simple as there is already a nice footprint for the
MEGA 2560 Pro here:

`https://robotdyn.com/mega-2560-pro-mini-atmega2560-16au.html`

See Figure 7-41.

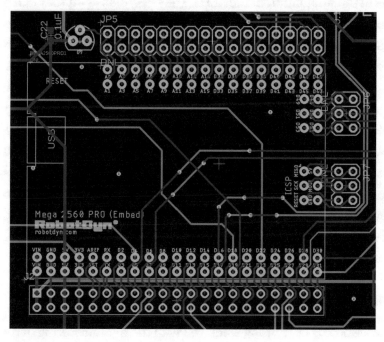

Figure 7-41. *Header layout*

IO on MEGA 2560:

The entire MEGA 2560 Pro

PCB Bill of Materials (BOM)

The PCB Bill of Material is included with this book online; make sure you get it if you plan on having PCBWay or some other board manufacturer. One thing to make sure you do is reply to the board manufacturer if they have any questions about the board. For example, they may ask for images of the orientation of the LEDs. They may also ask if they can use an alternative device. Another question could be about the footprints mismatching, which in the NatBot's case the Bluetooth module has those three extra pads, so I asked them to put some Kapton tape down over them, and PCBWay did exactly that. So just make sure you stay in contact with them as they will always have questions about the board you want manufactured. The BOM included with this book was the actual BOM I used with PCBWay in order to create the NatBot board. If you wanted to do this from scratch, you would need to source each of the components used on the NatBot; one thing to make sure is that the parts are in stock. This may seem like a simple task, but sometimes it is not trivial as parts go out of stock very often, and you will need to find another source for that or those components.

Finished Prototype

Alright, assuming everything went well with the manufacturing of the PCB, we should have a fully functioning NatBot PCB. Later on, we will test to make sure everything is working as expected, and if there are any issues, they will need to be fixed, and the PCB will need to be REVed. See Figures 7-42 and 7-43.

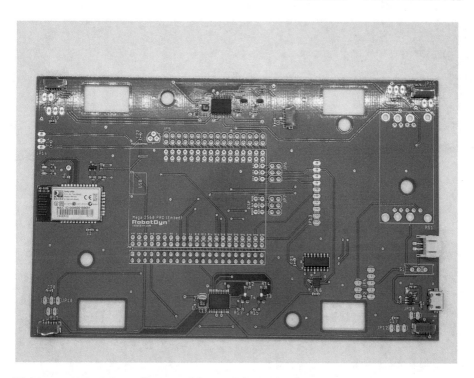

Figure 7-42. *Manufactured board from PCBWay*

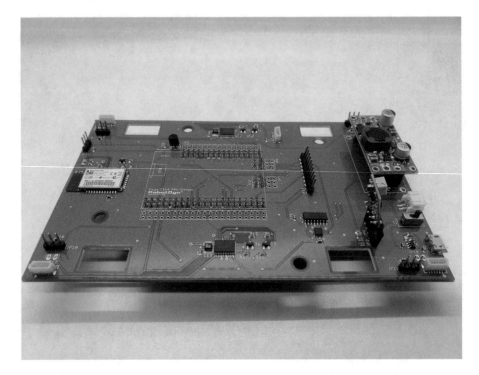

Figure 7-43. *Final board with all PCB level hardware soldered*

Summary

Well, this chapter started off with a review on making schematic sheets for the NatBot. We then dived headfirst into the requirements document for the NatBot; after that, we looked at how we will meet those requirements. Next, we looked at a few new functions that will help us make the dimensions of the NatBot as well as how to make sure nothing is routed under the Bluetooth antenna. Then we took a look at the main individual hardware that will be used for the NatBot; this included a discussion on what device would be used, what the schematic looks like, the layout of the hardware, and finally the pins used from the device to the MEGA 2560 Pro. I then discussed the BOM for the NatBot and some pointers on how to get it manufactured. Finally, we took a look at the prototype PCB that will be tested in the integration phase of this project.

CHAPTER 8

Final Project 3D Model

In this chapter, we will explore the 3D Modeling and printing of the NatBot. Just like the previous chapter, I will explain all new features used to create the 3D models. The first thing we will talk about is the requirements for the 3D chassis of the NatBot. Then we will look at the new functions used to create all the 3D models for the NatBot. Next, we will talk about each individual model and what measurements are important in order to make each of these mounts, brackets, and so on. After that, we will take a look at setting up the 3D printer to print each of these models using the Simplify3D slicer. Finally, we will look at the assembly of the NatBot which will include a short list of hardware needed in order to put together the NatBot. If you do have any issues with the model, don't worry; the full model is supplied with this book. If you need to reference it, that is perfectly fine. So, now that the introduction is completed, let us take a look at the requirements for the NatBot.

Final Project: NatBot

The NatBot requires a modular chassis that will allow for later updates to be implemented when necessary. This chassis should be able to be 3D printed on most standard 3D printers. The NatBot chassis should resemble a rover-style robot with four wheels that can be independently controlled. See Figure 8-1.

© Harold Timmis 2021
H. Timmis, *Practical Arduino Engineering*, https://doi.org/10.1007/978-1-4842-6852-0_8

Figure 8-1. *A fully assembled NatBot*

Requirements Gathering (3D Model)

Naticom has put together a requirements document for the 3D model portion of the design. They are

- Mounts for the motors should be independent of the chassis for easy printing and to make the NatBot more modular.

- The PCB should sit on top of the NatBot chassis for easy access.

- The GPS needs a mount hovering over the NatBot PCB.

- The LCD needs a mount hovering over the NatBot PCB.

- The Ultrasonic Sensor needs to be placed in the front of the NatBot chassis.

- The NatBot needs to have a rover-like appearance.

- The battery needs to be secure and located close to power input.

- The NatBot needs to have a panel mount micro USB port for ease of programming the robot.

- The NatBot should not be more than 200 x 150 x 175mm.

- Wheels should be modular and generic and do not exceed 60mm in diameter.

Okay! So, we have our requirements; we should be able to think through them and start to design the NatBot. In the next section, we will discuss each requirement and come up with a solution for each.

Outlining the 3D Model Requirements

Alright, we have several requirements; let us go through each of the bullet points and start putting together a robot chassis:

- Mounts for the motors should be independent of the chassis for easy printing and to make the NatBot more modular.

  This pretty much means we need to have the motor mounts separate from the main chassis to make them easy to print, and also if the customer (Naticom) wants to add or update the mounts later, they can. The motors need to be independent and should resemble a rover-style set of motor mounts.

- The PCB should sit on top of the NatBot chassis for easy access.

Another easy requirement, just make the PCB the "Lid" of the chassis; we will need to make sure that we have at least four of the five mounting holes on the PCB and have mounting posts, so the board is secured. We might even use brass inserts for more rigidity.

- The GPS needs a mount hovering over the NatBot PCB.

- The LCD needs a mount hovering over the NatBot PCB.

- The Ultrasonic Sensor needs to be placed in the front of the NatBot chassis.

We will need to create mounts for the GPS, LCD, and Ultrasonic Sensor; these can be fastened with hardware so the mounts should be able to handle vibration. We will also need to make sure each of these components is away from other hardware on the NatBot PCB. The Ultrasonic Sensor needs to be placed at the front of the NatBot which will also help with the rover appearance requirement.

- The NatBot needs to have a rover-like appearance.

As stated earlier, all features will give the appearance of a rover-style robot.

- The battery needs to be secure and located close to power input.

The battery will need to be in an easy access area and secured to the chassis; it should also be close to its input as the battery cable is not very long.

- The NatBot needs to have a panel mount micro USB port for ease of programming the robot.

The NatBot will have a panel mount micro USB port at the front of the robot to make it easier to program; without this panel mount, the user would have to remove the NatBot PCB every time they wanted to program it.

- The NatBot should not be more than 200 x 150 x 175mm.

    The NatBot cannot be more than 200mm long, 150mm wide, and 175mm tall. This will be a small rover, but it will still be a challenge to meet this requirement with such a large PCB.

- Wheels should be modular and generic and do not exceed 60mm in diameter.

They do not give us too much information on this, so we will just develop a simple 50mm wheel that will directly connect to the metal hubs we used for the previous project.

Fusion 360 Functions Explained

In order to create some of the 3D models, you will need to understand a few different functions in Fusion 360 that we have not used yet. The first function we will talk about is copying and pasting a 3D component, the second function is creating and using offset planes, and the third is using the Circular Pattern function. Let us get started with the first function, copying and pasting a 3D component.

1. First, open Fusion 360 if it is not already opened.

2. Create a new component and name it "Cube." See Figure 8-2.

Figure 8-2. *Create a new component named "Cube"*

3. Create a 5mm by 5mm by 5mm cube. See Figure 8-3.

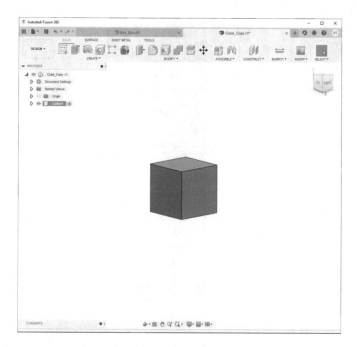

Figure 8-3. *5 x 5 x 5mm cube*

4. Right-click the cube component and select "Copy."

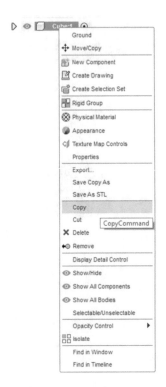

Figure 8-4. *Select "Copy"*

5. Then right-click the Cube_Copy assembly and
    select "Paste New." This will create a new body that
    is separate from the original cube. This is important
    if you want to modify just one of the components.
    This was used with the wheelbases of the rover.
    See Figure 8-5.

Figure 8-5. *Select "Paste New"*

6. Notice that if you select the copied cube and change
    it, the original does not change with it. See Figure 8-6.

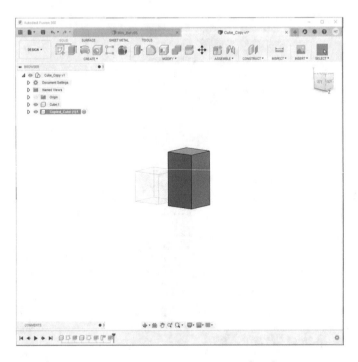

Figure 8-6. *The pasted component is a completely separate*
component

7. If you do want all of the components to match, then
all you need to do is select "Paste" instead of Paste
New." See Figure 8-7.

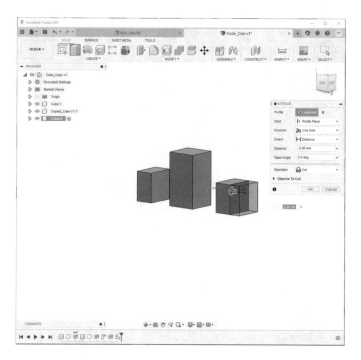

Figure 8-7. *If you just paste a component, both components will share dimensions*

So that is how you can copy a component; most of the time, you probably won't mind if all of the components are identical, but sometimes (like in the case of the wheelbase models) you will want to copy a model just to modify that specific model and not the original. Next, let us talk about how to create an offset plane.

1. Using the same example from the previous section, select one of the faces on a cube. See Figure 8-8.

441

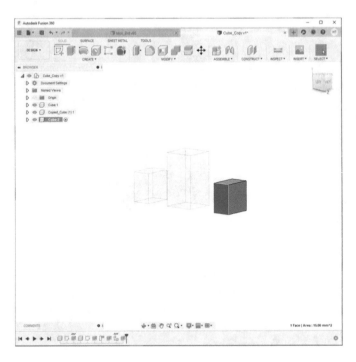

Figure 8-8. *Select a face on a cube*

2. Select Construct ➤ Offset Plane. See Figure 8-9.

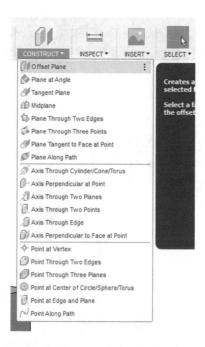

Figure 8-9. *Select the "Offset Plane"*

3.   Now move the offset plane to 10mm. See Figure 8-10.

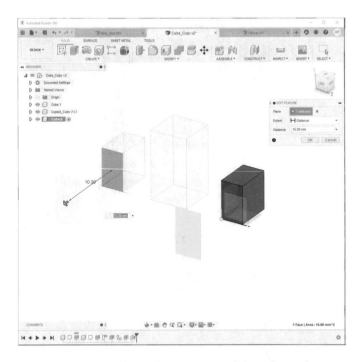

Figure 8-10. *Make the offset plane 10mm from the cube*

4. Now with this plane, you can create a sketch; you
    can even project faces onto the offset plane that can
    be used to make other bodies.

Offset planes can be used for a number of things for the rover; it was
used to create the rover wheels. It made it easy to capture a center point for
the motor shaft. Finally, we can talk about the last Fusion 360 function, the
Circular Pattern function.

1. Create a new model in Fusion 360.

2. Create a cylinder with a diameter of 50mm and a
    height of 10mm. See Figure 8-11.

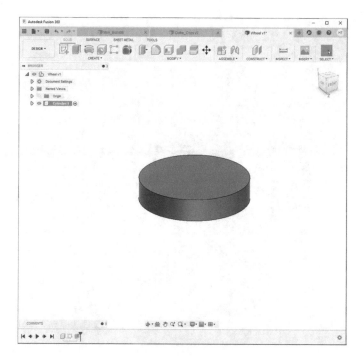

Figure 8-11. *Create a new component and make a cylinder*

3. Create a new sketch and make a 10mm circle
    around the center point of the top of the cylinder.
    See Figure 8-12.

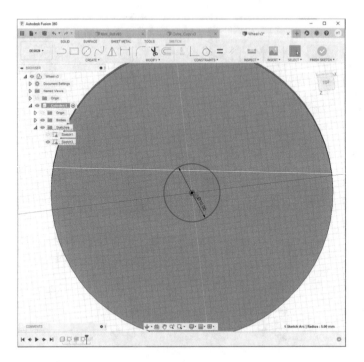

Figure 8-12. *Create a 10mm circle on the cylinder*

4. Make this circle a construction line by selecting it and pressing the "x" key.

5. Draw a 3mm circle on the perimeter of the 10mm circle. See Figure 8-13.

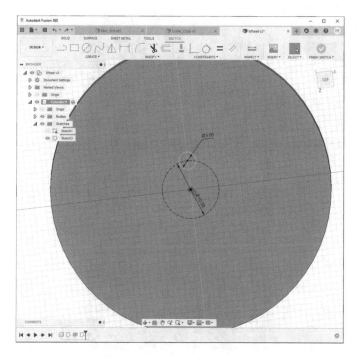

Figure 8-13. *Create a 3mm circle on the perimeter of the 10mm circle*

6. Select the Circular Pattern from the CREATE menu at the top. See Figure 8-14.

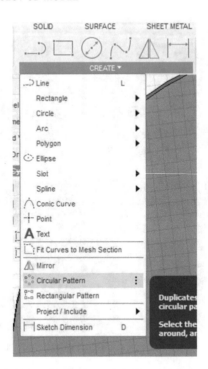

Figure 8-14. *Select "Circular Pattern"*

7. Select the 3mm circle as the "Object," and the
    "Center Point" will be the center of the 10mm circle.
    You will notice once you select these, you will have
    three circles on the screen; you can add more just by
    increasing the quantity. See Figures 8-15 and 8-16.
    Click "OK" when you are done, and you will see that
    these circles have been populated.

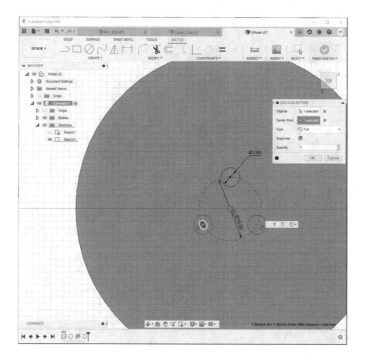

Figure 8-15. *Notice three circles populate on the cylinder*

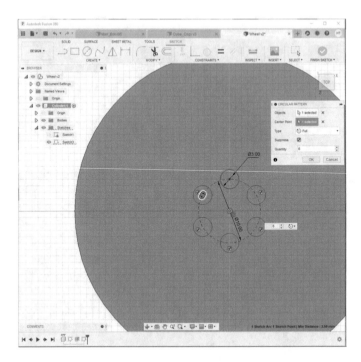

Figure 8-16. *For the quantity, put "6"*

8.   Click Finish Sketch.

9.   Select the six circles and press the "E" key. Extrude these holes to the bottom side of the cylinder. See Figure 8-17.

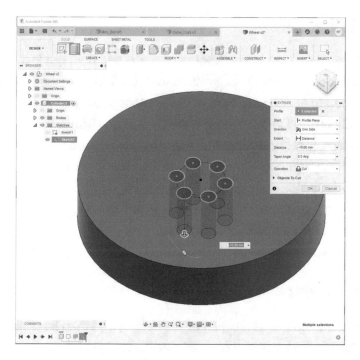

Figure 8-17.   *Extrude to make six holes*

Alright! That puts us in a good spot to start to talk about the various models you will be creating in this chapter. The next section will discuss each of these models.

Features of the NatBot 3D Model Explained

In this section, we will go through each 3D model that is needed to create the NatBot. Each part is explained, and each important dimension is discussed to make it easier to create the 3D model. Remember, you have some creative license here; you can make the NatBot exactly as this book does, or you can make the NatBot your own. It is entirely up to you. Let us get started.

NatBot Chassis

So the NatBot needs to have a few features that will hold the PCB and the battery in place. The motor assemblies and the GPS, LCD, and Ultrasonic mounts need to attach to it. Finally, there needs to be a place for a micro USB panel mount. The nice thing is the GPS, LCD, Ultrasonic Sensor, and the motor assembly mounts are all going to be designed by us, so we can make them any style we want. The same goes for the PCB, but we have already designed it a certain way, so we need to make sure we capture the PCB properly. The micro USB panel mount will need to have a spot made for it as we had to source that component.

Let us look at each section of the chassis.

Battery Holder

This is a simple holder as it captures the battery and then has four holes for zip ties to keep the battery contained. See Figure 8-18.

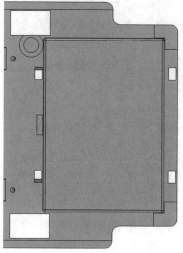

Figure 8-18. *Dimension of the battery holder on the NatBot chassis*

The key measurements are the batteries' length, width, and height.

Motor Assembly Mounts

The motor assemblies are our creation. Naticom has suggested they do want to keep it modular for future upgrades, and the PCB does include four servo motor channels, so we might want to make the mounts the same as a small servo, so if they want to use those mounts with servos, they can. See Figure 8-19.

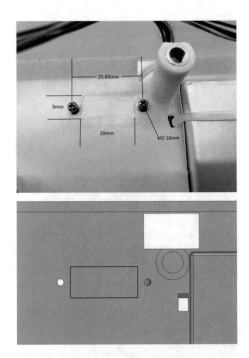

Figure 8-19. *Hole mount for wheelbase assemblies*

The key dimensions are the small Servo that could be used later for the NatBot. This includes the length, width, and height of the servo motor.

Ultrasonic Sensor Mount

To mount this, we can just use two holes that will attach the mount to the chassis. See Figure 8-20.

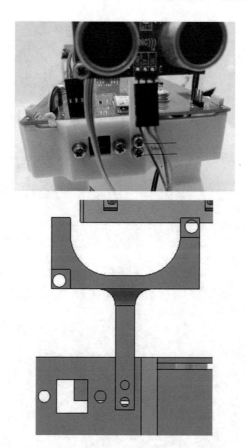

Figure 8-20. *Ultrasonic Sensor Mount chassis mount*

The key dimensions are the size of the screw.

LCD Mount

The LCD will be mounted on the top of the robot and needs to find a position on one of the PCB mounting posts and then be captured on one of the motor cable passthroughs. See Figure 8-21.

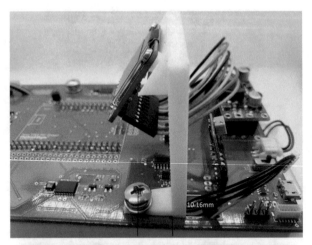

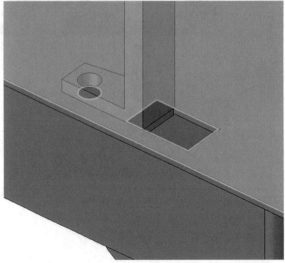

Figure 8-21. *LCD PCB mount*

The key dimensions are the M5 screw and the distance from the M5 hole to the motor cable passthrough.

Micro USB Panel Mount

The micro USB panel mount will need to have holes to mount it and a center hole that will give the user access to the micro USB port. See Figure 8-22.

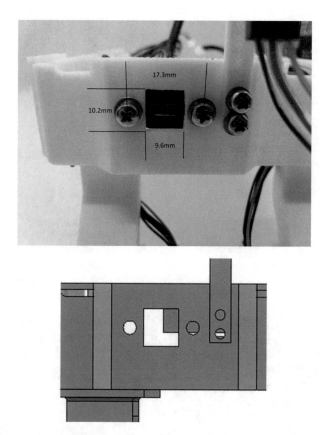

Figure 8-22. *Micro USB panel mount*

The key dimensions are the length between the two mounting holes and the height and width of the access hole.

PCB Mounting

The PCB will be mounted using brass inserts to all for more rigidity in case the PCB ever needs to be removed and then reassembled. The PCB will dictate how large this chassis is as it needs to be roughly the same size in the length and width. Four of the five holes used on the PCB will have a post that will attach the PCB to the chassis. See Figure 8-23.

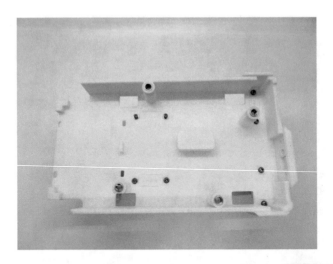

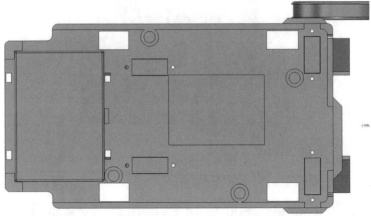

Figure 8-23. *Make sure to use a DXF export in order to get the exact dimensions of the NatBot PCB*

The key dimensions are the hole locations on the PCB, the motor passthrough locations, the length, height (with and without the Arduino attached), and width of the PCB. Using the DXF function to capture the PCB is a good practice as it will give you all of these dimensions minus the height of the PCB.

The last key dimension is the brass inserts that we plan to use for the project. See Figure 8-24.

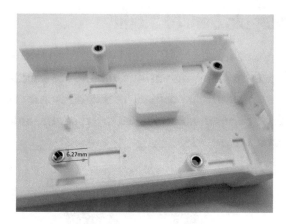

Figure 8-24. *Hole diameter of brass inserts*

This chassis will also need a post to hold the Arduino to the PCB. See Figure 8-25.

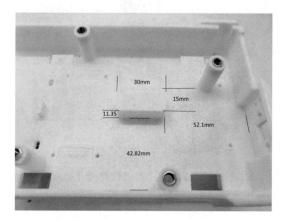

Figure 8-25. *Arduino post*

Finally, remember that the NatBot can only be so tall; the current height of the PCB is 28.22mm with a plastic thickness of 3mm, which should make the NatBot strong enough to withstand some impact.

NatBot Ultrasonic Sensor Mount

The ultrasonic mount should be light and require little to no support material for 3D printing. Key dimensions include the length and width of the ultrasonic sensor, the hole positions of the ultrasonic sensor, and the height of the tallest component on the back of the ultrasonic sensor. See Figures 8-26 and 8-27.

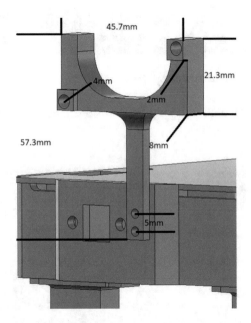

Figure 8-26. *Ultrasonic Sensor Mount dimensions*

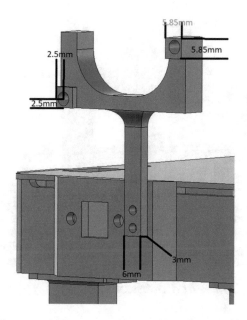

Figure 8-27. *Ultrasonic Sensor Mount dimensions (Cont.)*

This mount needs to attach to the front of the NatBot.

NatBot LCD Mount

The LCD will be mounted to the top of the PCB. The key dimensions are the position of the M5 PCB hole and the motor passthrough width. Also, we need to make sure the LCD is at an angle that will make it easy to see when looking down at it. We also need to make sure the mount is high enough so that it does not interfere with other components and can be connected to the PCB using a dupont connector. The hole positions on the LCD are also important. Finally, make sure there is clearance between the LCD and any components on the back, including but not limited to the SD card holder. See Figures 8-28 and 8-29.

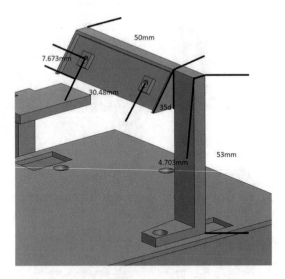

Figure 8-28. *LCD mount dimensions*

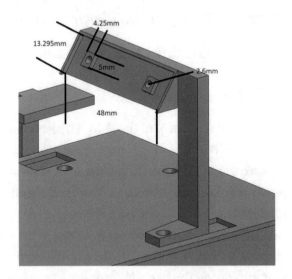

Figure 8-29. *LCD mount dimensions (Cont.)*

NatBot GPS Mount

The GPS mount will be above where the GPS connects. Key dimensions include the location of the GPS header on the NatBot PCB, the height from the PCB to the GPS module, the length and width of the GPS module, and hole positions on the NatBot chassis. See Figure 8-30.

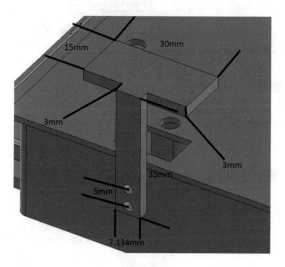

Figure 8-30. *GPS mount dimensions*

NatBot Front and Rear Wheelbase

We will need four separate wheelbases: front right, front left, rear right, and finally rear left. Take advantage of the copy and paste features discussed earlier in this chapter. The key dimensions will be the size of the micro geared motors (length, width, and height), the motor shaft length and width, the mounting hole positions of the micro motors, the total height of the wheelbase model, the motor cable passthrough position, and finally the chassis mounting dimensions created during the chassis portion of development. See Figures 8-31 through 8-34.

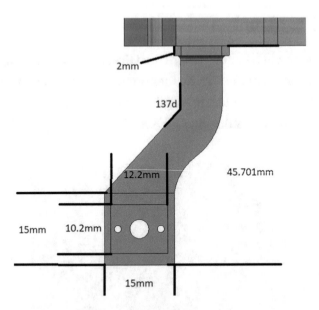

Figure 8-31. *Front wheelbase dimensions*

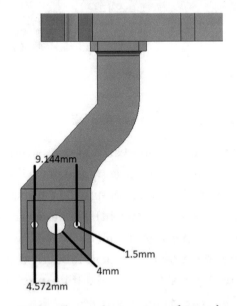

Figure 8-32. *Front wheelbase dimensions (Cont.)*

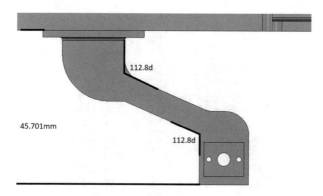

Figure 8-33. *Rear wheelbase dimensions*

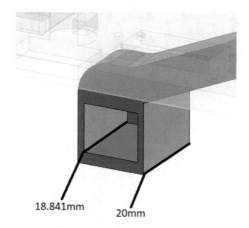

Figure 8-34. *Wheelbase motor depth*

The total height of the NatBot cannot exceed 175mm, so make sure you do not make these wheelbases too tall.

NatBot Wheels

These wheels will need to be attached to the same wheel couplers used in the first project of this book. Key dimensions include the motor coupler threaded holes and the distance between the wheel and the bottom of the NatBot chassis. See Figures 8-35 and 8-36.

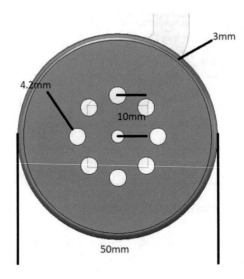

Figure 8-35. *Wheel dimensions*

Figure 8-36. *Wheel dimensions (Cont.)*

3D Printing the NatBot

Well, now it is time to test these dimensions and try to print the NatBot. In this section, I will explain what to print together, how to print, what infill % to use, and where to put support structures. Let us get started with printing the chassis:

Printing the chassis:

Infill % should be 25 to 30%.

Use PLA at 190 to 220C.

Estimated time to print: 4hrs.

You only really need to have support structures where the micro USB panel mount is because of the overhang. See Figure 8-37.

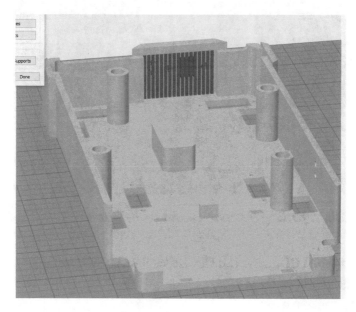

Figure 8-37. *Printing the NatBot chassis*

Printing the wheels and wheelbases:

Infill 25 to 35%.

Use PLA at 190 to 220C.

Estimated time to print: 7hrs.

Auto generate support material; use 2mm for the "Support Pillar Resolution" and 35 degrees as the "Max Overhang Angle."

Also, turn all the wheelbases 90 degrees so that the support structure inside the micro motor cavity can be removed easily. See Figure 8-38.

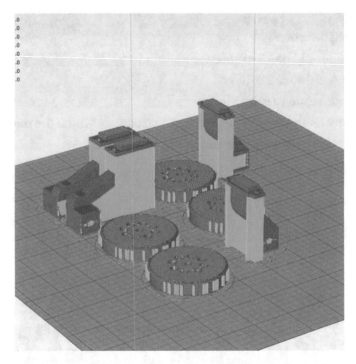

Figure 8-38. *Printing the wheels and wheelbases*

Printing the LCD, GPS, and Ultrasonic Sensor Mounts:

Infill % should be 25 to 30%.

Use PLA at 190 to 220C.

Estimated time to print: 1hr.

The only part that needs support structures is the LCD mount; use 2mm pillar resolution with a max overhang limit of 35 degrees. See Figure 8-39.

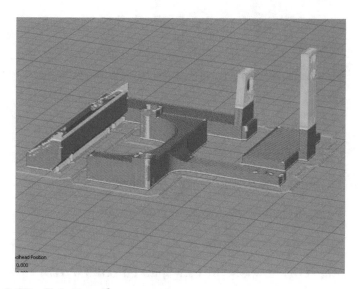

Figure 8-39. *Printing the mounts*

That should be all of the printable components. The next section will discuss assembling the robot.

Fit Check and Assembly

Let us first talk about some hardware you will need in order to assemble this robot:

> 4 x M5 10mm pan head screws (for PCB mounting)
>
> 4 x M5-0.8 OAL 5.83mm brass inserts (for PCB mounting)
>
> 12 x M2 10mm pan head screws (for wheelbase, Ultrasonic, GPS)
>
> 14 x M2 nuts
>
> 2 x M2 12mm pan head screws (for LCD mounting)

2 x M3 10mm pan head screws (for micro USB panel mount)

8 x M1.6 4mm (can be cut down from a longer M1.6 screw)

4 x 30mm gasket or rubber bands (for wheels)

1 x Adafruit micro USB panel mount cable (pn:)

4 x micro motor couplers (pn: Servo City 545348)

4 x micro geared motors (pn: Pololu 2209)

2 x 145 by 2.5mm zip ties

4 x JST SH Jumper Wire (pn: SparkFun GPS-09123)

1 x GPS module (pn:)

1 x Ultrasonic Sensor (pn:)

1 x Adafruit OLED LCD (pn:)

1 x 2Ahr Lithium Ion (pn: SparkFun PRT-13855)

2 x 10 position dupont housing

26 x female dupont crimps

2 x 3 position dupont housing

Small piece of Velcro

24 AWG wire

1. Press four of the brass inserts into the NatBot chassis using a small hammer or a vise to evenly push them into the PCB mounting posts. See Figure 8-40.

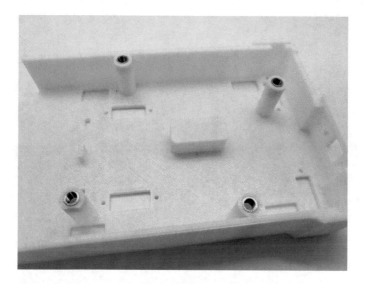

Figure 8-40. *Press the brass inserts into the chassis*

2.   Insert the micro motors into the wheelbases; they should fit snuggly. If they do not fit, try and use a file or X-Acto knife[tm] to clean the area around the motor housing on the wheelbase. If you have the rotary encoders for the motors, make sure they are already attached. See Figure 8-41.

471

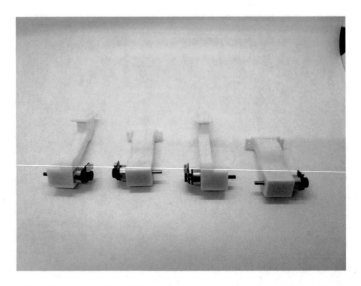

Figure 8-41. *Insert each of the geared motors into the wheelbases*

3. Using eight of the M1.6 4mm screws, attach the
    wheelbase to the micro motors. See Figure 8-42.

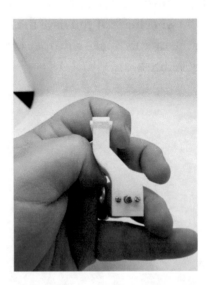

Figure 8-42. *Use the M1.6 4mm screws to attach the motor to the
wheelbase*

4. Attach the wheelbase prints to the NatBot chassis.
    They should be a bit of a tight fit, but if you are
    having trouble fitting them in, you can sand down
    the top a little to help them fit better. See Figure 8-43.

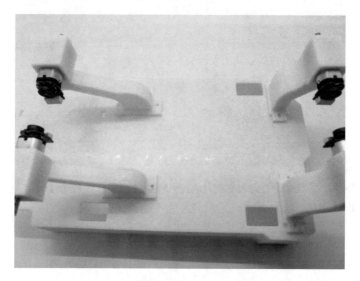

Figure 8-43. *Attach the wheelbases to the NatBot chassis*

5. Use eight of the M2 10mm bolts and eight of the
    M2 screws to secure the wheelbases to the chassis.
    See Figure 8-44.

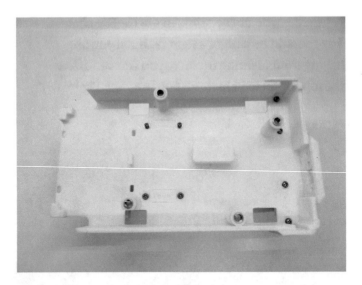

Figure 8-44. *Secure the wheelbases to the chassis using 8 x M2 10mm screws and nuts*

6. Attach the Ultrasonic Sensor to the Ultrasonic
    Sensor Mount using two of the M2 10mm screws
    and two M2 nuts. See Figure 8-45.

Figure 8-45. *Attach the Ultrasonic Sensor to the mount*

7.   Attach the GPS module to the GPS mount using a
     small piece of Velcro. Use scissors to cut the Velcro
     to size. See Figure 8-46.

Figure 8-46. *Attach the GPS module to the GPS mount using*
Velcro

8.   Attach the LCD to the LCD mount using two M2
     12mm screws and two M2 nuts. See Figure 8-47.

Figure 8-47. Attach the LCD to the LCD mount

9. Using crimpers, create a wire harness for the
    Ultrasonic Sensor. It will need 2 x 3 position dupont
    housings and 6 dupont female crimps. You will also
    need about 3 x 5in of 24 AWG stranded wire. See
    Figures 8-48 through 8-53.

Figure 8-48. *Cut off 1/8in insulation*

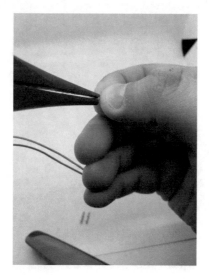

Figure 8-49. *Insert a wire and use pliers to gently squeeze the insulation crimp to hold the wire in place*

Figure 8-50. *Crimp the contact onto the wire*

Figure 8-51. *Finished crimp*

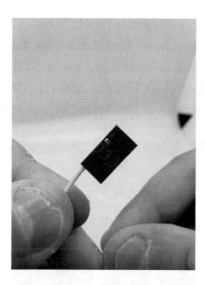

Figure 8-52. *Insert crimped wire into 3 position housing*

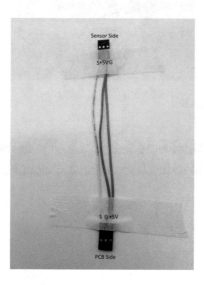

Figure 8-53. *Make sure the connector has this pinout*

10.   Create the wire harness for the LCD using 2 x 10 position dupont headers and 20 female dupont crimps. You will also need 10 x 3in 24 AWG stranded wire. See Figure 8-54. Use the same method to create the wiring harness as you did in the previous step.

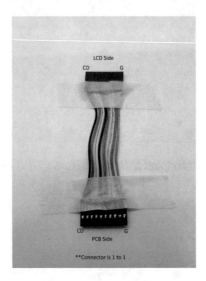

Figure 8-54. *LCD cable*

11.   Attach the Ultrasonic Sensor Mount to the chassis using 2 x M2 10mm screws and 2 x M2 nuts. See Figure 8-55.

Figure 8-55. *Attach the Ultrasonic Sensor Mount*

12. Put the battery into the battery holder and use the two zip ties to secure it to the NatBot chassis. See Figure 8-56.

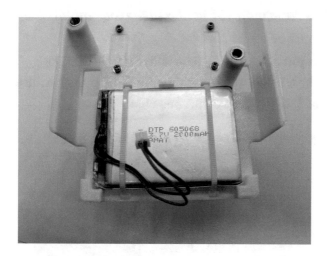

Figure 8-56. *Attach the battery to the chassis using two zip ties*

13. Attach the four JST cables to each of the four motors in the wheelbases and put them through the motor cable passthrough holes on the NatBot chassis. See Figure 8-57.

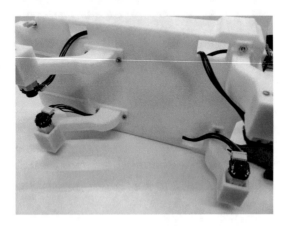

Figure 8-57. *Attach the JST cables to the four motors*

14. Wrap each of the JST wire with a zip tie to make them a bit shorter. Do not tighten too much because you can break the cable. See Figure 8-58.

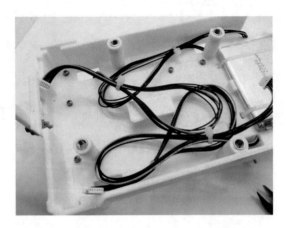

Figure 8-58. *Zip tie the JST cables to shorten them*

15. Mount the micro USB panel mount with 2 x M3
     10mm screws. See Figure 8-59. Then attach it to the
     MEGA 2560 Pro microcontroller. See Figure 8-60.

Figure 8-59. *Attach the micro USB panel mount*

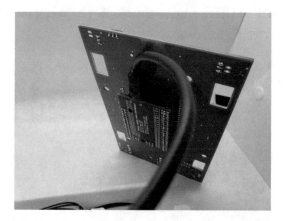

Figure 8-60. *Attach the panel mount to the MEGA 2560 Pro*

16. Attach the NatBot PCB to the NatBot chassis and
     use 3 x M5 screws to attach the PCB to the NatBot
     chassis. See Figure 8-61.

Figure 8-61. *Attach the PCB to the chassis using three M5 screws*

17. Attach the LCD mount to the NatBot by using an M5 screw. See Figure 8-62.

Figure 8-62. *Attach the LCD mount to the chassis*

18. Connect the other side of the LCD wiring harness to the PCB. Use a multimeter just to make sure all contacts are making the proper connection. See Figure 8-63.

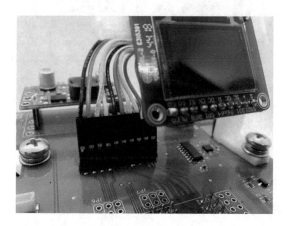

Figure 8-63. *Attach the LCD connector to the PCB*

19. Attach the GPS mount to the chassis using 2 x M2 10mm screws and 2 x M2 nuts. See Figure 8-64.

Figure 8-64. *Attach the GPS mount to the chassis*

20.   Attach the Ultrasonic Sensor wiring harness to the PCB. See Figure 8-65.

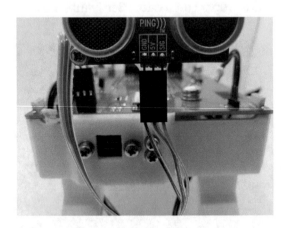

Figure 8-65. *Attach the Ultrasonic Sensor cable to the PCB*

21.   Connect all of the motor cables to the correct connector on the NatBot PCB. See Figure 8-66.

Figure 8-66. *Attach the JST cables to the motor headers on the PCB*

22.   Attach the motor couplers to the four motor shafts.
       See Figure 8-67.

Figure 8-67. *Attach the motor couplers to the geared motor shafts*

23.   Attach the four wheels to the motor couplers. See
       Figure 8-68.

Figure 8-68. *Attach the wheels to the couplers*

24.   Add the 30mm rubber bands or gaskets to the
       NatBot wheels. See Figure 8-69.

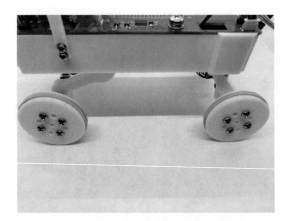

Figure 8-69. *Add 30mm rubber bands to give tires more traction*

Well, that should be it for the assembly of the NatBot; the only thing left is to write some software that will bring the NatBot to life. See you in the next chapter.

Summary

Alright, we covered a few things in this chapter. Let's take a look at them:

- Looked at the mechanical requirements for the NatBot chassis and mounts.

- Brainstormed how we can bring this robot to life and make it look like a rover.

- Took a look at all the important dimensions needed in order to create the NatBot chassis and mounts.

- Went into what it will take to print each of these components.

- Finally, we assembled the NatBot using a Bill of Materials (BOM).

CHAPTER 9

Final Project Software

Well, here we are ready to get started on the software portion of the final project. In this chapter, we will review the requirements for completing the software for the NatBot, as well as putting together a test plan to make sure each component works as expected. We will also explore a few APIs that will help us create the firmware for the NatBot. Finally, we will finish the NatBot's firmware and upload it to the NatBot. This chapter is going to have a lot of information and a lot of code, so take your time when reviewing the software. Let's get started by going over the software requirements for the NatBot.

Final Project: NatBot

The NatBot will require some sophisticated firmware that will control all of the various actions of the sensors, motors, and other peripherals. It also needs to be well documented so that if another developer/student wants to update the code, they could.

© Harold Timmis 2021
H. Timmis, *Practical Arduino Engineering*, https://doi.org/10.1007/978-1-4842-6852-0_9

Requirements Gathering (Firmware)

Naticom has put together a requirements document for the firmware portion of the design. They are

- The motors should be controlled with the following serial command: Motor 1 Direction, Motor 2 Direction, Motor 3 Direction, Motor 4 Direction, Motor 1 Speed, Motor 2 Speed, Motor 3 Speed, Motor 4 Speed. The string example will look like this:

  1,1,1,1,255,255,255,255
  Using serial communication over Bluetooth.

- Accelerometer should record the X, Y, and Z acceleration every time a "y" character is sent to the NatBot. It will also save this data to an SD card.

- The driving direction will be saved to the SD card every time an "x" command is received by the NatBot.

- GPS data will save to the SD card every time the "g" command is sent to the NatBot. It will save longitude and latitude data.

- When an "a" command is received by the NatBot, the Ultrasonic Sensor will tell the user if there is an object within 2 inches of the NatBot.

- The temperature will be displayed on the LCD every time the NatBot receives new trajectory commands.

Outlining the Software Requirements

Alright, we have several requirements; let us go through each of the bullet points and start putting together the firmware for the NatBot:

- The motors should be controlled with the following serial command: Motor 1 Direction, Motor 2 Direction, Motor 3 Direction, Motor 4 Direction, Motor 1 Speed, Motor 2 Speed, Motor 3 Speed, Motor 4 Speed. The string example will look like this:

  1,1,1,1,255,255,255,255
  Using serial communication over Bluetooth.
  This requirement talks about how the user will control each motor on the NatBot over Bluetooth. A single serial command will be used to control each motor's direction and speed. It may also make sense to print this string onto the serial monitor to make sure the correct functions are happening.

- Accelerometer should record the X, Y, and Z acceleration every time a "y" character is sent to the NatBot. It will also save this data to an SD card.

  Every time the NatBot receives the "y" character over Bluetooth, the NatBot will save the data to the SD card in the following format: X, Y, Z.

- The driving direction will be saved to the SD card every time an "x" command is received by the NatBot.

  Trajectory data will be saved to the SD card every time the "x" command is sent to the NatBot, in the following format: Motor A = 1 Motor B = 1 Motor C = 1 Motor D = 1

- GPS data will save to the SD card every time the "g" command is sent to the NatBot. It will save longitude and latitude data.

Longitude and latitude data will be saved to the SD card every time the "g" command is sent to the NatBot.

- When an "a" command is received by the NatBot, the Ultrasonic Sensor will tell the user if there is an object within 2 inches of the NatBot.

The Ultrasonic Sensor will send the user notification over Bluetooth that an object is within 2 inches of the NatBot.

- The temperature will be displayed on the LCD every time the NatBot receives new trajectory commands.

The temperature will be read and displayed onto the LCD every time new trajectory data is received.

Okay, now that we have a good idea of what we need to do, I want to introduce you to each of the libraries we will use to make this robot come to life. See you in the next section.

Reviewing the Arduino Libraries for the NatBot

In this section, we will discuss the various libraries used for the NatBot. I want to give a brief description of the library followed by some of the key functions that the NatBot will use.

ADXL362 Library

With this library, we will read data back from the accelerometer. Here are a few of the important commands:

ObjectName.Begin(): Sets up the SPI protocol

ObjectName.beginMeasure: Switches ADXL362 to measurement mode

ObjectName.readXYZData(X value, Y Value, Z Value, Temperature): Reads the values for the X, Y, and Z planes and then also reads the temperature

These are the main commands we will use for the NatBot when using the accelerometer. These commands should be enough to accomplish all of the requirements for the accelerometer besides the SD and LCD portions.

Adafruit SSD1331 Library

In this section, we will take a look at the SSD1331 Library; this library is used to control the OLED screen we have on the NatBot. There are two other libraries that you need in order to use this library; they are the Adafruit GFX and Adafruit BusIO.

> ObjectName.Begin(): This is used to start communication with the OLED display.
>
> ObjectName.setCursor(x position, y position): This will set the move of the cursor to the desired location.
>
> ObjectName.fillScreen(color): This will set the screen to a particular color.
>
> ObjectName.print("text"): This will put text on the OLED display.
>
> ObjectName.println("text"): This will put text on the OLED display and add a carriage return.
>
> ObjectName.setTextColor(color): Sets the text color.
>
> ObjectName.setTextSize(text size): Sets the text size.

These are the main functions that we will use for the NatBot project and should satisfy all of the requirements.

TinyGPS Library

The NatBot requires software that will parse NMEA data from a GPS module. To do this, we will use the TinyGPS library. Here are some commands we will use to meet the requirements:

> ObjectName.encode(): If encode returns "true" then a valid GPS sentence has been received.
>
> ObjectName.f_get_position(Latitude, Longitude, age): Returns the latitude, longitude, and age of the encoded data

These commands should give us everything we need to meet the requirements for Naticom.

SD Library

The SD Library will be used to store data onto an SD card. There are a few commands you need to be familiar with before we start to use this library; they are

> ObjectName.begin(ChipSelect Pin): This will start communication between the Arduino and the SD card reader.
>
> ObjectName.open(filepath, mode): This will open a file. If the file is being opened in write mode, then the file will be created if it does not exist.
>
> ObjectName.close(): Closes an opened file.

With these functions, we should be able to write to an SD card which will satisfy the requirements for this project.

These libraries will make up a lot of the functionality of the NatBot, and they all will be used to accomplish the requirements that are specified earlier.

Writing the NatBot Firmware

So, the code for this robot has some complexities to it, but it is actually rather quite simple. Here is the code for the NatBot:

```
#include <SPI.h>
#include <SD.h>
#include <ADXL362.h>
#include <Adafruit_GFX.h>
#include <Adafruit_SSD1331.h>
#include <TinyGPS.h>

// Adafruit Display
#define sclk 52
#define mosi 51
#define cs   31
#define rst  29
#define dc   28

// Color definitions
#define  BLACK           0x0000

int numCount = 0;

// Motor IO
const int fields = 8; // how many fields are there? right now 8
int motorPins[] = {42,44,40,46,25,12,26,13}; // Motor Pins
int index = 0;        // the current field being received
int values[fields];   // array holding values for all the fields

// Object Creation
TinyGPS gps;
ADXL362 accel;
```

```
Adafruit_SSD1331 display = Adafruit_SSD1331(cs, dc, mosi, sclk, rst);

// SD Card Chip Select
int SDCS = 30;

// Ultrasonic Sensor Pin
int pingPin = 22;

// Accelerometer variables
int16_t XValue, YValue, ZValue, Temperature;

// GPS data
char LatData[50];       // data buffer for Latitude
char LongData[50];

//Latching Variables
char prevState;
int prevAutoState;

// Data buffer for saving drive data
char driveData [50];

// TMP36 Variables
int tempPin = A0;
int sensorValue = 0;

void setup() {

  // Serial of Arduino, Serial of bluetooth, Fianlly Serial of GPS
  Serial.begin(9600);
  Serial1.begin(115200);
  Serial2.begin(4800);

  // CS Pins of SPI devices
  pinMode(SDCS, OUTPUT);
```

```
  pinMode(cs, OUTPUT);
  pinMode(27, OUTPUT);

  // set Motor pinMode to output
  for(int i; i <= 7; i++)
  {
    pinMode(motorPins[i], OUTPUT);
    digitalWrite(motorPins[i], LOW);
  }

  // Check for Card availability
  if (!SD.begin(SDCS)) {
    Serial.println("Card failed, or not present");
    // don't do anything more:
    while (1);
  }
  // Turn off SD Chip Select
  digitalWrite(SDCS, HIGH);

  Serial.println("card initialized.");

  Serial.println("The Format is: MotoADir,MotoASpe,MotorBDir,
  MotoBSpe\n");
}

void loop() {
  if( Serial1.available())
  {
    char ch = Serial1.read();

    if (ch == 'y' || prevState == 'y') // if Serial reads y
    {
      accel.begin(10);           // Setup SPI protocol, issue
                                 //   device soft reset
```

```
accel.beginMeasure();    // Switch ADXL362 to measure mode

// read all three axis in burst to ensure all
   measurements correspond to same sample time
accel.readXYZTData(XValue, YValue, ZValue, Temperature);
Serial.print("XVALUE=");
Serial.print(XValue);
Serial.print("\tYVALUE=");
Serial.print(YValue);
Serial.print("\tZVALUE=");
Serial.print(ZValue);
Serial.print("\tTEMPERATURE=");
Serial.println(Temperature);
delay(100);                      // Arbitrary delay to make serial
                                    monitor easier to observe

// Stop communication with accelerometer
digitalWrite(27, HIGH);

// Store data into SD card
// open the file. note that only one file can be open at
   a time,
// so you have to close this one before opening another.
SD.begin(SDCS);
File accelFile = SD.open("Accel.txt", FILE_WRITE);

// if the file is available, write to it:
if (accelFile) {
   accelFile.print(XValue);
   accelFile.print(" , ");
   accelFile.print(YValue);
   accelFile.print(" , ");
   accelFile.println(ZValue);
```

```
      accelFile.close();
      digitalWrite(SDCS, HIGH);
      }
    // if the file isn't open, pop up an error:
    else {
      Serial.println("error opening datalog.txt");
    }

    prevState = ch;
}
else if (ch == 'a') // if Serial reads a
{
  if (prevAutoState == 0)
  {
    prevAutoState = 1;
    // put your main code here, to run repeatedly:
    float duration, inches;

    pinMode(pingPin, OUTPUT);
    digitalWrite(pingPin, LOW);
    delayMicroseconds(2);
    digitalWrite(pingPin, HIGH);
    delayMicroseconds(2);
    digitalWrite(pingPin, LOW);

    pinMode(pingPin, HIGH);
    inches = duration / 74 / 2;

    if (inches >= 2)
    {
      Serial1.println("Object Near!!");
    }
  }
```

```
    else if (prevAutoState == 1)
    {
      prevAutoState = 0;
    }
  }
  else if (ch == 'g' || prevState == 'g') // if Serial reads g
  {
      if (Serial2.available() > 0) // now gps device is active
      {
        int c = Serial2.read();
        if(gps.encode(c))      // New valid sentence?
        {

          // Initialize Longitude and Latitude to floating
              point numbers
          float latitude, longitude;

          // Get longitude and latitude
          gps.f_get_position(&latitude,&longitude);

          Serial.print("Lat:    ");
          // Prints latitude with 5 decimal places to the
              Serial Monitor
          Serial.println(latitude,7);

          Serial.print("long: ");
          // Prints longitude with 5 decimal places to the
              Serial Monitor
          Serial.println(longitude,7);

          // Store data into SD card
          // open the file. note that only one file can be
              open at a time,
          // so you have to close this one before opening another.
```

```
        SD.begin(SDCS);
        File GPSFile = SD.open("GPS.txt", FILE_WRITE);

        // if the file is available, write to it:
        if (GPSFile) {
            GPSFile.print(latitude, 7);
            GPSFile.print(" , ");
            GPSFile.println(longitude,7);
            GPSFile.close();
            digitalWrite(SDCS, HIGH);
         }
        // if the file isn't open, pop up an error:
        else {
            Serial.println("error opening datalog.txt");
        }
    }
  }
  prevState = ch;
}
else if(ch >= '0' && ch <= '9') // If the value is a number
                                  0 to 9
{
  // add to the value array
  values[index] = (values[index] * 10) + (ch - '0');
}
else if (ch == ',') // if it is a comma
{
  if(index < fields -1) // If index is less than 4 - 1...
    index++; // increment index
}
else
{
```

```
for(int i=0; i <= index; i++)
{
  if (i == 0 && numCount == 0)
  {
    Serial.println("Motor A");
    Serial.println(values[i]);
  }
  else if (i == 1)
  {
    Serial.println(values[i]);
  }
  if (i == 2)
  {
    Serial.println("Motor B");
    Serial.println(values[i]);
  }
  else if (i == 3)
  {
    Serial.println(values[i]);
  }
  if (i == 4)
  {
    Serial.println("Motor C");
    Serial.println(values[i]);
  }
  else if (i == 5)
  {
    Serial.println(values[i]);
  }
  if (i == 6)
  {
```

```
    Serial.println("Motor D");
    Serial.println(values[i]);
  }
  else if (i == 7)
  {
    Serial.println(values[i]);
  }

  if (i == 0 || i == 2 || i == 4 || i == 6)
  // If the index is equal to 0 or 2
  {
    digitalWrite(motorPins[i], values[i]);
    // Write to the digital pin 1 or 0
    // depending on what is sent to the arduino.
  }

  if (i == 1 || i == 3 || i == 5 || i == 7)
  // If the index is equal to 1 or 3
  {
    analogWrite(motorPins[i], values[i]);
    // Write to the PWM pins a number between
    // 0 and 255 or what the person has entered
    // in the serial monitor.
  }

  values[i] = 0; // set values equal to 0

  sprintf(driveData, "Motor A = ", values[0], "Motor B = ",
  values[2], "Motor C = ", values[4], "Motor D = ", values[6]);

  // Send temperature to the LCD
  sensorValue = analogRead(tempPin);
```

```
        display.begin();
        display.fillScreen(BLACK);
        display.setCursor(0,0);
        display.print(sensorValue);
        digitalWrite(cs, HIGH);

    }


    index = 0;
    numCount = 0;
  }
  if (ch == 'x' || prevState == 'x') // if Serial reads x
  {
        SD.begin(SDCS);
        File driveFile = SD.open("Drive.txt", FILE_WRITE);

        // if the file is available, write to it:
        if (driveFile) {
            driveFile.println(driveData);
            driveFile.close();
            digitalWrite(SDCS, HIGH);
         }
        // if the file isn't open, pop up an error:
        else {
            Serial.println("error opening datalog.txt");
        }
        prevState = ch;
    }
  }
}
```

The first bit of code is all the includes for the program; these includes allow us to use various functions from other libraries. You will notice the libraries for SPI, SD, ADXL362 accelerometer, and the TinyGPS library are all accounted for.

```
#include <SPI.h>
#include <SD.h>
#include <ADXL362.h>
#include <Adafruit_GFX.h>
#include <Adafruit_SSD1331.h>
#include <TinyGPS.h>
```

The next section of code will define and initialize all of the global variables we need in order to control the NatBot. The first variables are defined with the define directive which will set each of these variables to a specific value. The next section deals with creating new instances of objects; these objects are then used with the API to call certain functions, for example:

```
gps.f_get_position(&latitude,&longitude);
```

This function will return the longitude and latitude data. Finally, we start to declare the global variables. These variables can be used anywhere in the program which is great, but if you don't want somebody accessing this variable, your best bet would be to use a local variable which would be placed within that function instead of on the outside of the setup() and loop() functions. You will notice several variables have integers associated with them; these are the pin numbers assigned to the Arduino.

```
// SD Card Chip Select
int SDCS = 30;

// Ultrasonic Sensor Pin
int pingPin = 22;
```

```
// Accelerometer variables
int16_t XValue, YValue, ZValue, Temperature;

// GPS data
char LatData[50];       // data buffer for Latitude
char LongData[50];

//Latching Variables
char prevState;
int prevAutoState;

// Data buffer for saving drive data
char driveData [50];

// TMP36 Variables
int tempPin = A0;
int sensorValue = 0;
```

Now in the setup loop, we will find several different functions and variables that we need in order to get the NatBot up and running. First, serial ports 0 through 2 are started. The first serial port is set to a baud rate of 9600, which is okay for the main RX/TX lines. The second serial port is for the Bluetooth module, and the third serial port is for the GPS module. Next, the CS (chip select pins) are set up as outputs, and the motor pins are all set to LOW. The next bit of code checks that an SD card is present, if it is the code will continue and if it is not the program will send out an SD card failed command. Then the SDCS (SD card chip select pin) is set to high, which will stop communication between the Arduino and the SD card. Finally, the card will say it is initialized and will also ask the user to enter trajectory information in a particular manner.

```
void setup() {

  // Serial of Arduino, Serial of bluetooth, Fianlly Serial of GPS
  Serial.begin(9600);
```

```
Serial1.begin(115200);
Serial2.begin(4800);

// CS Pins of SPI devices
pinMode(SDCS, OUTPUT);
pinMode(cs, OUTPUT);
pinMode(27, OUTPUT);

// set Motor pinMode to output
for(int i; i <= 7; i++)
{
  pinMode(motorPins[i], OUTPUT);
  digitalWrite(motorPins[i], LOW);
}

// Check for Card availability
if (!SD.begin(SDCS)) {
  Serial.println("Card failed, or not present");
  // don't do anything more:
  while (1);
}
// Turn off SD Chip Select
digitalWrite(SDCS, HIGH);

Serial.println("card initialized.");

Serial.println("The Format is: MotoADir,MotoASpe,MotorBDir,
MotoBSpe   MotoCDir,MotoCSpe,MotorDDir,MotoDSpe \n");
}
```

Now we enter the loop structure which is the main portion of the software for the NatBot. The first small section of this code relates to checking the availability of bytes coming in from Serial1; if there are bytes, then they will be passed through all of the if statements within the loop structure.

```
void loop() {
  if( Serial1.available())
  {
    char ch = Serial1.read();
```

The next section of code runs if the "y" command is received over Serial1. If it is, the accelerometer is enabled with a begin function, and the readXYZData() function is called to read the X, Y, Z, and temperature data. Then the accelerometer is disabled by setting its CS pin to "High." Next, the SD card is enabled with a begin function; a file is created called Accel.txt. Then the X, Y, and Z data is sent to the SD card. Finally, the previous state is monitored so that this block of code only runs once.

```
if (ch == 'y' || prevState == 'y') // if Serial reads y
  {
    accel.begin(10);          // Setup SPI protocol, issue
                              //   device soft reset
    accel.beginMeasure();     // Switch ADXL362 to measure mode

    // read all three axis in burst to ensure all measurements
    //   correspond to same sample time
    accel.readXYZTData(XValue, YValue, ZValue, Temperature);
    Serial.print("XVALUE=");
    Serial.print(XValue);
    Serial.print("\tYVALUE=");
    Serial.print(YValue);
    Serial.print("\tZVALUE=");
    Serial.print(ZValue);
    Serial.print("\tTEMPERATURE=");
    Serial.println(Temperature);
    delay(100);               // Arbitrary delay to make serial
                              //   monitor easier to observe
```

```
// Stop communication with accelerometer
digitalWrite(27, HIGH);

// Store data into SD card
// open the file. note that only one file can be open at
    a time,
// so you have to close this one before opening another.
SD.begin(SDCS);
File accelFile = SD.open("Accel.txt", FILE_WRITE);

// if the file is available, write to it:
if (accelFile) {
   accelFile.print(XValue);
   accelFile.print(" , ");
   accelFile.print(YValue);
   accelFile.print(" , ");
   accelFile.println(ZValue);
   accelFile.close();
   digitalWrite(SDCS, HIGH);
   }
// if the file isn't open, pop up an error:
else {
   Serial.println("error opening datalog.txt");
}

prevState = ch;
}
```

The next section of code will only run if the "a" command is received. If it is received over Serial1, then the ultrasonic sensor will pulse once and check the distance to the nearest object. If 2 inches or less is detected, Serial1 will be sent a message "Object Near!!"

```
else if (ch == 'a') // if Serial reads a
    {
      if (prevAutoState == 0)
      {
        prevAutoState = 1;
        // put your main code here, to run repeatedly:
        float duration, inches;

        pinMode(pingPin, OUTPUT);
        digitalWrite(pingPin, LOW);
        delayMicroseconds(2);
        digitalWrite(pingPin, HIGH);
        delayMicroseconds(2);
        digitalWrite(pingPin, LOW);

        pinMode(pingPin, HIGH);
        inches = duration / 74 / 2;

        if (inches >= 2)
        {
          Serial1.println("Object Near!!");
        }
      }
      else if (prevAutoState == 1)
      {
        prevAutoState = 0;
      }
```

This section focuses on the GPS; it will be activated if the "g" command is received over Serial1. Two floating-point local variables are created called the latitude and longitude; these variables are fed into the f_get_position(&latitude, &longitude) function. We then print latitude and longitude data to the main serial port for debugging purposes. Finally, we initialize the SD card again and save the latitude and longitude data to the

SD card. One thing to also note is we shut down the SD card again with a digitalWrite(SDCS, HIGH).

```
else if (ch == 'g' || prevState == 'g') // if Serial reads g
    {
        if (Serial2.available() > 0) // now gps device is active
        {
          int c = Serial2.read();
          if(gps.encode(c))      // New valid sentence?
          {

              // Initialize Longitude and Latitude to floating
                  point numbers
              float latitude, longitude;

              // Get longitude and latitude
              gps.f_get_position(&latitude,&longitude);

              Serial.print("Lat:    ");
              // Prints latitude with 5 decimal places to the
                  Serle ial Monitor
              Serial.println(latitude,7);

              Serial.print("long: ");
              // Prints longitude with 5 decimal places to the
                  Serial Monitor
              Serial.println(longitude,7);

              // Store data into SD card
              // open the file. note that only one file can be
                  open at a time,
             // so you have to close this one before opening another.
              SD.begin(SDCS);
              File GPSFile = SD.open("GPS.txt", FILE_WRITE);

              // if the file is available, write to it:
```

```
         if (GPSFile) {
             GPSFile.print(latitude, 7);
             GPSFile.print(" , ");
             GPSFile.println(longitude,7);
             GPSFile.close();
             digitalWrite(SDCS, HIGH);
          }
         // if the file isn't open, pop up an error:
         else {
             Serial.println("error opening datalog.txt");
         }
      }
   }
   prevState = ch;
}
```

The next section will parse out any numbers 0 to 9 and store that value into the values array which will be used later to control the motors.

```
else if(ch >= '0' && ch <= '9') // If the value is a number 0 to 9
   {
     // add to the value array
     values[index] = (values[index] * 10) + (ch - '0');
   }
```

This else if section will parse out the "," character; they will not be needed to control the NatBot.

```
else if (ch == ',') // if it is a comma
   {
     if(index < fields -1) // If index is less than 4 - 1...
        index++; // increment index
   }
```

The final section will print a script out of each of the motors' direction and speed. Then, each of the indexes will be parsed into a direction bit which will go to a digitalWrite function or will be passed into an analogWrite function for the speed of the motors. Next, a sprintf function is used to concatenate all of the motor directions into a string that will later be sent to the SD card. Finally, the TMP36 is read, and the LCD is initialized; then the sensorValue (which is the analog temp value) is displayed on the LCD.

```
else
    {

      for(int i=0; i <= index; i++)
      {

        if (i == 0 && numCount == 0)
        {
          Serial.println("Motor A");
          Serial.println(values[i]);
        }
        else if (i == 1)
        {
          Serial.println(values[i]);
        }
        if (i == 2)
        {
          Serial.println("Motor B");
          Serial.println(values[i]);
        }
        else if (i == 3)
        {
          Serial.println(values[i]);
        }
```

```
if (i == 4)
{
  Serial.println("Motor C");
  Serial.println(values[i]);
}
else if (i == 5)
{
  Serial.println(values[i]);
}
if (i == 6)
{
  Serial.println("Motor D");
  Serial.println(values[i]);
}
else if (i == 7)
{
  Serial.println(values[i]);
}

if (i == 0 || i == 2 || i == 4 || i == 6)
// If the index is equal to 0 or 2
{
  digitalWrite(motorPins[i], values[i]);
  // Write to the digital pin 1 or 0
  // depending on what is sent to the arduino.
}

if (i == 1 || i == 3 || i == 5 || i == 7)
// If the index is equal to 1 or 3
{
  analogWrite(motorPins[i], values[i]);
  // Write to the PWM pins a number between
```

```
    // 0 and 255 or what the person has entered
    // in the serial monitor.
  }

  values[i] = 0; // set values equal to 0

  sprintf(driveData, "Motor A = ", values[0], "Motor B = ",
  values[2], "Motor C = ", values[4], "Motor D = ", values[6]);

  // Send temperature to the LCD
  sensorValue = analogRead(tempPin);

  display.begin();
  display.fillScreen(BLACK);
  display.setCursor(0,0);
  display.print(sensorValue);
  digitalWrite(cs, HIGH);

  }

  index = 0;
  numCount = 0;
}
```

The final section of this code will activate if the "x" character is received by Serial1. If it is, the SD card will activate, and the trajectory data will be saved to the SD card. Finally, the SD card is closed with the digitalWrite(cs, HIGH).

```
if (ch == 'x' || prevState == 'x') // if Serial reads x
  {
          SD.begin(SDCS);
          File driveFile = SD.open("Drive.txt", FILE_WRITE);
```

```
    // if the file is available, write to it:
    if (driveFile) {
        driveFile.println(driveData);
        driveFile.close();
        digitalWrite(SDCS, HIGH);
     }
    // if the file isn't open, pop up an error:
    else {
        Serial.println("error opening datalog.txt");
    }
    prevState = ch;
}
```

Alright, so that is the code for the NatBot; the only thing left to do is to upload it to your Arduino. The next section will go over that process.

Uploading and Testing the NatBot Firmware

Just like you did with the previous projects, you will need to make sure the Arduino is plugged into your computer and the correct COM port is selected. If you are having trouble finding the correct COM port, use the device manager and look for the port named USB-SERIAL CH340 (COM#). Then select the correct board which is an Arduino Mega or Arduino MEGA 2560; the processor should be an Atmega2560. Once all of that is settled, click the "Upload" button and the code will be sent to the Arduino.

Summary

Alright! The firmware portion of this project is completed, but we will still use some of it to help us create an application on a computer to control the NatBot, but first let's review what we covered in this chapter:

- Learned how to send string commands over the serial port (Bluetooth)

- Learned how to send text to an LCD and change it at a rapid pace

- Learned how to use multiple SPI connections in order to talk to several devices

- Learned how to use the TinyGPS library and get longitude and latitude data

- Learned how to get accelerometer data by using the ADXL362 library

- Learned how to use the Ping Ultrasonic sensor

CHAPTER 10

Final Project Putting It All Together

In this chapter, you will learn about a new piece of software (LabVIEW) that will allow us to integrate the NatBot with a computer and an Xbox controller, per our Naticom's requirements document. LabVIEW is a very powerful programming language, as well as a powerful testing tool. In this chapter, we will use LabVIEW to interface with the Xbox controller so that we can control the NatBot's movements. We will not need to write any new Arduino code for this chapter, as we will be using the same code from Chapter 9, so we will first go over the basics of the LabVIEW environment and programming language so that you are more comfortable with the Naticom's project for this chapter.

Note I suggest visiting www.ni.com, as they will have a large selection of tutorials and videos.

Introduction to the LabVIEW Environment

We will first need to install the LabVIEW Student Edition onto a computer. You can get a great bundle from SparkFun at www.sparkfun.com/products/10812. If you don't want to buy the bundle, you can download a 30-day trial from www.ni.com/labview. This process is very

© Harold Timmis 2021
H. Timmis, *Practical Arduino Engineering*, https://doi.org/10.1007/978-1-4842-6852-0_10

straightforward. Simply put the LabVIEW CD into your DVD-ROM drive, and follow the onscreen instructions.

Now that we've installed the LabVIEW Student Edition, we can start using it for various projects, but first let's take a look at some of the fundamentals of LabVIEW. The next section will discuss the various parts of the LabVIEW environment that we will use in this chapter. They are the Front Panel, the Controls Palette, the Block Diagram, the Functions Palette, and the Tools Palette.

Note   If you ever need help in LabVIEW, all you need to do is press Ctrl-H, and a help box will pop up. Anything you run your mouse over—a control, indicator, function, structure, and so on—the help box will give you information on.

The Front Panel

After you open LabVIEW, a screen will open. Click the "Blank VI" option on the screen, and two windows will open, one of them being the Front Panel. The Front Panel is where we will put all of the controls and indicators for our projects. When we are finished with the design of the Front Panel, we will have completed our GUI. You can also align the controls and indicators on the Front Panel by using Align Functions buttons at the top of the Front Panel. You will be starting your program from the Front Panel using the white arrow button in the upper-left corner of the window (you must click this white arrow in order for the program to start). Figure 10-1 shows the Front Panel.

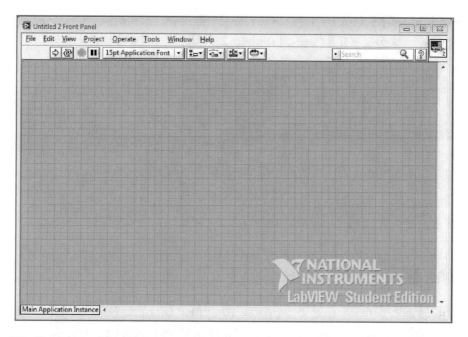

Figure 10-1. *The Front Panel*

Note   If you have a broken arrow instead of a solid white arrow in the Front Panel, that means that your code has an error and will not run. If you click the broken arrow, an error dialog box will pop up and tell you what errors you have.

The Controls Palette

In this palette, you will find all of the controls and indicators that you will use to create your GUI. Some of these controls and indicators include toggle switches, numerical indicators, string controls and indicators, and much more (I suggest playing around with this palette). To get to this palette, go to View ➤ Controls Palette. We will be using only a few controls and indicators in this chapter, but if you want to learn more, I suggest visiting www.ni.com, as they have a large selection of tutorials and videos. Figure 10-2 shows the Controls Palette.

Figure 10-2. *The Controls Palette*

The Block Diagram

This is where all the magic happens. The Block Diagram is where we code the application and make the Front Panel do something (this can range from turning on an LED to GPS data analysis). It contains the white arrow button to run the program, and it also has a few debugging functions (we will talk about those later). The Block Diagram also has a palette that we will discuss in the next section. Figure 10-3 shows the Block Diagram.

Figure 10-3. *The Block Diagram*

The Functions Palette

This palette has all of the various functions that you might or might not
need. We will be going over only a few functions, but it is also a good
idea to play around with this palette. You can find this palette by going to
View ➤ Functions Palette. You will find functions for strings, numerical,
Boolean, comparison, serial communication, and much more. Figure 10-4
shows the Functions Palette.

Figure 10-4. *The Functions Palette*

Next, we will discuss the Tools Palette, which is used to control what your mouse will do.

The Tools Palette

This palette can be used in either the Front Panel or the Block Diagram, although most of the options will work only in the Block Diagram. You can view this palette by clicking the View ➤ Tools Palette. For the most part, we will not be using this palette because it defaults to Automatic Tool Selection, which means it will automatically select the best tool for what you are doing. Figure 10-5 shows the Tools Palette.

Figure 10-5. *The Tools Palette*

Now that you are a bit more familiar with the LabVIEW environment, let's go over some of the functions we'll be using in this chapter.

LabVIEW Functions Explained

LabVIEW uses a different approach to programming; it uses the Data Flow Process, which means data will "flow" from left to right on the screen. This makes code very easy to read and understand. The following functions will be used in the project for this chapter, as we will be creating software to scale values from the Xbox controller.

Note   It is always a good idea to wire error clusters and error wires to keep data flow moving from left to right. We will see an example of this later in this chapter.

To find the first function that we will discuss, go to Block Diagram ➤ Functions Palette ➤ Programming ➤ Structures. Here, you will see several types of loops and conditional structures. We will be using the While Loop, the Case Structure, and the Sequence Structure for this chapter. The next section will discuss the While Loop.

The While Loop

This loop operates like any other While Loop, except that it is a visual While Loop. In order to use it with other functions, you simply place the functions within the While Loop. The While Loop will run at least one time, and has many uses, just as in our Arduino programs. We can use a conditional terminal to stop the While Loop, and we can use an iteration terminal to check what iteration the While Loop is on. Figure 10-6 shows the While Loop.

Figure 10-6. *A While Loop*

In the next section, we will discuss the Case Structure and its functions.

The Case Structure

This is a conditional structure much like the switch statement or the if-else-if statements. You can have a true or false Case Structure, or you can use enumerated data to have multiple case statements, such as a State Machine; however, we will not go over State Machines in this book. To use a Case Structure, you will need to select the Case Structure from the Functions Palette ➤ Programming ➤ Structures, and drag the Case Structure to the appropriate size that you need. You can then switch from the true case to the false case by clicking the arrow at the top center of the Case Structure. The Case Structure uses the Selector Terminal to select the case that the Case Structure will call (we will see an example of this in the project for this chapter). Figure 10-7 shows a Case Structure.

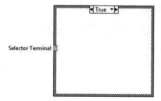

Figure 10-7. *A Case Structure*

The Sequence Structure

This structure is used to force code to flow in a sequential manner (as the name suggests). It is not a good LabVIEW programming practice to have multiple Sequence Structures or Stacked Sequences, as they hide code and alter the Data Flow Process. However, a one-frame Sequence Structure used well, such as for initializing values, is not a bad practice. You can find the Sequence Structure by going to the Functions Palette ➤ Programming ➤ Structures. Figure 10-8 shows a Sequence Structure.

Figure 10-8. *A Sequence Structure*

Now that we have discussed the While Loops, Case Structures, and Sequence Structures, we can move on to the rest of the functions we will use for this chapter.

Numerical Functions

We will use a few Numerical Functions that will help us in the final project. To get to the Numerical Functions, we need to first go to the Block Diagram, then go to the Functions Palette ➤ Programming ➤ Numeric. Figure 10-9 shows the Numeric Palette.

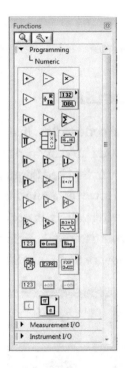

Figure 10-9. *The Numeric Palette*

In here, you will see functions ranging from decrementing to a random number function. We will use these functions to scale values from the Xbox controller to work with the Arduino. Now, we need to discuss a few functions from this palette that we will use in this chapter:

- Divide: This function is used to divide numerical values (see Figure 10-10(a)).

- Multiply: This function is used to multiply numerical values (see Figure 10-10(b)).

- Decrement: This function is used to subtract by one or decrement by one (see Figure 10-10(c)).

Figure 10-10. *(a) The Divide Function, (b) the Multiply Function, and (c) the Decrement Function*

String Functions

We use String Functions to manipulate strings. We will use a few of these functions to create the protocol so that the Xbox controller can communicate with the Arduino. You can find the String Functions by going to the Functions Palette ➤ Programming ➤ String (see Figure 10-11).

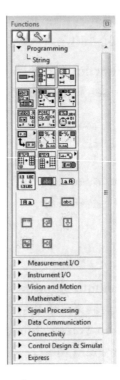

Figure 10-11. *The String Palette*

We'll be using the following String Functions for this chapter:

- Concatenate String: This function is used to combine two or more strings (see Figure 10-12(a)).

- Number to Decimal String: This function converts a numerical value to a string value (see Figure 10-12(b)).

Figure 10-12. *(a) The Concatenate String Function and (b) the Number to Decimal String Function*

Comparison Functions

We use Comparison Functions to compare types to one another, for example, whether 2 > 1. You can find the Comparison Functions by going to the Functions Palette ➤ Programming ➤ Comparison (see Figure 10-13).

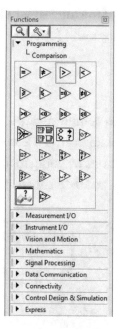

Figure 10-13. *The Comparison Palette*

We will be using the following Comparison Functions:

- Less?: This function compares a value x to a value y and tests whether x is less than the y value (see Figure 10-14(a)).

- Greater?: This function compares a value x to a value y and tests whether x is greater than y (see Figure 10-14(b)).

- Less than 0?: This function compares a value x to zero (see Figure 10-14(c)).

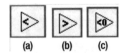
(a)   (b)   (c)

Figure 10-14. *(a) The Less? Function, (b) the Greater? Function, and (c) the Less than 0? Function*

Now that we have some of the fundamentals of LabVIEW covered, we can move on to Serial Functions and Input Device Control Functions.

Serial Functions

We can use these functions to communicate with USB devices. We will use these functions to write data from the Xbox controller to the Arduino. You can find the Serial Functions by going to the Functions Palette ➤ Instrument I/O ➤ Serial. Figure 10-15 shows the Serial Palette.

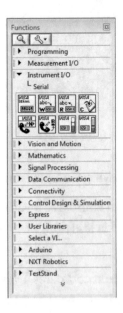

Figure 10-15. *The Serial Palette*

In this chapter, we will use the following Serial Functions:

- Virtual Instrument Software Architecture (VISA) Configure Serial Port: This function sets up the serial port's resource name, baud rate, parity, stop bits, flow control, and data bits (see Figure 10-16(a)).

- VISA Flush I/O Buffer: This function deletes the data that is stored on the buffer, allowing for more information to take its place (see Figure 10-16(b)).

- VISA Write: This function writes data to the serial port you specified in the VISA Configure Serial Port Function (see Figure 10-16(c)).

- VISA Close: This function closes out the serial communication session (see Figure 10-16(d)).

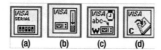

Figure 10-16. *(a) The VISA Configure Serial Port Function, (b) the VISA Flush I/O Buffer Function, (c) the VISA Write Function, and (d) the VISA Close Function*

Now that we understand the functions that we will need to communicate with a serial port, we can move on to understanding the functions that are necessary for the Xbox controller to work with the application for this chapter.

Input Device Control Functions

We can use these functions to communicate with HIDs (Human Interface Devices), such as a mouse, keyboard, or joystick. We will use these functions to communicate with the Xbox controller. You can find the Input

Device Control Functions by going to the Functions Palette ➤ Connectivity ➤ Input Device Control. Figure 10-17 shows the Input Device Control Functions.

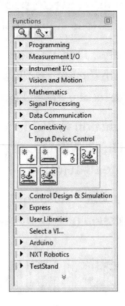

Figure 10-17.   *The Input Device Control Palette*

In this chapter, we will use the following Input Device Control Functions:

- Initialize Joystick: This function starts the communication between the computer and the joystick that you selected with the device index (see Figure 10-18(a)).

- Acquire Input Data: This function gets the data from the joystick device, such as button information and axis information (see Figure 10-18(b)).

- Close Input Device: This function closes out the input device session (see Figure 10-18(c)).

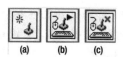

Figure 10-18. *(a) The Initialize Joystick Function, (b) the Aquire Input Data Function, and (c) the Close Input Device Function*

With a primer of the LabVIEW software environment under our belts, we can apply our newfound knowledge to our customer's project. Let's first gather the requirements and then address hardware and software details.

Gathering Requirements and Creating the Requirements Document

Naticom wants an application that can control the NatBot from a computer using an Xbox controller; this application needs to control the movements of the NatBot and also be able to send the various commands that will save data to the SD card or check if an obstacle is in the NatBot's way.

Software

Here are the software requirements for this project:

- Write LabVIEW software that allows the Xbox controller to control the Arduino's motion, and control the x, a, y, and g commands that can be sent to the NatBot.

- The NatBot will also send a message back to the LabVIEW application if the "a" command is sent to the NatBot and will say if an object is too close to the NatBot.

- Display scaled data from the joystick in a String Indicator in the following format: 1,255,1,255,1,255,1,255.

- Use the same code from Chapter 9 for the Arduino.

We should now have everything we need to move forward with this project. In the next section, we will begin writing the application software that will control the NatBot.

Writing the Software

This section is a bit different from what you normally see in this book; this is because we will not be writing any Arduino code. Instead, we will be writing code in LabVIEW, which will let us use the Xbox controller with the Arduino.

Getting Started

Use the following steps to get started writing the software in LabVIEW:

1. First, you will need to start LabVIEW by double-clicking the LabVIEW icon.

2. After LabVIEW starts, click the "Blank VI" option. Figure 10-19 shows this process.

3. A Front Panel and a Block Diagram should appear on the screen, ready to be added to. Figure 10-20 shows the Front Panel and Block Diagram.

Note   A black-outlined box within a figure indicates where you should click with your mouse, or it denotes new code that has been added.

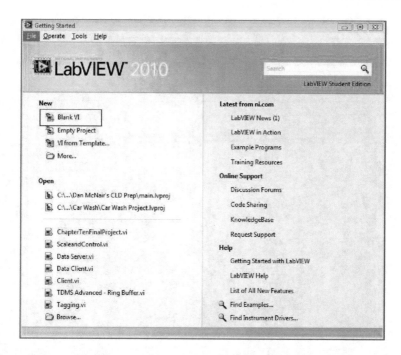

Figure 10-19. *The start screen for LabVIEW (double-click "Blank VI")*

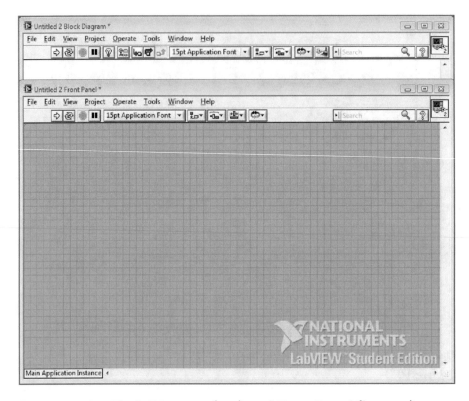

Figure 10-20. *Block Diagram (top) and Front Panel (bottom)*

Designing the GUI

Now we need to design the GUI for this project:

1. First, go to the Controls Palette ➤ Modern ➤ Boolean ➤ Stop Button, and click the Stop Button and drag it to the Front Panel.

2. After that, we need to add the String Indicator to the Front Panel. Go to the Controls Palette ➤ Modern ➤ String & Path ➤ String Indicator, and drag the String Indicator to the Front Panel. If you want to resize

any controls or indicators, simply hover your mouse
over the edge of the control or indicator and drag it
out to the size that you want.

3. Next, add the Write Button to the Front Panel by
    going to the Controls Palette ➤ Modern ➤ Boolean
    ➤ OK Button and dragging the OK Button to the
    Front Panel.

4. Then, you can rename the OK Button by clicking
    the text and changing it to "Write." After that, right-
    click the Write Button, and a pop-up menu should
    appear; click Mechanical Action ➤ Switch when
    Pressed.

Programming the Application

For now, the Front Panel is complete, and we are going to move on to
programming our LabVIEW application. Figure 10-21 shows the GUI for
this project.

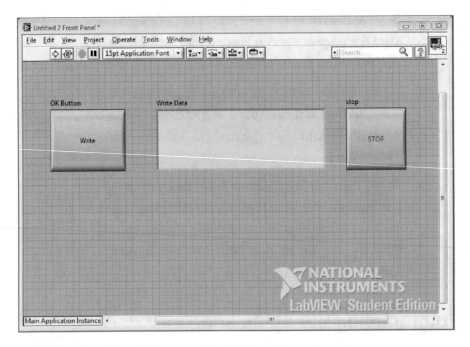

Figure 10-21. *Partially completed Front Panel*

1. Go to your Block Diagram. You should have three controls on it because we added them on the Front Panel.

2. First, go to the Functions Palette ➤ Programming ➤ Structures ➤ While Loop, and drag the While Loop onto the Block Diagram. Figure 10-22 shows this process.

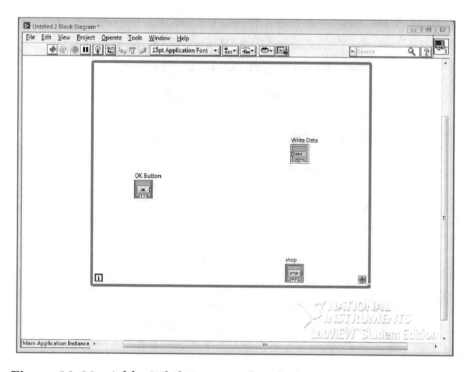

Figure 10-22. *Add a While Loop to the Block Diagram*

3. Next, go to the Functions Palette ➤ Connectivity ➤ Input Device Control ➤ Initialize Joystick. Drag this function to the Block Diagram on the outside of the While Loop. Then, click the device ID terminal on the Initialize Joystick Function and drag the wire to the While Loop.

4. Next, click the error out terminal and drag the wire to the While Loop.

5. After that, go to the Functions Palette ➤ Connectivity ➤ Input Device Control ➤ Acquire Input Data, and drag this function to the Block Diagram, inside the While Loop.

6.   Then, attach the device ID from the Initialize Joystick Function that we wired to the While Loop to the device ID terminal on the Acquire Input Data Function.

7.   Then, attach the error wire from the Initialize Joystick Function to the error in (no error) terminal on the Acquire Input Data Function.

8.   Finally, go to the Functions Palette ➤ Connectivity ➤ Input Device Control ➤ Close Input Device, and drag this function to the Block Diagram to the outside of the While Loop on the right.

9.   Then, connect the device ID from the Acquire Input Data Function to the device ID terminal on the Close Input Device Function. These terminals are on the edges of the functions. This particular terminal controls which device will be used.

10.   After that, connect the error out terminal on the Acquire Input Data Function to the error in (no error) terminal on the Close Input Device Function.

11.   After that, right-click the device ID on the left side of the Initialize Joystick Function, and a pop-up menu should appear. Go to Create ➤ Control on the pop-up menu; this will add a control to your Block Diagram and Front Panel. Figure 10-23 shows adding the Input Device Control Functions to the Block Diagram. (Make sure you leave plenty of space on the Block Diagram, as we still have some functions to add to it.)

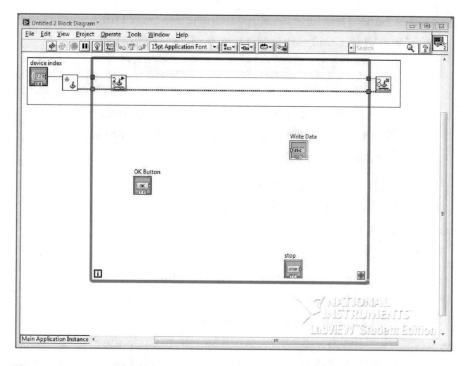

Figure 10-23. *Add Input Device Functions to the Block Diagram*

Adding Serial Functions

Now that we have our Input Device Control Functions added and connected on the Block Diagram, we can move on to adding the Serial Functions to the Block Diagram.

1. First, go to the Functions Palette ➤ Instrument I/O ➤ Serial ➤ VISA Configure Serial Port, and drag this function to the outside of the While Loop on the left.

2. Then, go to the Functions Palette ➤ Instrument I/O ➤ Serial ➤ VISA Flush I/O Buffer, and drag this function to the right side of the While Loop, after the VISA Configure Serial Port Function.

543

3. Connect the VISA resource name out terminal from the VISA Configure Serial Port Function to the VISA resource name terminal on the VISA Flush I/O Buffer Function.

4. Connect the error out (no error) terminal from the VISA Configure Serial Port Function to the error in terminal on the VISA Flush I/O Buffer Function.

5. Add a Case Structure to the Block Diagram inside the While Loop. Go to the Functions Palette ➤ Programming ➤ Structures ➤ Case Structure, and drag it out a little on the Block Diagram.

6. Connect the Write Button to the conditional terminal on the Case Structure (it is the small square with a question mark in it). In the true case, we will need to add a VISA Write Function. Go to the Functions Palette ➤ Instrument I/O ➤ Serial ➤ VISA Write, and drag this function to the inside of the Case Structure to the True Condition.

7. Now we need to connect the VISA resource name out terminal on the VISA Flush I/O Buffer Function to the VISA resource name terminal on the VISA Write Function. Connect the error out terminal on the VISA Flush I/O Buffer Function to the error in (no error) terminal on the VISA Write Function.

8. Wire the VISA resource name out terminal on the VISA Write Function to the right wall of the Case Structure, and do the same for the error out terminal on the VISA Write Function. You will notice that there are two white squares on the right wall of the Case Structure; this is because your false statement

has not been wired yet. Go to the false case of the Case Structure and wire from the VISA resource name out terminal on the VISA Flush I/O Buffer Function to the right wall of the Case Structure where the white square is located (these squares are called tunnels). Do the same thing for the error out terminal in the false case of the Case Structure.

9. Add a Sequence Structure to the Block Diagram. To do this, go to the Functions Palette ➤ Programming ➤ Structures ➤ Sequence Structure, and drag this function out a little, inside the While Loop next to the Case Structure.

10. Add a Wait(ms) Function to the inside of the Sequence Structure. To do this, go to the Functions Palette ➤ Programming ➤ Timing ➤ Wait(ms), and drag it to the inside of the Sequence Structure.

11. Right-click the milliseconds to wait terminal on the Wait(ms) Function; a pop-up menu will appear. Go to Create ➤ Constant; a small constant box will appear next to the Wait(ms) Function. Double-click this box and type in "100."

12. Now wire the data that is coming from the Case Structure through the Sequence Structure (both error out and VISA reference name out).

13. Then, add another VISA Flush I/O Buffer Function after the Sequence Structure. To do this, go to the Functions Palette ➤ Instrument I/O ➤ Serial ➤ VISA Flush I/O Buffer, and drag it to the Block Diagram, after the Sequence Structure.

14.   Connect the wires from the Sequence Structure to the VISA Flush I/O Buffer Function.

15.   Add a VISA Flush I/O Buffer Function to the outside of the While Loop, on the right side of the While Loop.

16.   Add a VISA Close Function after the VISA Flush I/O Buffer Function. You can find this function by going to the Functions Palette ➤ Instrument I/O ➤ Serial ➤ VISA Close.

17.   Right-click the VISA resource name terminal on the left side of the VISA Configure Serial Port Function; a pop-up menu will appear. Go to Create ➤ Control on that pop-up menu, and a control will be created on the Block Diagram and the Front Panel. Figures 10-24 and 10-25 illustrate adding the Serial Functions to the Block Diagram.

18.   Then, right-click the error on the left side of the VISA Configure Serial Port Function; a pop-up menu will appear. Go to Create ➤ Control on the pop-up menu, and a control will be created on the Block Diagram and Front Panel. Figures 10-24 and 10-25 show the process of adding the error cluster to the Block Diagram.

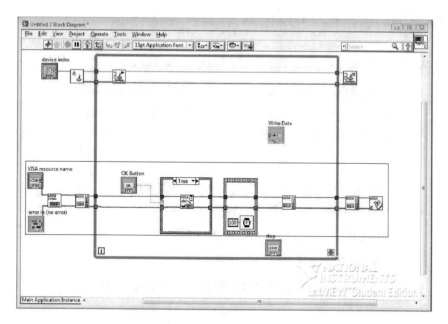

Figure 10-24. *Add serial communication to the Block Diagram (part 1 of 2)*

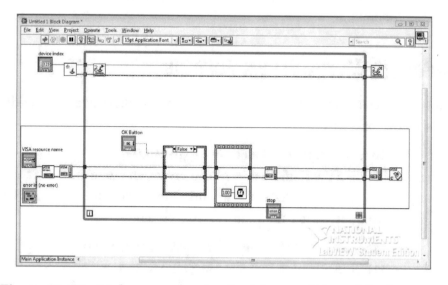

Figure 10-25. *Make sure you wire the false condition of the Case Structure (part 2 of 2)*

Completing the While Loop Condition

Now, we need to complete the While Loop condition:

1. First, add an Or Function to the Block Diagram. To do this, go to the Functions Palette ➤ Programming ➤ Boolean ➤ Or, and drag it next to the conditional terminal of the While Loop.

2. Then, connect the x.or.y? terminal to the conditional terminal on the While Loop.

3. After that, connect the Stop Button to the bottom terminal on the Or Function.

4. Next, add an Unbundle by Name Function to the Block Diagram. To do this, go to the Functions Palette ➤ Programming ➤ Cluster, Class, & Variant ➤ Unbundle by Name, and drag it to the Block Diagram, next to the top terminal on the Or Function.

Adding a Merge Errors Function

Now, we need to add a Merge Errors Function to the Block Diagram. To do this, follow these instructions:

1. Go to the Functions Palette ➤ Programming ➤ Dialog & User Interface ➤ Merge Errors, and drag it to the Block Diagram and connect the error out terminal to the Unbundle by Name Function.

2. Then, connect the status terminal of the Unbundle by Name Function to the top terminal on the Or Function.

3. Connect the error out terminal from the Acquire
    Input Data Function to the first terminal on the
    Merge Errors Function.

4. Then, attach the error out terminal from the VISA
    Flush I/O Buffer Function (the one inside the While
    Loop) to the second terminal on the Merge Errors
    Function. Figure 10-26 shows the completed While
    Loop condition.

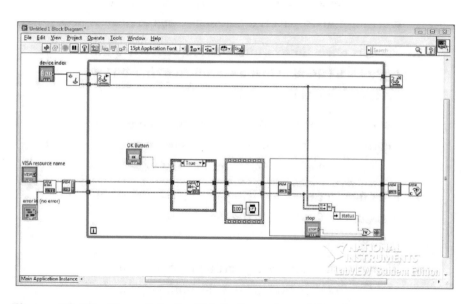

Figure 10-26. *Complete the While Loop by adding in stop
conditions*

Next, we need to add a SubVI to our program.

Adding a SubVI

A SubVI is much like the subroutines we create when we program with the Arduino IDE. Every function that we have put on the Block Diagram has been a SubVI, but we are about to add a SubVI that LabVIEW does not come with. You can find this SubVI with the source code from Chapter 10 at www.apress.com.

1. Once you have downloaded the SubVI (the SubVI's name is ScaleandControl.vi) to your desktop, you can drag and drop it onto the Block Diagram.

2. Then, connect the axis info terminal on the Acquire Input Data Function to the axis info terminal on the Scale and Control Function.

3. Next, connect the button info terminal on the Acquire Input Data Function to the button info terminal on the Scale and Control Function.

4. After that, connect the string terminal on the Scale and Control Function to the Write Data String Indicator.

5. Finally, connect the string terminal on the Scale and Control Function to the write buffer terminal on the VISA Write Function. Figure 10-27 shows the completed SubVI.

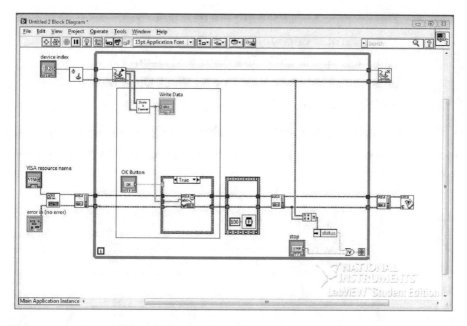

Figure 10-27. *Add a SubVI to the Block Diagram that will scale the Xbox controller's values and dictate which direction to move the robot*

Error Handling

Now, we need to complete the error handling for this project.

1. First, add a Merge Errors Function to the outside of the While Loop, after the VISA Close Function.

2. Next, attach the error out terminal on the VISA Close Function to the second terminal on the Merge Errors Function.

3. Then, attach the error out terminal on the Close Input Device Function to the first terminal on the Merge Errors Function.

4. Finally, right-click the error out terminal on the
   Merge Errors Function, and a pop-up menu should
   appear. Go to Create ➤ Indicator, and an error
   indicator should be added to your Block Diagram
   and Front Panel.

Now, you can modify the Front Panel as you see fit because we have no
more controls or indicators to add to it. That should do it for the LabVIEW
software. See Figure 10-28.

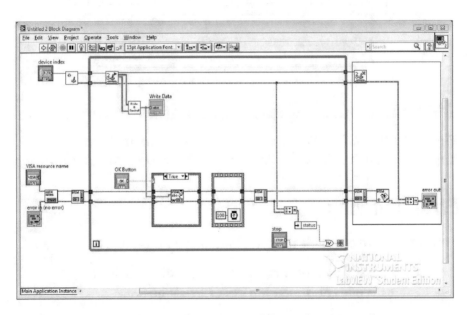

Figure 10-28. *Finish error handling of the LabVIEW software to
finish the program*

Read Function

Now, we need to complete the error handling for this project.

1. First, let's expand the Front Panel a bit to accommodate
   the new string indicator that we will need.

2. Now add another string indicator onto the Front
    Panel and name it "Serial Read."

3. Go ahead and stretch it to be the same width as the
    "Write Data" string indicator and about half of its
    height. See Figure 10-29.

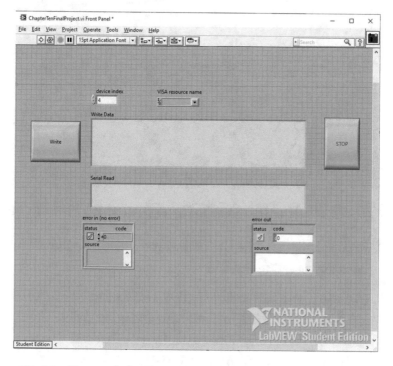

Figure 10-29. *Expand the Front Panel*

4. Add a little flare to the Front Panel by double-
    clicking the Front Panel and writing "NatBot
    Interface" onto the Front Panel. See Figure 10-30.

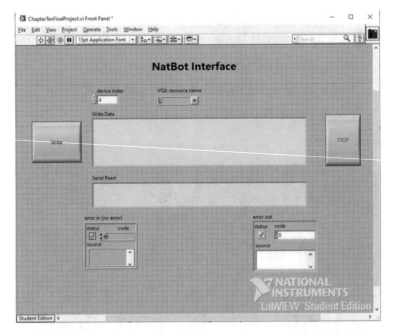

Figure 10-30. *Add the text "NatBot Interface" to the Front Panel*

5. You can increase the size of the text by selecting the text and pressing Ctrl and +.

6. To add a vertical scrollbar to the "Serial Read" indicator, right-click the indicator and go to Visible Items ➤ Vertical Scrollbar, and the scrollbar will appear. See Figures 10-31 and 10-32.

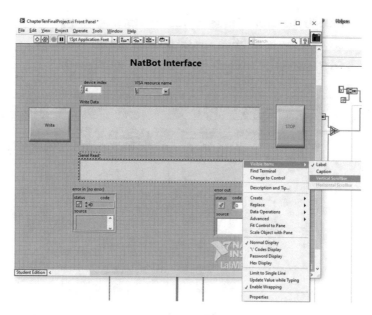

Figure 10-31. *Make the vertical scrollbar visible*

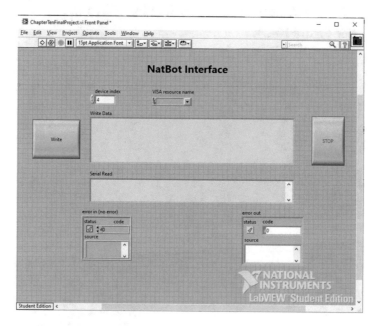

Figure 10-32. *Vertical scrollbar*

7. Move to the Block Diagram and remove the wires
    between the sequence structure and the flush buffer,
    and expand the while loop a bit. See Figure 10-33.

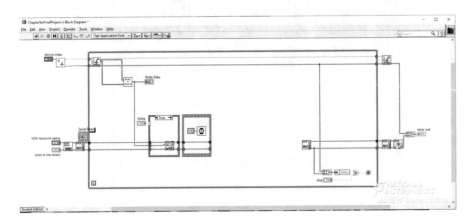

Figure 10-33. *Expand the while loop*

8. Add a VISA Read Function to the Block Diagram.
    See Figure 10-34.

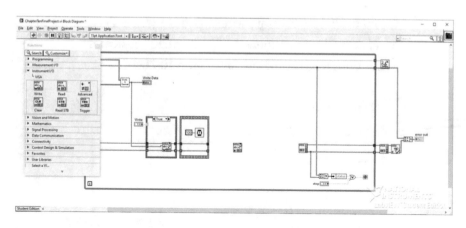

***Figure 10-34.** Add a VISA Read Function*

9. Add a VISA Property Node to the Block Diagram. This will be a "Bytes at Port" function which will set the size of the buffer that we will be looking for on the serial port. See Figure 10-35.

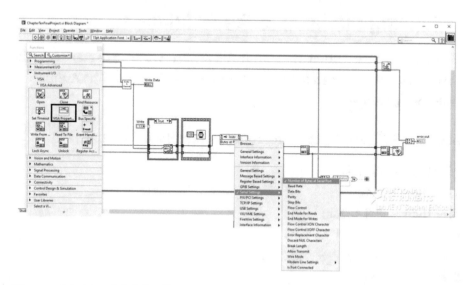

***Figure 10-35.** Add the "Bytes at Port" property*

10.   Connect all the necessary wires for the "Bytes at Port"
function and also connect the "Serial Read" indicator
to the VISA Read Function. See Figure 10-36.

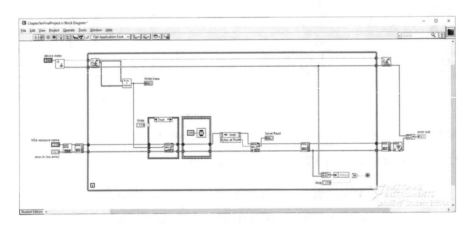

Figure 10-36. *Make sure your Block Diagram looks like this*

Uploading the Code to the Arduino

Now that we have written our LabVIEW software, we need to make sure the
correct code is uploaded to the Arduino. Listing 10-1 shows the Arduino
code for this project.

Listing 10-1. Same firmware from Chapter 9 will be used

```
#include <SPI.h>
#include <SD.h>
#include <ADXL362.h>
#include <Adafruit_GFX.h>
#include <Adafruit_SSD1331.h>
#include <TinyGPS.h>

// Adafruit Display
#define sclk 52
```

```
#define mosi 51
#define cs   31
#define rst  29
#define dc   28

// Color definitions
#define  BLACK            0x0000

int numCount = 0;


// Motor IO
const int fields = 8; // how many fields are there? right now 8
int motorPins[] = {42,44,40,46,25,12,26,13}; // Motor Pins
int index = 0;        // the current field being received
int values[fields];   // array holding values for all the fields

// Object Creation
TinyGPS gps;
ADXL362 accel;
Adafruit_SSD1331 display = Adafruit_SSD1331(cs, dc, mosi, sclk,
rst);

// SD Card Chip Select
int SDCS = 30;

// Ultrasonic Sensor Pin
int pingPin = 22;

// Accelerometer variables
int16_t XValue, YValue, ZValue, Temperature;

// GPS data
char LatData[50];      // data buffer for Latitude
char LongData[50];
```

```
//Latching Variables
char prevState;
int prevAutoState;

// Data buffer for saving drive data
char driveData [50];

// TMP36 Variables
int tempPin = A0;
int sensorValue = 0;

void setup() {

  // Serial of Arduino, Serial of bluetooth, Fianlly Serial of GPS
  Serial.begin(9600);
  Serial1.begin(115200);
  Serial2.begin(4800);

  // CS Pins of SPI devices
  pinMode(SDCS, OUTPUT);
  pinMode(cs, OUTPUT);
  pinMode(27, OUTPUT);

  // set Motor pinMode to output
  for(int i; i <= 7; i++)
  {
    pinMode(motorPins[i], OUTPUT);
    digitalWrite(motorPins[i], LOW);
  }

  // Check for Card availability
  if (!SD.begin(SDCS)) {
    Serial.println("Card failed, or not present");
    // don't do anything more:
```

```
    while (1);
  }
  // Turn off SD Chip Select
  digitalWrite(SDCS, HIGH);

  Serial.println("card initialized.");

  Serial.println("The Format is: MotoADir,MotoASpe,MotorBDir,
  MotoBSpe\n");
}

void loop() {
  if( Serial1.available())
  {
    char ch = Serial1.read();

    if (ch == 'y' || prevState == 'y') // if Serial reads y
    {
      accel.begin(10);        // Setup SPI protocol, issue
                              //   device soft reset
      accel.beginMeasure();   // Switch ADXL362 to measure mode

      // read all three axis in burst to ensure all
      //   measurements correspond to same sample time
      accel.readXYZTData(XValue, YValue, ZValue, Temperature);
      Serial.print("XVALUE=");
      Serial.print(XValue);
      Serial.print("\tYVALUE=");
      Serial.print(YValue);
      Serial.print("\tZVALUE=");
      Serial.print(ZValue);
      Serial.print("\tTEMPERATURE=");
      Serial.println(Temperature);
```

```
    delay(100);                // Arbitrary delay to make serial
                                  monitor easier to observe

    // Stop communication with accelerometer
    digitalWrite(27, HIGH);

    // Store data into SD card
    // open the file. note that only one file can be open at
      a time,
    // so you have to close this one before opening another.
    SD.begin(SDCS);
    File accelFile = SD.open("Accel.txt", FILE_WRITE);

    // if the file is available, write to it:
    if (accelFile) {
       accelFile.print(XValue);
       accelFile.print(" , ");
       accelFile.print(YValue);
       accelFile.print(" , ");
       accelFile.println(ZValue);
       accelFile.close();
       digitalWrite(SDCS, HIGH);
       }
     // if the file isn't open, pop up an error:
     else {
       Serial.println("error opening datalog.txt");
     }

     prevState = ch;
  }
  else if (ch == 'a') // if Serial reads a
  {
     if (prevAutoState == 0)
```

```
{
   prevAutoState = 1;
   // put your main code here, to run repeatedly:
   float duration, inches;

   pinMode(pingPin, OUTPUT);
   digitalWrite(pingPin, LOW);
   delayMicroseconds(2);
   digitalWrite(pingPin, HIGH);
   delayMicroseconds(2);
   digitalWrite(pingPin, LOW);

   pinMode(pingPin, HIGH);
   inches = duration / 74 / 2;

   if (inches >= 2)
   {
      Serial1.println("Object Near!!");
   }
}
else if (prevAutoState == 1)
{
   prevAutoState = 0;
}
}
else if (ch == 'g' || prevState == 'g') // if Serial reads g
{
   if (Serial2.available() > 0) // now gps device is active
   {
      int c = Serial2.read();
      if(gps.encode(c))      // New valid sentence?
      {
```

```
// Initialize Longitude and Latitude to floating
    point numbers
float latitude, longitude;

// Get longitude and latitude
gps.f_get_position(&latitude,&longitude);

Serial.print("Lat:    ");
// Prints latitude with 5 decimal places to the
    Serle ial Monitor
Serial.println(latitude,7);

Serial.print("long: ");
// Prints longitude with 5 decimal places to the
    Serial Monitor
Serial.println(longitude,7);

// Store data into SD card
// open the file. note that only one file can be
    open at a time,
// so you have to close this one before opening
    another.
SD.begin(SDCS);
File GPSFile = SD.open("GPS.txt", FILE_WRITE);

// if the file is available, write to it:
if (GPSFile) {
    GPSFile.print(latitude, 7);
    GPSFile.print(" , ");
    GPSFile.println(longitude,7);
    GPSFile.close();
    digitalWrite(SDCS, HIGH);
  }
  // if the file isn't open, pop up an error:
```

```
        else {
            Serial.println("error opening datalog.txt");
        }
    }
  }
  prevState = ch;
}
else if(ch >= '0' && ch <= '9') // If the value is a number
                                 0 to 9
{
  // add to the value array
  values[index] = (values[index] * 10) + (ch - '0');
}
else if (ch == ',') // if it is a comma
{
  if(index < fields -1) // If index is less than 4 - 1...
    index++; // increment index
}
else
{

  for(int i=0; i <= index; i++)
  {

    if (i == 0 && numCount == 0)
    {
      Serial.println("Motor A");
      Serial.println(values[i]);
    }
    else if (i == 1)
    {
      Serial.println(values[i]);
```

```
    }
    if (i == 2)
    {
      Serial.println("Motor B");
      Serial.println(values[i]);
    }
    else if (i == 3)
    {
      Serial.println(values[i]);
    }
    if (i == 4)
    {
      Serial.println("Motor C");
      Serial.println(values[i]);
    }
    else if (i == 5)
    {
      Serial.println(values[i]);
    }
    if (i == 6)
    {
      Serial.println("Motor D");
      Serial.println(values[i]);
    }
    else if (i == 7)
    {
      Serial.println(values[i]);
    }

    if (i == 0 || i == 2 || i == 4 || i == 6)  // If the
                                               index is
                                               equal to
                                               0 or 2
```

```
      {
        digitalWrite(motorPins[i], values[i]); // Write to
                                      the digital
                                      pin 1 or 0
        // depending on what is sent to the arduino.
      }

      if (i == 1 || i == 3 || i == 5 || i == 7)
// If the index is equal to 1 or 3
      {
        analogWrite(motorPins[i], values[i]);  // Write to
the PWM pins a number between
        // 0 and 255 or what the person has entered
        // in the serial monitor.
      }

      values[i] = 0; // set values equal to 0

      sprintf(driveData, "Motor A = ", values[0], "Motor B = ",
      values[2], "Motor C = ", values[4], "Motor D = ", values[6]);

      // Send temperature to the LCD
      sensorValue = analogRead(tempPin);

      display.begin();
      display.fillScreen(BLACK);
      display.setCursor(0,0);
      display.print(sensorValue);
      digitalWrite(cs, HIGH);

    }

    index = 0;
    numCount = 0;
  }
```

```
if (ch == 'x' || prevState == 'x') // if Serial reads x
{
        SD.begin(SDCS);
        File driveFile = SD.open("Drive.txt", FILE_WRITE);

        // if the file is available, write to it:
        if (driveFile) {
            driveFile.println(driveData);
            driveFile.close();
            digitalWrite(SDCS, HIGH);
          }
        // if the file isn't open, pop up an error:
        else {
            Serial.println("error opening datalog.txt");
        }
        prevState = ch;
    }
  }
}
```

If you would like to read the discussion of this program, please read the "Writing the Software" section in Chapter 9's final project.

Note   Make sure the Arduino and the Xbox controller are connected to your computer.

Operation

The following steps will guide you through the operation of this project:

1. To operate the LabVIEW software, you will need to first know the serial com port to which the Arduino is connected. Go to the Front Panel of the LabVIEW software and click the arrow on the VISA resource name control; a drop-down menu will appear, and you can select the correct serial port to which the Arduino is connected.

2. After that, you need to select the correct number ID with which the Xbox controller is associated. To do this, click inside the white area of the device index control and type in the number (the best thing to do is type in 1; if that doesn't work, type in 2; if that doesn't work, type in 3; repeat these steps with a larger number each time).

3. Then, click the white arrow at the top left of the screen. After that, your program should run. Click the Write Button, and the robot should move when you move the joystick up, down, left, and right.

Now that we have written the LabVIEW software and Arduino software, we can move on to fixing any bugs or issues we might have had with both the hardware and software. In the next section, we will discuss how to debug the software.

Debugging the LabVIEW Software

LabVIEW has several built-in debugging tools. I will explain only two of them: Highlight Execution and probes.

Highlight Execution is used to see the flow of your program and to find where errors are occurring. It slows the program down considerably and runs through the code function by function. To use this debugging method, click the Highlight Execution button at the top of the Block Diagram (the button has a light bulb on it). If you click this function while the program is running, you will see bright lines showing you where you are in the code.

Probes are used to see specific values that controls or indicators are giving or receiving. For instance, if you wanted to see at what point a logical error is occurring in your code, you could use a probe to view data on the wires to figure out where the mistake is. To use probes, right-click any wire on the Block Diagram. A pop-up menu will appear. Click probe, and a display will pop up with an indicator showing you the value on that wire.

We can use these tools to figure out issues that the LabVIEW software might be having. If you have a broken arrow, you might have connected something incorrectly, or you forgot to connect a terminal on one of the functions. Make sure your code is exactly like that shown in Figure 10-36. Now, if you have a white arrow, and you are still having issues with your LabVIEW software, you might have encountered a logical error. Use probes and Highlight Execution to find these issues. Because every Xbox controller will have different calibration, you might need to adjust the limits on the Xbox controller. To do this, double-click the Scale and Control SubVI, and the Block Diagram for this SubVI should appear. Then adjust the constants, shown in Figure 10-37, to a higher or lower value, depending on what your Xbox controller is doing.

Figure 10-37. *Change the constants on these functions to set the limits for vertical and horizontal movements of the joystick on the Xbox controller*

If the software is working, and you are still having issues, refer to the next section on troubleshooting the hardware.

Finished Prototype

Well, if everything is working, you have a finished prototype ready to deliver to the customer. Figure 10-38 shows the finished prototype.

Figure 10-38. *The NatBot*

Summary

That's it! But before you leave, let us recap what we have gone over in this chapter:

- Learned about the LabVIEW environment

- Learned how to use serial communication to control the NatBot with a LabVIEW application

- Learned how to structure your code on the Block Diagram and how to arrange your Front Panel (GUI)

- Learned about various functions in LabVIEW

- Created your own Serial Interface using LabVIEW

Index

A

Accelerometer, 8, 409, 410, 491
Adafruit SSD1331
    library, 493
ADXL362 library, 492
Allen wrenches, 135, 136
Analog communication, 46
Arduino boards, 2, 184
Arduino engineering process
    configuring hardware, 20, 21
    creating requirements
        document, 19
    debugging software, 23
    finished prototype, 25
    gathering hardware, 19
    hardware components
        ArduinoBT/Bluetooth
            Mate Silver, 3
        Arduino Duemilanove/
            UNO, 2
        Arduino shields, 5
        GPS shield, 6
        miscellaneous
            components, 10
        Motor shield, 6
        servos and motors, 9
        solderless breadboard, 4, 5
        wire, 5

requirements document,
    creation, 18
tools, 10–17
troubleshooting hardware, 24
writing software, 22
Arduino microcontroller, 2
Arduino shields, 5
Arrays, 31

B

Bluetooth Mate Silver, 3, 4

C

Calipers, 137, 161, 343
Capacitors, 10, 185, 281
Case structure, 526–527
Comparison functions, 531–532
Conditional statements, 31–33, 53
Control board, 142, 143
Cura, 145
Cutters, 11, 15

D

DesignSpark Mechanical, 58
Digital calipers, 137
Digital commands, 45

© Harold Timmis 2021
H. Timmis, *Practical Arduino Engineering*, https://doi.org/10.1007/978-1-4842-6852-0

I, J, K

L

M

O

P, Q

Printed in the United States
by Baker & Taylor Publisher Services